0-07-041793-9	B. Merrow	*VSE/ESA: Performance Management and Fine Tuning*
0-07-054977-X	J. Savit	*VM/CMS: Concepts and Facilities*
0-07-018994-3	T. Eddolls	*ASO: Automated Systems Operations for MVS*
0-07-018303-1	T. Baritz/D.Dunne	*AS/400: Concepts and Facilities*
0-07-035869-9	J. LeBert	*CICS Essentials for Application Developers and Programmers*
0-07-050623-X	J. Porter	*AS/400 Information Engineering*
0-07-006565-9	K. Bosler	*MVS TSO/ISPF: A Guide for Users and Developers*
0-07-033783-7	T. Keller	*CICS: Capacity Planning and Performance Management*
0-07-039825-9	S. Malik	*CSP: A Devloper's Guide*
0-07-041984-1	L. Trindell	*NetView: A Professional's Guide to SNA Network Management*
0-07-067175-3	A. Varsegi	*MVS COBOL Application Developer's Toolbox*
0-07-054972-9	J. Savit	*VM and CMS: Performance and Fine Tuning*
0-07-096425-4	M. Gopaul	*IBM Mainframe Programmer's Desk Reference*
0-07-024128-7	F. Graubart-Cervone	*VSE/ESA JCL: Utilities, POWER, and VSAM*
0-07-049654-4	D. Peterson	*ENTERPRISE NETWORK MANAGEMENT: A Guide to IBM's NetView*

D1523344

Enterprise Network Management

DATE DUE

Enterprise Network Management

A Guide to IBM's NetView

David M. Peterson

McGraw-Hill, Inc.

New York   San Francisco   Washington, D.C.   Auckland   Bogotá
Caracas   Lisbon   London   Madrid   Mexico City   Milan
Montreal   New Delhi   San Juan   Singapore
Sydney   Tokyo   Toronto

Library of Congress Cataloging-in-Publication Data

Peterson, David M.
    Enterprise network management : a guide to IBM's NetView / David
M. Peterson.

       p.   cm. — (J. Ranade IBM series)
    Includes index.
    ISBN 0-07-049654-4
    1. IBM Netview. 2. Local area networks (Computer networks)
—Management. I. Title. II. Series.
    TK5105.7.P487 1993
    004.6'12—dc20   93-41525
                                                   CIP

1 2 3 4 5 6 7 8 9 0 DOC/DOC 9 0 9 8 7 6 5 4

ISBN 0-07-049654-4

The sponsoring editor for this book was Jerry Papke.

Printed and bound by R. R. Donnelley and Sons Company.

To my parents, who always thought that I might want to someday write a book. And to Madeleine, for her patience.

Contents

Part 3   Major Functional Components   169

Chapter 10.   Command Facility   171

Preface

Why a NetView book ?

The early IBM network management products provided adequate support for the host-based computing environment. Over the past decade, both the nature and component elements of enterprise-wide computing have grown very rapidly in variety and complexity. A wide range of hardware platforms and software is now available to allow many types of applications to be distributed throughout the network. This situation has created many new challenges. In particular, end users and vendors alike are wrestling with the task of implementing an enterprise-wide management and control strategy.

The NetView product, first introduced in 1986, forms the centerpiece of the IBM systems and network management strategy in the mainframe arena. In recent years, the product's features have been significantly upgraded and enhanced, allowing it to grow well beyond its original SNA network management roots. Recent enhancements allow for a wider role within the enterprise, focusing on automation, non-SNA resource management, and improved display capabilities. NetView has also been integrated more tightly into IBM's systems management framework, SystemView.

Despite its shortcomings and perceived inadequacies, NetView is still the most comprehensive network management product currently available for most large, "industrial strength" users.

Purpose of the Book

This is a huge subject area. There are literally dozens, perhaps hundreds, of manuals, redbooks, articles, and IBM Information Network (IBMLINK) entries that have been examined during the course of writing this book.

After starting on the project, it became clear that it would not be possible to completely replace all of the detailed and ever-changing reference manuals distributed by IBM. Therefore, the book has steered clear of attempting to be a complete operational, vocationally oriented text satisfying every reader's needs.

Rather, the purpose of the book is to present a comprehensive introduction and guide to the NetView product. Perhaps most importantly, it clearly illustrates, through a detailed examination of the individual product features, how NetView implements and embodies the major architectural standards. Indeed, behind the functions, there is a reason and method that continues to guide the product's development.

This book is therefore a tutorial on IBM's vision with respect to hetergeneous enterprise network management, with an emphasis on how NetView can be used to support these goals.

NetView for MVS

IBM provides NetView on several of its popular operating systems. The most advanced, production-oriented of these is MVS. Consequently, the control of the majority of the largest networks is carried out using NetView on MVS.

In fact, there is a consistent pattern where new NetView features are first introduced with the MVS versions, and then (possibly) migrated to the other platforms as well.

This book therefore focuses on NetView as implemented in the MVS environment. While the product actually remains much the same across the other operating systems, the users of NetView for MVS will derive the most benefit. The latest version of NetView (as of this writing), is version 2.3, which will be used as a basis for the book.

Stylistic Matters

Part of my work in creating the NV/Monitor product involved examining NetView's internal processing in detail, including the various modules and data areas. Coming from such a development environment, there is of course a tendency to become too narrowly focused on the bits and bytes. Recognizing this hazard, and with encouragement from my previous published writing, I set out to create a text that would benefit as wide an audience as possible.

In doing this, I established three major goals regarding the style and content. These include:

- Broad coverage of the subject matter.
- Consistent level of detail throughout.
- Clear, objective, and useful descriptions.

As mentioned above, it is easy to dwell on a particular aspect of NetView (e.g., internals, operations, administration). Instead, I decided to provide a broad explanation of the product and its features. Since NetView supports a wide range of architectures and standards, these would also need to be included.

A consistent level of detail is desirable in order to make the book more uniform and usable throughout. This approach is further strengthened by a clear description of each aspect of the product.

Organization

The nineteen chapters include the most important aspects of the NetView product. These chapters have been arranged into four major parts, which, when read sequentially, gradually develop and strengthen the reader's grasp of the subject matter.

The first part provides a foundation for many of the features and facilities presented later by establishing the architectural framework. Part 2 introduces the basic configuration tasks and operational aspects of the product. The third part includes a chapter dedicated to each of the major internal components, focusing on their functions and features. The last part of the book includes a description of the more advanced capabilities and how they can be used to implement enterprise-wide network management.

Audience

One of the book's strengths is its ability to illustrate how the features and functions of NetView fit within the architectural frameworks such as SNA Management Services and SystemView. It provides a broad coverage of the product capabilities.

Therefore, this book will be of use to a wide range of professionals. It is designed first to be read by those new to NetView, or perhaps only familiar with one aspect of it. This would include, for example, junior network systems programmers or operators who desire a more complete understanding of the product. Others in the mainframe area will include non-NetView systems programmers, automation specialists, network analysts and planners, and managers.

In addition, there will undoubtedly be other readers outside of the mainframe area who would benefit from the book. This is especially true as IBM continues to extend NetView's reach into the enterprise, connecting it to more platforms for improved management and control.

Completeness and Accuracy

As mentioned above, the material included is designed to be as complete as possible within the confines of a book of this size, without diminishing its detail and usefulness. The text strives to provide the complete picture, cutting across several subject areas.

In the process of performing the research and writing, I have worked to maintain a high degree of accuracy. In the end, however, I must accept responsibility for the content of this book and any mistakes or inaccuracies.

If when reading the book, you have any comments, suggestions, or corrections, please contact the author directly. As an alternative, you can send this information to:

McGraw-Hill
P.O. Box 338
Grand Central Station
New York, NY 10163-0338

And of course, as NetView continues to evolve, there will be new features and uses for the product. I look forward to the possibility of a second edition, at which time new information can be included and any errors corrected.

Future Network Management Directions

With all of IBM's recent financial troubles, and a common drive among customers toward "open systems," it seems difficult to predict with absolute certainty what the future holds. NetView will undoubtedly be enhanced, further advancing it as the ultimate network management platform.

However, the mainframe is facing challenges from all sides. This includes competition from inside as well as outside of the IBM product line. For example, the NetView/6000 product, designed for the management of TCP/IP networks, is rapidly expanding with the aim of possibly replacing the mainframe version of NetView as the central point of control. The LAN NetView family will also be available to support the LAN-based OS/2 machines.

IBM will continue to support all three environments, providing communication and cooperation as much as possible. However, in the case where the mainframe version of NetView is available, the strategy will be to position NetView at the center, with remote operation and control functions carried out with the other supporting products.

David Peterson

Acknowledgments

Writing this book has proved to be quite an experience. I would like to thank those individuals who helped along the way to make it more enjoyable, and also to improve the accuracy and usefulness of the end result.

I would like to thank George Sackett of ASAP Technologies for his review and helpful suggestions. His wide network experience, especially with SNA and TCP/IP, has allowed him to make a solid contribution.

Joby O'Brien at Enterprise Software Corporation also reviewed the manuscript. Thank you for your attention to detail, and several helpful insights. I wish you the best with the new Net/Overview (NetView-based) product.

Looking back on life at Peregrine, it now seems to be a blur of nothing but long hours and hard work. I would like to thank Rifai Apin who worked with me in producing the NV/Monitor product, something we did together in under one year. The work allowed both of us to better understand NetView and its internal operations.

At Candle, I would like to thank Steve Samson for first introducing me to Jay Ranade, and for initially encouraging me to write this book. Little did he realize, however, that I would very soon after decide to leave for Peregrine. Also, the late James Greenlee, former editor of the Candle Computer Report, was especially helpful. I learned quite a bit from Dr. Greenlee in the area of organization and editing, and actually published my first articles with his help and direction.

I would also like to thank Jeff Pulver and Fred Blakely, both of whom I worked for as a programmer at Westinghouse Elevator in New Jersey, in the summers during college. I first began working closely with IBM technology in those days in the "silver palace" data center, a converted warehouse behind the manufacturing plant in Randolph.

Finally, thanks go out to my editor at McGraw-Hill, Jerry Papke, for his encouragement and patience as the deadline for this book seemed to continually slip.

IBM Network Management Framework

1

Evolution of IBM Network Management

Over the last two decades, both the complexity and usage of data communication networks have grown rapidly. In the early days of mainframe computing, only a handful of protocols were sufficient to support the small number of terminals attached to any single host. But as networks began to expand in size and scale, the need arose for a single, unified method which would guide the development of networking products and services. In 1974, IBM solidified their approach to the implementation of networking systems with the announcement of Systems Network Architecture (SNA).

SNA provides a set of communication protocols which allows for the efficient and error-free transmission of data through the network. The SNA specifications serve as a blueprint for the construction of hardware and software products. With this model in place, IBM and third party vendors have been able to create a wide variety of products that are used in networks throughout the world.

The architecture has continually expanded to meet the growing challenges of managing and administering enterprise communication networks. These enhancements have been driven by, among other things, the rapid increase in computer capabilities and the subsequent divergence of CPU power away from the center. More and more, businesses are turning to distributed processing models where hundreds or thousands of workstations and other devices are used to supplement (or even replace) the central mainframe glasshouse.

One area of SNA which IBM has paid particular attention to when addressing this evolving computer landscape is network management, or what was originally named Communication Network Management

(CNM). CNM is both a philosophy and collection of formats and protocols woven into the early SNA model; it provides for the explicit management of network resources by an application residing on the central host. With CNM, we see the beginnings of a division between the underlying structures designed to enable network management and the function of the applications which use them to control the network.

The next major step towards meeting customer requirements was taken shortly after NetView was announced in 1986, when IBM introduced its Open Network Management (ONM) strategy. ONM allows for the management of SNA as well as non-SNA devices through the use of the service point architecture, thus extending the reach of central, controlling applications. The accompanying SNA Management Services (SNA/MS) specifications more clearly defined the capabilities and interactions of the networking products, with a particular emphasis in later releases on the growing peer-to-peer networks.

Finally, SystemView was introduced in 1990 as a comprehensive systems management framework. With this major new initiative, the role of network management was more closely integrated with the larger task of managing system resources throughout the enterprise. The Networking Blueprint, released in the fall of 1992, provides further emphasis on systems and network management within the SystemView framework.

This chapter begins with a brief introduction to SNA. It then proceeds chronologically through the most important developments along the evolution of IBM's network management strategy.

1.1 Basic SNA Concepts

Before approaching the subject of SNA network management, it is first necessary to review the basic concepts of SNA. Of course, this is a very large subject area which cannot possibly be covered in a single section. The interested reader should refer to the appendix for several good books, as well as the latest IBM manuals on the subject.

A Layer Architecture

The features and functions of SNA are specified in a detailed Format and Protocol Language (FAPL). These FAPL specifications are grouped as subsets and arranged in a layered structure. This allows changes and updates to be isolated, thus facilitating enhancement with minimal disruption.

The original or "traditional" SNA model includes only five layers. With the advent of Advanced Peer-to-Peer Communications (APPC), also known as logical unit type 6.2, the top SNA layer was essentially divided and expanded into two layers. Transaction and Presentation Services support the execution of transaction programs within the APPC framework.

At the same time, IBM began including the bottom physical control layer, thus creating a seven-layer model. While a necessary part of an actual network, the physical connectivity specifications (e.g., RS-232) were never collected together and published as a part of SNA (at least not publicly). However, they are now included, a practice which more closely aligns SNA with the OSI model. Refer to Figure 1.1 for an illustration of the evolution of SNA's layered architecture.

While the protocols in the older model are still in use today, the network products are clearly in transition to the seven-layer stack as usage of APPC-based systems become more widespread.

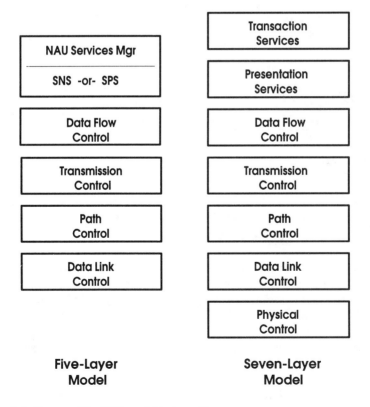

Figure 1.1 Layers of the SNA model in transition.

NAUs and the PC Network

The Network Addressable Units (NAU) are comprised of the upper SNA layers, beginning with Transmission Control. As the name implies, each NAU has a unique address by which it is known throughout the network. The NAUs engage in temporary connections between each other called sessions. Figure 1.2 provides a list of the NAUs in the SNA network.

Network Addressable Unit	Description
Systems Services Control Point (SSCP)	The SSCP is implemented within VTAM on the host. It provides network control and assistance to the other NAUs in establishing sessions.
Physical Unit (PU)	The PU controls a node's physical environment, supporting the local resources with a session to the SSCP.
Logical Unit (LU)	An end user gains access to the network through the LU. Each node usually contains several LUs, such as terminals or applications.

Figure 1.2 SNA Network Addressable Units.

One type of NAU, the logical unit, provides end-user access to the network. There are four basic categories of NAU-to-NAU sessions in the traditional SNA network. These include:

- SSCP-to-SSCP. This is implemented as a VTAM-to-VTAM connection which is used to assist in establishing cross-domain sessions. In the newer distributed processing nodes, the equivalent is the CP-to-CP session.
- SSCP-to-PU. VTAM manages the physical resources of the network by communicating with the PUs in its domain.
- SSCP-to-LU. Access to the network must be made by an end user through an LU, with the assistance of VTAM.

■ LU-to-LU. The ultimate goal of the SNA network is
for end users to share data, which is accomplished
through this session category.

There are several different types of LU-to-LU sessions, each of
which is tailored to meet the needs of a particular device or technology.
For example, the LU type 2 session is used between an SNA 3270
terminal and a host-based application.

Supporting the NAUs is the Path Control (PC) network, which is
made up of protocols in the bottom layers of the model. Once an SNA
session has been established between two NAUs, the underlying PC
network accepts session traffic and routes it across the network between
the NAUs.

The Path Control layer includes specifications describing the Virtual Route (VR), Explicit Route (ER), and Transmission Group (TG).
Together, these protocols provide for the transmission and routing of
data among the SNA nodes. The Data Link Control layer supports the
management and control of the individual links between adjacent devices.

This division of functionality, between the NAUs and the underlying transport protocols, helps to more clearly illustrate the two most
basic operational characteristics of the SNA network.

Logical Unit Type 6.2

The variety of LU session types found in SNA had been an impediment
to interoperability among network resources. Announced by IBM in
1983, LU type 6.2 represents the culmination of several attempts to
develop a single, unified communication standard. LU 6.2, or APPC as
it is also known, provides a flexible and dynamic model which includes
the best elements of the other session types. It formally defines a basic
set of services in the LU which support the execution of Transaction
Programs (TP), thus providing a layer of abstraction. It is portrayed as
the ultimate communication vehicle and perhaps will be the final LU
type created by IBM. Its use is especially appropriate within the
distributed processing and dynamic peer-to-peer networks found in
many corporations today.

APPC can be utilized at all levels of the network by providing users
access to the network through an architected set of generic TP verbs.
These verbs form a protocol boundary with the underlying data flow and
transmission capabilities of the LU. LU 6.2 is an open protocol that is
published and available to third party vendors and users.

Traditional Subarea Network

SNA resources are grouped together to form nodes. These nodes vary in complexity and function. Figure 1.3 presents the node types defined by SNA. In the traditional SNA model there are two major categories of nodes: subarea and peripheral.

Node Number	Node Type	Description
5	SUBAREA	The type 5 node contains the SSCP. It is implemented as VTAM on the host. The SSCP controls all resources in its SNA domain.
4	SUBAREA	The communication controller running the Network Control Program (NCP) represents an implementation of a type 4 node.
2	PERIPHERAL	The type 2 node is usually implemented as a 3274 or 3174 control unit with multiple 3270 terminals.
1	PERIPHERAL	This is an older peripheral node which supports certain line-mode devices, such as a teletype.
2.1	LEN; APPN	PU 2.1 protocols form the basis for Low Entry Networking (LEN), and the later Advanced Peer-to-Peer Networking (APPN) nodes.

Figure 1.3 Node types defined by the SNA architecture.

The subarea nodes, each identified by a unique subarea number, have more function and complexity than the peripheral nodes. They are usually implemented as host mainframes running the VTAM product (node type 5), and as communication controllers executing the Network Control Program (node type 4). The type 5 node forms the center of an SNA domain and manages all other NAUs within its domain.

Peripheral nodes are less sophisticated, requiring support from the subarea nodes to which they are attached; this is accomplished with the subarea node's boundary function (BF) component. A peripheral node is typically a control unit consisting of a group of 3270 display terminals.

Within the subarea network, each NAU is represented by its unique network address, consisting of the subarea plus element number. A peripheral node utilizes a local addressing scheme, and must rely on the attached subarea node for address conversion and support.

Advanced Peer-to-Peer Networking

In 1983, along with APPC, IBM introduced the node type 2.1, or PU 2.1. This node diverges from the traditional SNA model, providing the basis for more dynamic network configuration, session establishment, and routing within an Advanced Peer-to-Peer Networking (APPN) environment.

There are three nodes which can participate in an APPN network:

- Low Entry Networking (LEN) end node.
- APPN end node.
- APPN network node.

The LEN architecture allows for the connection of adjacent nodes, with predefined definition parameters, and was first announced by IBM in 1986.

Soon after this, IBM began distributing the APPN products to support their midrange computers (e.g., S/36). The dynamic nature of APPN provided several advantages, and was subsequently established as a formal architecture in 1991.

The APPN network and end nodes together form the basis for what has been called the "new SNA." These nodes, and the LUs they support, engage in dynamic, peer-to-peer connections without the need for a central SSCP. Instead, each node includes a Control Point (CP). The CP-to-CP sessions between APPN nodes allow for the distribution and execution of the required command and control functionality. Figure 1.4 provides a list of the major functions provided within an APPN network.

The APPN network nodes include a robust level of functionality, enabling them to form the backbone of the APPN network. Some of the APPN protocols, such as intermediate routing, are only supported by the network nodes.

The APPN end nodes are more limited, and implement a subset of the protocols. End nodes can establish connections with other directly attached end nodes. However, for a wider participation in the APPN network, each end node must rely on a network node. In this way, the APPN end node acts as a client to a network node server.

APPN Feature	Description
Distributed Directories	Dynamically determine, through a distributed search, the node location of a remote LU.
Topology and Route Selection	Allows for the best route to be selected for a session, based on certain user input.
Adaptive Pacing and Transmission Priority	Dynamically adjusts flow based on changing conditions; sessions can also be assigned a priority based on performance objectives.
Intermediate Session Routing	The network node can route session traffic when neither LU is resident in the node.

Figure 1.4 Major features available with the APPN network.

Advanced Architectures

Within SNA, there are several discreet sets of advanced functional specifications that are implemented in conjunction with LU type 6.2 to extend the architecture for APPC distributed processing. SNA/MS is one such architecture, which is discussed in Chapter 2. Another extension to the APPC model is the SNA Distribution Services (SNA/DS) architecture. SNA/DS is a store-and-forward service used in several areas to distribute documents and other files.

1.2 Communication Network Management

CNM is a relatively simple, yet well-defined structure which enables the management of the traditional subarea networks. It was designed to fulfill the basic management requirements for networks which, at the time, were dominated by the large system platforms. As such, CNM has a definite hierarchical nature with the command and control features executed exclusively from the central mainframe.

In CNM we find a discernible split between the definition of the functions as performed by a central management application (i.e., what is done) and the underlying format and protocol structures (i.e., how it is done). This division is important to recognize because, over time, it is clear that IBM has enhanced and matured both aspects of their network management structure.

Early Goals of Network Management

The designers of the CNM specifications were faced with the task of managing and controlling a subarea network with a powerful host at the center and a collection of subservient devices out in the network. At this stage, CNM was initially focused on the physical aspects of the communication network.

The first goal was the detection of error conditions arising in the network. This was accomplished by defining data flows and procedures which supported the ability to monitor, interrogate, and test devices in the network. Data would arrive as the solicited response to a request initiated at the host, or in an unsolicited fashion when conditions in the network justified the host's involvement.

CNM had to be constructed to provide a flexible base which could be expanded as required. In the SNA model, the PU is responsible for controlling a node's local physical environment. It must, therefore, be involved in the process. These basic parameters, plus the SNA restriction which disallowed an LU-PU session, helped form the basic design. As a result, the CNM procedures on the host were placed in an application outside of the SSCP (i.e., VTAM).

Structure of CNM

CNM defines two basic entities designed to carry out the execution of network management functions. The CNM application component on the host is implemented as an application program which gains access to the network through a logical unit connected to VTAM. A CNM services component resides within each of the nodes in the network, and interfaces with the PU in the node. Refer to Figure 1.5 for a diagram depicting the basic CNM structure.

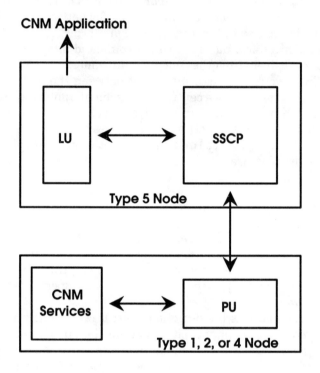

Figure 1.5   Basic structure of Communication Network Management.

The host application appears as an LU and must communicate with the PUs (and ultimately the CNM service components) in order to provide the network management capability. However, since there is no direct LU-PU session defined, the connection is made indirectly through the SSCP. That is, the CNM application has a session with VTAM, while VTAM has a single session with each of the PUs in the domain. With this arrangement, for example, the application can send a request to VTAM which is then forwarded to the desired PU. The reply is returned in the reverse direction. Note that the type 5 node also includes a PU to manage its own local environment (although not shown in the figure).

Data Flows

Originally, there were several categories of Request Units (RUs) used in CNM, including management and maintenance. The management RUs would flow between the CNM application and VTAM, providing an envelope for the network management data. There were two important RUs used by a CNM application for this purpose:

- Forward - carried requests from the application (LU) to VTAM (SSCP).
- Deliver - passed replies and other data from VTAM back to the CNM application.

The maintenance RUs, on the other hand, would flow between VTAM and the PUs in the network. For example, the Record Maintenance Statistics (RECMS) flowed from PUs in the network to report statistics to VTAM (and ultimately to the target CNM application).

However, the maintenance category of RUs was retired, with many of the remaining RUs consolidated into the management services category. A single RU, the Network Management Vector Transport (NMVT), is now being used to manage the peripheral nodes in the traditional subarea network. The NMVT was first introduced with the announcement of version 3.2 of the Network Problem Determination Application (NPDA) in 1984, one of the predecessors to NetView. It is designed to be a general purpose transport mechanism for both network and systems management data, primarily on the SSCP-to-PU sessions. With the introduction of the NMVT, IBM signaled the beginning of a more unified approach toward SNA network management.

Some of the older RUs, reclassified under management services, are still in active use. These include:

- Record Formatted Maintenance Statistics (RECFMS) - flows from PU to SSCP.
- Request Maintenance Statistics (REQMS) - flows from SSCP to PU.

In addition to retiring the many network-related flows, both the Forward and Deliver RUs were also being augmented by product specific flows. Namely, the CNM Header data area, maintained and documented by VTAM, is now used by a CNM application.

CNM Application

The CNM application on the host can gain access to the devices in its domain through the CNM interface, an API implemented by VTAM. The application must first open its Access Method Control Block (ACB). This ACB corresponds to an Application ID (APPLID), which must have been defined with CNM authorization. Once the ACB is opened, the application can then exchange requests and responses over the CNM interface with VTAM.

There can be several CNM applications active concurrently, making requests over the interface and receiving solicited replies. However, there can be only one CNM application per VTAM domain receiving a specific type of unsolicited CNM data from VTAM.

In fact, the NetView program contains several VTAM applications that utilize the CNM interface.

Managing the Logical Network

As the number of network users has grown, management of the corresponding growth of SNA sessions has become more of a concern. These sessions make up the "logical" network. A major enhancement was made in this area in 1984. IBM announced an LU-to-LU parallel session connection between VTAM V2.2 and release 2 of the Network Logical Data Manager (NLDM) product, another predecessor of NetView.

VTAM sends a session awareness (SAW) data request to NLDM whenever an SNA session is established or terminated. The VTAM APPLID ISTPDCLU within VTAM is used to connect to NLDM; this same connection exists with NetView today (APPLID DSIAMLUT). Figure 1.6, the result of a VTAM display command, shows the connection between NetView version 2.3 and VTAM.

```
   NCCF                     N E T V I E W    CNM23 OPER1     08/03/93 14:32:51
   * CNM23     D NET,E,ID=ISTPDCLU
     CNM23       IST097I  DISPLAY  ACCEPTED
   ' CNM23
   IST075I  NAME = ISTPDCLU          , TYPE = APPL
   IST486I  STATUS= ACTIV      , DESIRED STATE= ACTIV
   IST977I  MDLTAB=***NA*** ASLTAB=***NA***
   IST861I  MODETAB=***NA*** USSTAB=***NA*** LOGTAB=***NA***
   IST934I  DLOGMOD=ISTNLDM
   IST597I  CAPABILITY-PLU ENABLED  ,SLU ENABLED  ,SESSION LIMIT NONE
   IST654I  I/O TRACE = OFF, BUFFER TRACE = OFF
   IST271I  JOBNAME = VTAM33  , STEPNAME = NET
   IST171I  ACTIVE SESSIONS = 0000000002, SESSION REQUESTS = 0000000000
   IST206I  SESSIONS:
   IST634I  NAME        STATUS        SID          SEND RECV VR TP NETID
   IST635I  DSIAMLUT ACTIV-P    F21B7D141E3AAC8E 024C 0000   0  0 MACH03
   IST635I  DSIAMLUT ACTIV-P    F21B7D141E3AAC8D 0000 0000   0  0 MACH03
   IST314I  END
   --------------------------------------------------------------------------


   ???
```

Figure 1.6 Display command showing NetView's sessions with VTAM.

Note, however, that in an MVS/ESA environment VTAM passes this data (as well as trace data) to NetView through the dataspace buffers.

1.3 Announcement of NetView

The announcement of NetView in 1986 was a turning point in IBM's network management strategy. It signaled the beginning of what would be a rapid series of enhancements to both the SNA architectural framework and the features of the various networking products. Since its introduction, NetView has become one of the strategic products in the implementation of IBM's network and systems management plan.

Previous Product	NetView Component	Description
Network Communication Control Facility (NCCF)	Command Facility	Provides a base for the implementation of other functions; includes command and message capabilities.
Network Problem Determination Application (NPDA)	Hardware Monitor	Receives, filters, records, and displays data from the network dealing with problem management and resolution.
Network Logical Data Manager (NLDM)	Session Monitor	Provides a view of the logical network, which revolves around SNA sessions; includes SAW and trace data.
VTAM Node Control Application (VNCA)	Status Monitor	Accepts and displays information from several sources which describes the status of network resources.
Network Management Productivity Facility (NMPF)	Help Desk Facility	On-line guide to assist with network operations. As with other components, can be customized.

Figure 1.7 Major NetView components and their predecessors.

Collection of Existing Products

NetView is not a new product. Rather, it is a collection of previously existing network management products that were assembled and repackaged together as a single product. Refer to Figure 1.7 for a list of the major NetView components and their respective predecessors.

Since its original announcement, NetView has been improved and enhanced. New functions have been added, and it has recently assumed a greater role in the management of resources in the enterprise. The interested reader should refer to the appendix for a summary of the NetView announcement letters for the various releases of the program product.

Execution Environments

The original announcement letter provided NetView for the MVS/XA, MVS/370, and VM environments. The most current version, V2.3, executes on the MVS/XA and MVS/ESA platforms, as well as VM/ESA and VSE/ESA.

IBM has chosen to focus on improving the MVS releases, largely because of the sophistication of the operating system and its widespread use in production environments. Consequently, most of the recent enhancements are found first, and sometimes exclusively, in the MVS products.

1.4 Open Network Management

On September 18, 1986, IBM announced Open Network Management (ONM) as a part of the Open Communication Architectures initiative. ONM further improved and defined the IBM network management strategy by providing a cohesive umbrella for SNA network management. It contains a collection of protocols and products, and is at the same time a statement of direction and purpose with respect to network management. At the heart of the original ONM announcement was the ability to provide management support for a more heterogeneous network, including non-SNA equipment, thereby extending the reach of SNA network management from the central mainframe. ONM also laid the groundwork for a more flexible response to the needs of the peer-to-peer processing of the future.

Network Management Architecture

ONM provides a conceptual structure which extends the earlier CNM model. Control is maintained at one or more centrally located focal point applications. The exact specifications are detailed in the SNA Management Services architecture, described in Chapter 2. This focal point model is generally referred to as the SNA Network Management Architecture (e.g., see the original NetView announcement letter 286-205). In the Network Management Architecture, there are three defined entities. Figure 1.8 presents the basic structure as defined by ONM.

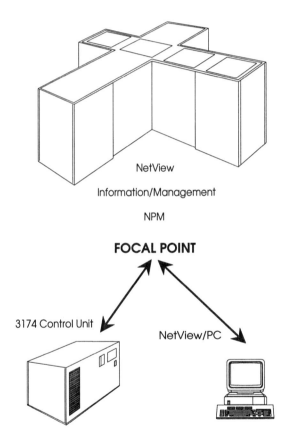

NetView

Information/Management

NPM

FOCAL POINT

3174 Control Unit

NetView/PC

Figure 1.8 Basic focal point architecture as defined by ONM, showing NetView/PC as one of the available service points.

The focal point was originally implemented as the central, controlling CNM application on the host. This has been expanded by defining the focal point as more of a logical entity, with flexibility as to its location and implementation. There can be several focal points within the same domain or network, each implementing one or more of the disciplines defined by the SNA/MS. NetView is one prominent example of a focal point, and supports operations control, network automation, response time monitoring, and problem determination.

An entry point is an SNA-addressable element, which provides support for itself and any attached devices. An example of an entry point is the IBM 3174 control unit. The entry point communicates with a designated focal point, in this case within the NetView application region through the SSCP.

The service point can be thought of as a protocol converter for network management data. That is, it supports one or more attached non-SNA devices by translating between the SNA network management requests and the local format used by the equipment being supported. With the service point, a central focal point can provide the non-SNA devices with the required network management support. Both the AIX Service Point product on the RS/6000 workstation, and NetView/PC can act as service points.

NetView/PC

NetView/PC is an example of one of the available products which act as a service point. It is customizable, providing the Application Programming Interface for Communication Services (API/CS). The product, currently distributed at the version 1 release 2 level, has been successfully integrated with dozens of non-SNA products, such as the ROLM PBX phone system.

While helping to fulfill a legitimate need, the technology used in NetView/PC and its underlying SSCP-to-PU session structure is gradually being superseded by the direct LU-to-LU type 6.2 connection described in the next chapter.

1.5 Impact of SystemView

On September 5, 1990, IBM unleashed a barrage of announcements that would align and reshape its product plans. At the center was something called SystemView, a comprehensive strategy for enterprise-wide systems management. Network management is, of course, a key element of the overall systems management picture. As a consequence, the IBM network management strategy has been strongly influenced by SystemView. Below is a discussion of the enhancements made to Open Network Management designed to accommodate SystemView. Refer to Chapter 4 for a more complete discussion of SystemView, as well its direct relation to the NetView product releases.

Open Network Management Revisited

ONM was positioned primarily as a technology that would enable the support of non-SNA devices by the SNA management applications on the mainframe. Since its announcement, the growth in non-SNA networking and network management protocols has continued to accelerate. Because of this, IBM has no longer been able to dictate to a customer base which is continually demanding more of an open, non-proprietary approach to providing network solutions. It was therefore in IBM's best interests to respond to market pressures and reach beyond its proprietary SNA. In 1990, IBM announced an expansion of the Open Network Management framework, with an emphasis on the word "open."

The revised ONM was enhanced to include support for protocols found in the model for Open Systems Interconnection (OSI) and the TCP/IP standards. At the same time, and in conjunction with SystemView, ONM would emphasize more application integration and consolidation, better automation facilities, and a more sophisticated user interface.

Open System Interconnection

In the late 1970's, the International Standards Organization (ISO) began assembling a collection protocols that today forms the basis of the model for Open Systems Interconnection (OSI). This framework represents an attempt to develop a comprehensive set of standards which better facilitates communication and interoperability between computers. IBM, together with other vendors, has been active in the design work as well as helping to influence its acceptance. This is particularly evident with respect to the OSI Network Management (OSI/NM) forum, an organization from which IBM is accepting and implementing several technologies. Some of the newer network management technologies found in NetView are based on standards drawn from the OSI framework.

The OSI model is a seven-layer structure similar to SNA. However, it is designed to support a wider variety of products and services. Perhaps because of its comprehensive and complex nature, there has been a relatively slow development and deployment of OSI-compliant products. On the positive side, OSI is assimilating many of the recent advances in operating system and programming technologies. For example, the OSI systems management specifications reply heavily upon the use of object-oriented technologies.

TCP/IP

Transmission Control Protocol / Internet Protocol (TCP/IP) is a simple, yet effective and widely used, protocol stack for routing data between nodes in a computer network; its creation was based on the early Department of Defense ARPANET project. The transport layer (i.e., TCP), roughly equivalent to the fourth layer of the OSI model, provides a connection-oriented link to other nodes in the network. It rests on top of the Internet Protocol (IP) layer, responsible for sending and receiving data in a connectionless fashion while utilizing a minimum of error detection and correction.

Network management within the TCP/IP framework is carried out through the aptly named Simple Network Management Protocol (SNMP). These basic protocol specifications have been refined in recent years based upon user requirements. The second generation, named SNMP version 2 (SNMPv2), includes several enhancements in the area of security and distributed management.

Because of its widespread usage, IBM has been forced to acknowledge and support the protocol. In fact, it is becoming more common on all of the IBM platforms, including MVS. As will be seen in a later chapter, IBM supports the management of TCP/IP devices in one of two main ways. Both currently involve an SNMP-to-SNA protocol conversion, which is carried out on the mainframe through the use of MVS TCP/IP product, or with the more remote support found in the recent NetView/6000 offering.

1.6 The Networking Blueprint

In September 1992, IBM announced a major initiative which would help clarify its networking and network management strategy. The letter, entitled "The Networking Blueprint," is an ambitious attempt by IBM to provide a framework for interoperability and network management for the many users with heterogeneous network compositions. It provides a layered model where multiple networking architectures and hardware protocols from different sources can be used in a manner that is effectively transparent to the application users.

There are four key elements to the plan, around which the development effort is focused:

- Structure for multivendor application support
- Integration of multiple networking protocols into an efficient network
- Subnetworking, which allows for the newly emerging protocols to be seamlessly absorbed and applied
- Systems and network management

In approaching this task, IBM has acknowledged and adopted several "open" standards, which have been created and advanced outside of its direct control.

With respect to systems and network management, IBM re-emphasizes its reliance on the evolving SystemView framework. Included will be the SNA/MS specifications, as well as support for TCP/IP and OSI-based networks. The Distributed Management Environment (DME) architecture will also influence IBM's direction to some extent. Although it seems unlike that IBM will rely completely upon DME, relevant sections of the technology might be extracted for use (i.e., as soon as it is completed). DME is an object-oriented, comprehensive structure for systems management under control by the Open Software Foundation (OSF).

2

SNA Management Services

The SNA Management Services (SNA/MS) architecture was released in May of 1986 along with the original NetView product announcement. Since that time, SNA/MS has evolved through several major revisions (i.e., the reference manual has been updated five times) to become one of the major implementation blueprints within IBM's overall network and systems management plan. As such, it is a strategic element in the delivery of the management and control functionality required for the enterprise networks of the 1990's.

The Management Services architecture is loosely based on elements found within the earlier CNM designs. The concepts of a central network management application and service element within the network nodes have been made more dynamic and robust. Also, the Management Services Unit, with its wide range of major vectors and subvectors, has replaced the "retired" CNM maintenance request unit flows. Although the architecture has absorbed the CNM host-based management of peripheral nodes, its main focus for the future is to provide support for the management of APPN networks.

SNA/MS includes the detailed workings which implement the Open Network Management focal point architecture described in Chapter one. SNA/MS provides for the management of peripheral nodes, as well as the APPN end nodes; the SSCP-to-SSCP control and management flows are currently not documented. The most recent update to the SNA/MS reference also includes documentation for some of the APPN network node specifications.

SNA Management Services is positioned for the future. It exploits the dynamic and flexible nature of the LU 6.2 protocols in order to provide the type of connectivity and advanced functionality required.

The formats and protocol logic for network management, as well as the role of the focal point application, have been greatly expanded.

2.1 SNA Network Management for the 1990's

The typical hierarchical subarea networks that have long dominated the data processing world are rapidly giving way to the interconnection of a multitude of smaller, more powerful alternative computing platforms. In this transition, the nature of computer networks and the requirements for their management have changed. For many of the devices that are now being installed, it is no longer appropriate to require the type of support traditionally provided by the host. Such nodes can operate independently, establishing sessions and exchanging data without the need for assistance from VTAM. In the IBM-SNA world, the workstations, midrange platforms, and personal computers communicate using LU type 6.2 protocols as supported by the APPN nodes. The development of these dynamic peer-to-peer networks creates an opportunity to apply some of the newer network management technologies and techniques. This section lists the major aspects of any IBM network and systems management solution that might be proposed for the 1990's, and specifically describes the characteristics of the SNA/MS architecture.

Support for Peer-to-Peer Networks

For many years, IBM has prepared its customer base for a transition from the traditional subarea SNA networks to Advanced Peer-to-Peer Networking (APPN). The APPN networks, as compared to subarea networks, are composed of a large number of node resources, each of which is generally more capable than their subarea counterparts (e.g., an OS/2 workstation versus a 3270 terminal). These APPN nodes can independently establish sessions and dynamically route traffic, adjusting its flow as required. In fact, many of the APPN protocols have been patented by IBM. The network management requirements for the large APPN networks are considerably more complex than those of traditional host-based networks.

While the architecture provides a high level of sophistication (e.g., directory services and route selection), IBM has been slow in delivering the actual APPN-compliant products. This delay, combined with the rapid growth of non-IBM networking standards such as TCP/IP, has spawned some debate as to the level of APPN's acceptance. In fact, a forum of vendors proposed an APPN alternative: the Advanced Peer-to-Peer Internetworking (APPI) model. Although this initiative gained widespread support and momentum, it gradually faded as IBM moved quickly to support APPN and respond to the concerns and complaints of the vendors involved.

One of the most appealing aspects of APPI was its use of TCP/IP to transport SNA data, and the fact that its design specifications were intended to be made available at little or no charge. This contrasts sharply with IBM's original intentions of charging, what would be for many vendors, a significant APPN licensing fee. Despite any perceived problems with APPN or IBM's administration of the technology, APPI was in fact, a validation of APPN concept.

A Flexible Center for Network Management

The older CNM structure allowed for a controlling application on the central host. As networks have expanded and grown, regardless of their routing protocol, there is now more of a requirement for flexibility in terms of how and where control is administered. The idea of some type of centralized management still has several advantages, including:

■ With central, standard operational policies in place, redundancies in both staff and procedures can be avoided. This reduces cost and improves efficiency.
■ Network management data, such as alert and performance information, can be collected and analyzed in a more comprehensive manner at one location.
■ The majority of application processing will still revolve around a central processor, whatever its eventual form. This is reaffirmed by such recent concepts as client-server computing.

While some form of central management is desirable, the shape and form of the focal point center should be flexible. That is, a "logical" rather than physical center can better meet today's network management needs.

IBM customers need the option of performing network management from the platform of their choice. And based on recent enhancements to the NetView product, users of the most current releases will have the option to manage both their traditional subarea as well as APPN networks from the mainframe.

Exploit LU Type 6.2 Protocols

APPC is IBM's best and brightest model for how LU-to-LU (or more generally, any-to-any) communication should be accomplished. With SNA/MS, we see a major initiative which recognizes and exploits the advantages of the LU 6.2 protocols. It represents another example of IBM's commitment to the APPC model and the fulfillment of a promise made long ago as to its eventual importance.

The earlier CNM communication relied on the SSCP-to-PU session, which has severe limitations affecting network management. First, a session with VTAM (i.e., an SSCP) is, by definition, required. The protocols used by this session have several restrictions, including the maximum RU size and the ability to have only one request (e.g., operator command) outstanding at a time. Also, the techniques used to route the incoming RUs, particularly unsolicited data, are very basic in that the RU is examined and routed by type to the appropriate network management application.

LU type 6.2, with its larger RU size, parallel session support, TPs, flexible implementation options, and availability in both subarea and APPN networks (to mention just a few advantages), provides an ideal base for the communication of network management data. It is a widely used, open, and well-documented implementation choice for the future.

Need for Advanced Functionality

As the delivery of CPU processing power has accelerated, networks and applications are becoming more complex. This creates a need for a corresponding level of sophistication in the network management capabilities. While performance is important, even this can become secondary in some cases to the required type and level of service. A common, scalable structure is needed which supports the implementation of a diversity of network and systems management disciplines across the enterprise network.

Alignment with Systems Management

It is becoming increasingly obvious that network and systems related management tasks are very similar. Many years ago, the concentration of computing power was at the central mainframe, with the main network management objective being the control of the physical resources. While this aspect of network management is still important, it is being augmented as networks grow richer in applications and function. Network management is becoming the management of distributed system resources.

2.2 Focal Point Control Structure

The focal point architecture was introduced as part of the Open Network Management (ONM) initiative, first mentioned in Chapter 1. SNA/MS precisely defines the protocol functions and data formats used to support ONM. This section discusses the focal point framework and its relation to the SNA/MS specifications.

Focal Point Architecture

The focal point concept is a continuation of the CNM philosophy and product implementations. At the same time it is flexible, so as to support the newer APPN networks. At the core of the architecture is the concept of centralization. Network and systems management tasks are consolidated at a central site. This type of centralization, particularly with respect to operations, has several advantages, as outlined in the previous section.

SNA/MS identifies several major categories of services which define the required tasks and therefore serve as a guide for implementation. These MS services are implemented through the use of a two-level command and control structure:

- Focal Point
- Entry Point

The focal point provides the highest level of control within the network. It works with the entry points in its domain to provide the specified network and systems management support.

Because of the definition and division of the MS functions, it becomes possible to allocate responsibility for their execution among multiple focal points within one network. For example, one focal point can handle alerts while another deals with managing network configuration. In addition, the focal point nodes contain one or more applications which assist in implementing the SNA/MS services.

At a secondary layer, the entry point is implemented to manage the local resources within its own node. It reports to, and relies on, one or more focal point nodes to provide assistance and control within the SNA/MS framework.

The service point, also defined by ONM, is really a special case of the entry point; it is designed to support attached non-SNA devices. Although defined by ONM, the service point has been de-emphasized within the SNA/MS specifications.

Focal Point and Entry Point Pairings

In a network situation, an entry point reports to one or more of the available focal points. A Management Services pairing is therefore established between a focal point and entry point during an architected MS capabilities exchange. This exchange is only supported in the APPN environment; the subarea SSCP-to-PU session has not been updated to use these flows.

After determining each other's characteristics, the two nodes are connected and speak the same language. There are two major types of focal points operating in the network:

- Primary
- Backup

Maintaining a record of the focal point relationships can be important for several reasons, including the ability to deal with the loss or failure of a focal point.

SSCP in the Subarea Network

In the subarea network, the System Services Control Point (SSCP) manages the resources in its domain, serving as a focal point. The VTAM product implements the SSCP and is therefore the focal point for network management in the subarea network. Some of the designated focal point applications, which rely upon the SSCP, include: NetView, Information/Management, and NetView Performance Monitor (NPM).

The physical unit acts as the entry point. A common example of an entry point is the 3174 control unit configured as a peripheral node (i.e., PU type 2.0).

APPN Network Nodes

The APPN network node acts as a focal point, while an end node is the entry point. The availability of the network node specifications, including the SNA/MS definitions, have been restricted by IBM in the past.

This is beginning to change, as IBM is responding to vendor and user complaint in an effort to popularize the APPN architecture.

A focal point and its entry points define a single APPN domain. In a larger network, it is possible to have more than one focal point. In this case, one focal point can support the other focal points in a sort of "king among kings" structure. The managed focal points form the sphere of control for the managing focal point. In this situation, a "nesting" of the control takes place.

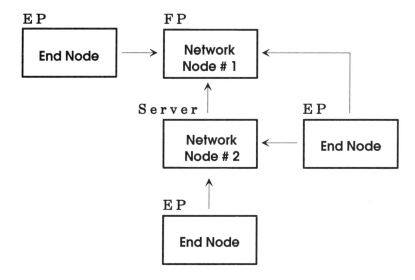

Figure 2.1 An APPN network highlighting the focal point to entry point pairings.

Figure 2.1 shows an APPN network which highlights the focal to entry point relationships. Here, network node #2 acts as an APPN server to the attached end nodes, providing intermediate routing and access to the larger APPN network. By default, network management data flows to the server over the CP-to-CP sessions, thus improving efficiency and overall performance.

By default, the server registers with the focal point at network node #1, using an LU-to-LU type 6.2 session. Node #1 can also directly connect using LU type 6.2 with end nodes that are served by other network nodes (as shown).

2.3 Functional Characteristics

SNA/MS has arranged its functionality into five major categories which are briefly described below. Support and responsibility for each of the major categories or their subclasses can be implemented by one or more focal point applications. In addition, there is a set of common services which enable the administration and delivery of these major categories.

Problem Management

The detection, definition, containment, and resolution of problems in the network is an important, original, aspect of network management. Problems can develop not only in hardware devices, but also in software, media (e.g., disk or tape), or as a result of environmental situations. Problem management defines several subcategories, or elements, including:

- Identification/Determination
- Diagnosis
- Bypass and Recovery
- Resolution
- Tracking and Control

Performance and Accounting Management

Performance is an important part of providing networking services to end users. This major category defines the processes for monitoring, measuring, reporting, and controlling the performance of the network, including aspects of the network's usage and availability. Performance management defines several elements, including:

- Response-Time Monitoring
- Availability Statistics
- Utilization Monitoring
- Component Delay
- Performance Tuning
- Tracking and Control
- Accounting

Configuration Management

Configuration management is the ability to record and track the physical and logical network resources, as well as their connectivity relationships. This includes, for example, the type, location, and users of equipment in the network. Some of this information can be collected and stored through the Vital Product Data (VPD) capability contained within NetView.

Configuration data is used to complement and augment the other SNA/MS categories of service, including:

- Problem management. When a problem occurs, the configuration information for the resources involved can assist in its resolution.
- Change management. By determining a network's current configuration, the result of a previously executed change can be analyzed. Also, the configuration management discipline can help implement change.

It can be seen from the above example how closely related the systems management categories are.

Change Management

The management of change within a network is an important aspect of SNA/MS which allows users to gain better control of their resources. Through a close relation with the configuration management major category, the additions, deletions, and modifications to system resources can be better planned and administered. The types of resources can be changed include software programs, microcode, and hardware.

Changes can be deliberate and planned, or can happen as the result of some bypass of an unexpected error condition. There are two major operations involved with change management:

- Change control and execution
- Node activation

Change management is also closely related to the operations management major category.

Operations Management

With the dispersion of information processing power, it becomes necessary to provide for a common operational framework. A basic philosophical principle used in the design of the operations management category is skills centralization: operators manage a distributed network from a central location. Network automation is also provided to help reduce the manual workload for the operations staff. Either the Common Operations Services (COS) or Operations Management function set, which together form this major discipline, can be utilized.

The COS function is implemented to manage adjacent nodes through a generic command enveloping mechanism; it allows for the support of resources not explicitly defined by the architecture. The two main subfunctions within COS include the execute command and resource management services.

The operations management function provides for the control of resources in a distributed network. To summarize, the following examples illustrate how operations management is carried out:

- Activation of resources
- Deactivation of resources
- Sending commands and receiving replies
- Updating remote clocks

The operations management discipline is, of course, an important aspect of network management and control. Through formally defined formats and protocols, this area can benefit from integration with other application technology (e.g., automation).

Focal Point and Security Services

There are two types of common services which provide for the delivery of the five major categories of Management Services function described above: focal point services and security.

A focal point supports one or more of the major categories specified within SNA/MS. There can be one or more focal points supporting a network. Because of this flexibility, the need arises to track and maintain the focal point to entry point relationships for the purpose of backup and recovery.

Also, security is a well-known need within communication networks, especially for network management. The security services allow for the protection of equipment and software resources from accidental or purposeful destruction or compromise.

2.4 Node Elements

The elements within the SNA nodes participating in the Management Services framework have their roots in the older CNM structures. The function and flexibility of the management services elements have been expanded to support the evolving network management requirements. This includes absorbing the CNM structures, as well as providing a basis for the support of large APPN networks.

Physical Unit Management Services

The PUMS is part of a peripheral node's PU, and represents a redefinition and enhancement of the earlier CNM services component. The PUMS serves as a means of providing network management support for the traditional subarea networks within the new Management Services framework.

The PUMS component communicates with other elements in the peripheral node and the controlling SSCP (via the SSCP-to-PU SNA session). It sends unsolicited management RUs, as well as responses to requests, up to the host. When a type 2.1 node is supported by the boundary function of a subarea node, it functions as if it were a type 2.0 node. In this case, the node's control point performs the PUMS function on behalf of the node.

Control Point Management Services

The newer APPN nodes, as discussed in the first chapter, have a control point. The CPMS resides within the CP and provides Management Services support for the APPN node. CPMS communicates with local elements within the node, as well as with other CPMS elements throughout the network over the CP-to-CP and LU-to-LU sessions.

The CPMS component is more complex than the PUMS. It provides the functional basis for distributing MS support within the APPN network.

Local Management Services

The Local Management Services (LMS) components reside within the peripheral and APPN nodes. The LMS elements represent a distribution of MS functionality within the node to support the overall SNA/MS structure.

There are several derivatives of the LMS. Each communicates with the node's PUMS or CPMS component to provide access to the data as specified by the architecture. The LMS elements include:

- Physical Resources Manager LMS - provides unsolicited notification of problems with the node's physical resources.
- Logical Unit LMS - sends unsolicited problem notifications and supports response time measurement (peripheral nodes).
- Program Supervisor LMS - alters software and microcode components within the node as requested.

Each LMS elements acts as a type of micro agent, embedded within the node to support the SNA/MS framework.

Implementing Function Sets

A network is composed of a collection of hardware and software resources with a wide range of capabilities and network management requirements. Each device participates to some extent in helping to manage the network as a whole. The implementation of one or more SNA/MS function sets within each node enables their participation in the MS framework.

A function set is a collection of services and features which performs a specific MS function for the node. Each function set usually contains a large and varied number of specifications, which would be difficult to implement in all situations. Therefore, every function set has a single base subset which must be included by developers when implementing that function set. This ensures that a common level of communication is possible between like nodes. In addition, one or more optional subsets within a given function set are usually available for selection.

There are two major categories of function sets provided and documented by IBM: those which are general in nature and commonly used in different types of nodes (including focal points), and the function sets designed for entry points. Refer to Figure 2.2 for a list of the general function sets available with the SNA/MS architecture.

Entry point function sets follow a common naming standard. In this case, each begins with "EP_", and has a unique suffix. See Figure 2.3 for a list of function sets specifically designed for entry point implementation.

Function Set	Description
Multiple Domain Support	MULTIPLE_DOMAIN_SUPPORT provides the basic transport mechanism for APPN nodes over CP-to-CP and LU-to-LU sessions.
Management Services Capabilities	MS_CAPS is a common enabling function set which tracks and maintains the focal point to entry point relationships for backup and recovery.
File Services	FILE_SERVICES_SUPPORT supports the transfer of bulk MS data using SNA/DS; SNA/FS agent objects and files are also utilized.
Basic Peripheral Node Support	SEND_DATA_SSCP_PU is required by peripheral nodes to forward information (e.g., alerts) to the SSCP on the central host.
Advanced Peripheral Node Support	RECEIVE_REQUEST_SSCP_PU is a more advanced set of functions implemented to support requests from the SSCP.

Figure 2.2 General function sets defined by the SNA/MS architecture.

The decision over which function sets and subsets to implement is determined by the role of the node in the network and also by certain elective choices available in each case. The architecture identifies each participating SNA node by category. For each type of node (e.g., peripheral node), specific base subsets must be included, along with one or more optional subsets.

2.5 Function Sets Enabling MS Infrastructure

Many of the SNA/MS function sets implement services which fall into one of the major categories of function as described above in section three. However, some function sets are more general in that they are required to establish an infrastructure enabling the basic MS operation. This section presents the most common function sets in this latter category.

Function Set	Description
Alerts	EP_ALERT sends problem and resolution notifications to the node's focal point.
Response Time Measurement	EP_RTM provides response time measurement capability for the LUs within a node.
Query Product ID	EP_QPI allows a node to be physically identified, as well as dependent resources.
Change Management	EP_CHANGE_MGMT implements functionality to support the control of changes in the network.
Common Operations Services	EP_COMMON_OPERATIONS_SERVICES supports the execution of node-specific commands.
Operations Management	EP_OPERATIONS_MGMT enables network operators to control remote nodes from a central site.

Figure 2.3 Function sets defined by the SNA/MS architecture which are specific to entry points.

A peripheral node is required to provide an implementation of the SEND_DATA_SSCP_PU function set, while an APPN end node must provide support for MDS and MS_CAPS. Both node types must include the EP_ALERT function set. These function sets establish a basic level of capability and service throughout the network. The recent update to the SNA/MS reference includes APPN network node specifications for the MDS and MS_CAPS function sets.

Multiple Domain Support

MDS is a key Management Services function set which, in its basic form, supports the transport of non-bulk MS data between peer APPN nodes. The data is transferred over a CP-to-CP and/or the LU-to-LU session utilizing LU type 6.2 protocols. The CPMS component of the node's control point interfaces with an MDS Router, which is responsible for executing the LU 6.2 services TPs as required.

The High Performance optional subset provides an extension to the basic MDS capabilities. It can be used to enhance the performance of node-to-node communication by, among other things, allowing for persistent conversations over dedicated sessions and eliminating the need for a confirmation response for every request.

Management Services Capabilities

The MS capabilities (MS_CAPS) function set allows nodes to establish focal point to entry point relationships, which are then tracked and recorded. This function becomes important in the large and complex APPN networks, especially when securing backup and recovery focal points. It helps to enable a high degree of flexibility as to the location of network control.

Supporting Traditional Peripheral Nodes

The support provided with the earlier CNM protocols has been absorbed into SNA/MS. Keeping with the architectural model, there are two functions sets which enable the SSCP-to-PU operability. The base subset SEND_DATA_SSCP_PU is required in peripheral nodes; it provides the basic ability to send information to the host SSCP. The RECEIVE_REQUEST_SSCP_PU function set is optional and provides a more advanced capability in responding to requests from the host. Also, the EP_QPI set allows the host to determine the physical characteristics of a node, including any attached, dependent resources.

Alert Processing

EP_ALERT is the base function set required for sending problem notifications (i.e., alerts) and resolutions to a focal point. The exact form of the implementation depends on the node. This function set is required for both peripheral and APPN nodes.

2.6 Data Transport

Within an SNA node, Management Services data flows between the node's components through protocol boundaries. In particular, there are seventeen such interfaces defined by the SNA/MS architecture for use between function sets. For example when the EP_ALERT function within a peripheral node must forward an unsolicited alert to the focal point at the host, it must interact with the SEND_DATA_SSCP_PU function set. In the process, the address of an NMVT buffer must be provided by EP_ALERT.

Externally, data is exchanged between the nodes over SNA sessions. There are three types of node-to-node connections used for exchanging data as outlined by the SNA/MS architecture; Figure 2.4 provides a summary of these sessions.

Management Services Unit

The Management Services Unit (MSU) is a very precisely formatted data structure used to communicate SNA/MS information. Its exact form depends upon the particular usage and the nodes involved in the exchange. There are three MSUs defined by the SNA/MS architecture:

- Network Management Vector Transport (NVMT). The NMVT is used primarily over the SSCP-to-PU session to support the attached peripheral nodes. It can also be passed to NetView directly from within the same host using the Program-to-Program Interface (see Chapter 7).
- Control Point MSU (CP-MSU). The CP-MSU is an LU type 6.2 GDS variable used to envelope alerts and other major vectors. It can be sent over the CP-to-CP or LU-to-LU session.

■ Multiple Domain Support Message Unit (MDS-MU).
Like the CP-MSU, the MDS-MU is a GDS variable. It
is the main vehicle for communicating SNA/MS
between APPN nodes, as outlined by the MDS function set.

Each MSU is composed of control and major vectors, as well as
additional GDS variables in some cases. The major vectors are constructed using one or more subvectors which can be further broken down
into individual fields. All of these data formats are defined and documented by IBM.

SNA Session	Description
SSCP-to-PU	The SNA/MS peripheral node support utilizes the SSCP-PU session, and transports MS data using the NMVT request unit.
CP-to-CP	MS data can be sent over the shared APPN CP-to-CP sessions, thus reducing the number of dedicated LU type 6.2 sessions required by instances of MDS.
LU-to-LU	LU type 6.2 sessions are used by MDS to send MS data and also by the SNA/DS service.

Figure 2.4   SNA sessions used to transport Management Services encodings.

Non-Bulk versus Bulk Data Transfer

The architecture differentiates between two major types of Management
Services data: non-bulk and bulk data. Non-bulk data transferred
through the network is characterized by its relatively small size and the
more immediate operational importance. This type of information is
carried by the NMVT, and the MDS-MU within an APPN network.

Bulk MS data, on the other hand, consists of larger messages, or entire files, which have less of an immediate impact on system operations. Bulk data is transferred over LU type 6.2 sessions using the SNA/DS protocols; MDS is not required. An example of bulk data transfer can be found in the Change Management major discipline, described above.

Managing the Subarea Network

An important aspect of SNA/MS is its support of the large number of installed subarea networks. Here, the MS data is exchanged over the SSCP-to-PU session using the NMVT. On the host, the data flows through VTAM to the designated CNM application. Although the CNM interface is still used, the maintenance category of RUs has been retired.

The use of the management service NMVT has helped to extend the capabilities of the SSCP-to-PU session and overcome some of its limitations. For example, multiple NMVTs can be grouped together through a correlation field, but sent separately over the session.

Managing the APPN Network

The MDS function set provides the basis for exchanging data with brief conversation over shared sessions between APPN nodes. The MDS function set includes the MDS router, a type of transaction processing engine. A set of MS application programs within the node can interface with the MDS router, which then executes the actual APPC transaction programs.

APPN nodes exchange the MDS-MU data structure over the LU-to-LU sessions. CP-to-CP sessions are also utilized and, in this case, a performance improvement can be realized. Since these sessions are also needed in the normal operation of the APPN network, a large number of LU-to-LU sessions can be eliminated by sharing the CP-to-CP sessions for the purpose of network management.

APPN Management from the Subarea Network

In addition to the NMVT, the Management Services (MS) transport, featuring an implementation of the MDS function set, has been included with NetView version 2.2 (and above). This can be used to bypass the traditional SSCP-to-PU connection altogether, thus allowing NetView to have a wider access to a variety of network management data through a more direct LU type 6.2 connection.

In addition to connecting to other host nodes, the MS transport can be used to manage the APPN networks. In this case, NetView can directly connect to any of the following nodes:

- APPN end node.
- APPN network node server.
- APPN focal point.

This technology clearly positions NetView to control both the older subarea resources, as well as the newer APPN nodes. While the MS transport enables this APPN management, a future release of NetView must be designed to provide its actual implementation.

3

Alert Major Vector

The SNA Management Services architecture precisely defines the formats used for the communication of network management information. These data structures are exchanged within the Open Network Management framework.

The management data is arranged into major vectors, each of which is designed for a specific purpose. This chapter describes the alert major vector, an important Management Services encoding used to notify a central location of a specific problem in the network.

An alert is always sent in an unsolicited fashion to a focal point which is providing problem management support. It is used to report a problem, and contains additional information which identifies the location of the error as well as indications as to its probable cause.

In older releases of VTAM and the network management products, alert information was conveyed in a non-generic manner. The data structure utilized hardcoded references to display panels at the central host; this approach had several inherent restrictions regarding the alert's display and processing. The method of sending non-generic data has been improved upon and superseded with the definition of a generic alert in which architectural defined code points are used. This chapter describes the techniques for creating an alert and sending it to the central host.

3.1 Alert Structure

The alert major vector follows the encoding scheme used for all other SNA/MS major vectors, as described in the previous chapter. Using this common format facilitates a much wider usage and provides more options for the alert's transfer, processing, and display.

Basic Format

The major vector begins with a two-byte length field, specifying the length of the entire data structure, including the length field itself. Immediately following the length field is a two-byte key, which uniquely identifies the major vector. In the case of an alert, the key contains the value of hex 0000 (X'0000').

The body of a major vector is composed of several subvector structures, again defined by the MS architecture. Figure 3.1 illustrates the format of a major vector with multiple subvectors. Most subvectors use a fixed or variable format. With the fixed format, the entire subvector has been defined together as one entity. The variable format subvector, on the other hand, uses one or more subfields. This method allows a greater degree of flexibility, where subfields can be added or removed without affecting other aspects of the subvector.

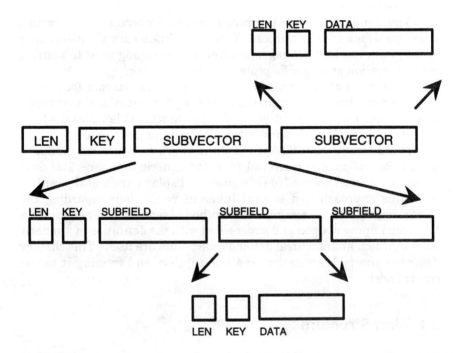

Figure 3.1 Example of an MS major vector showing the two main types of subvectors.

Both the subvector and subfield begin with a length, followed by a key. Unlike the major vector, however, these values are each only one byte long. In theory, this imposes a limit on a single subvector or subfield such that neither can exceed 255 bytes (including the length and key fields).

The subvectors within a major vector, and the subfields within a subvector, can usually be arranged in any order. This is a result of the common length-key header used, which allows for easy identification and separation. There are a few exceptions to this arrangement, which are noted later in the chapter.

Subvectors

The MS subvectors are used to convey information which describes the alert, the sender's characteristics, the most probable cause of the problem, as well as suggestions for a resolution. The subvectors available for use with the alert major vector fall into one of two major categories:

- Common subvectors, which can be used in any of the MS major vectors.
- Alert-specific subvectors, which have been created specifically for the alert major vector.

Common Subfields

Just as there is a set of subvectors shared among the MS major vectors, there is also a group of subfields which can be used by several of the alert-specific subvectors. These subfields are shown in Figure 3.2.

3.2 Sending the Alert

Once an alert has been constructed, it must be sent to the focal point which is providing support for problem management, as specified according to the SNA/MS architecture. An alert major vector is always packaged within an envelope for transmission to the focal point. The exact format used depends on the sender's position in the network.

Within the SNA/MS structure, there are three main methods for sending an alert to the central host for processing by NetView. Each case is described below. There are slight differences in the exact subvectors contained with the alert major vector, based on the envelope utilized. Where appropriate, these differences are noted throughout the chapter.

KEY (hexadecimal)	Subvector Name
81	Recommended Actions
82	Detailed Data
83	Product Set ID Index
84	Resource List Index
85	Detailed Data Extended

Figure 3.2 Subfields that are shared by the subvectors used with the alert major vector.

Peripheral Node Support

A peripheral node within the traditional SNA subarea network is supported by VTAM on the host. For example, the 3174 control unit operates as a type 2.0 node and communicates with VTAM over the architectural defined SSCP-to-PU session. In this case, an alert is packaged within the NMVT request unit. Figure 3.3 shows the NMVT data format, including an alert major vector.

The NMVT is a general transport envelope, 8 bytes in length. The first three bytes identify the RU. The procedure related identifier (PRID), contained in the lower 12 bits of the 2-byte field, is used by VTAM when a solicited request must be correlated with the expected reply. In the case of an unsolicited alert, this value is not used and contains zero.

The flag byte consists of several indicators, such as chaining information when multiple NMVTs are sent by the peripheral node all with the same PRID. There is also a flag signaling whether the SNA Address List subvector is included with the data. Following this fixed header, there can be one or more major vectors, such as the alert shown.

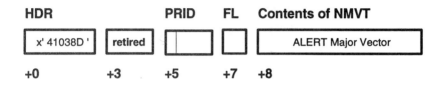

Figure 3.3 An example of the Network Management Vector Transport (NMVT) request unit.

APPN Network

As discussed in Chapter two, the Management Services data is formatted differently for the APPN network. Dedicated LU-to-LU sessions can be used, as well as the shared CP-to-CP sessions. In an APPN network, the alert major vector is packaged and transmitted within the CP-MSU, which is in turn contained within the MDS-MU.

As of version 2.2, NetView includes an implementation of the MDS function set as designed for use in the APPN networks. The MS transport, as it is referred to, allows NetView to establish a direct LU-to-LU connection with other nodes in the network. This session, based on LU type 6.2 protocols, positions NetView to bypass the restrictive SSCP-to-PU session and provide better management of the distributed peer-to-peer nodes.

NetView includes a set of MS transport applications, one of which provides support for problem management focal point services. When a device or platform in the network connects to the host over the MS transport, it can send alerts directly to NetView for processing. The CP-MSU, packaged in a MDS-MU, is accepted by the hardware monitor and processed in the same way as any of the other alerts that are received.

NetView PPI

Another technique that can be used to send an alert to NetView is through the program-to-program interface (PPI). The NetView PPI was introduced with version 1.3, and provides a general method for any two programs on the same MVS host to communicate. The data is exchanged in a store-and-forward fashion through the NetView subsystem (SSI) address space.

Alert processing is a special case of PPI usage. The alert receiver task within NetView, once activated, waits on its PPI queue for data to arrive. Each data buffer is an alert wrapped in the NMVT and can be sent by any of the programs on the same MVS machine; several IBM products have been enhanced to use this facility. For example, the NetView Performance Monitor (NPM) product sends alerts to NetView over the PPI when performance thresholds have been exceeded, indicating a problem.

3.3 Code Points

As part of the architecturally defined framework for conveying problem information, the generic alert makes use of fields called code points. A code point is a value used to convey information, without text, in a language independent manner. It serves as an index into a table or module. When a search is done with the code point, the result is an actual textual description or message.

Using code points in this manner establishes a consistency for communicating specific information, but allows flexibility in terms of its actual use and display. For example, the code points are pre-defined and fixed by IBM, but the corresponding text stored at the central problem management location (i.e., NetView) can be modified as required. This might need to be done across different countries in order to maintain language compatibility.

Code points are used by several of the alert subvectors and subfields, most notably those which describe the actual problem and attempt to identify its cause and possible resolution.

Format

The most common code points used by NetView are two bytes in length, and commonly depicted as four hexadecimal digits. They are divided into groups, first according to the high-order digit, then further based on the full high-order byte. Figure 3.4 lists the major categories for the code points in the alert descriptor field. Figure 3.5 shows a further resolution under the HARDWARE category.

Code Point Categories (hexadecimal)	Description
1xxx	HARDWARE
2xxx	SOFTWARE
3xxx	COMMUNICATIONS
4xxx	PERFORMANCE
5xxx	CONGESTION
6xxx	MICROCODE
7xxx	OPERATOR
8xxx	SPECIFICATION
9xxx	INTERVENTION REQUIRED
Axxx	*** RETIRED ***
Bxxx	NOTIFICATION
Cxxx	SECURITY
Exxx	RESERVED
Fxxx	UNDETERMINED

Figure 3.4 Arrangement of the alert description code points into categories.

Code Point Sub-groupings (hexadecimal)	Description
10xx	EQUIPMENT MALFUNCTION
11xx	INPUT DEVICE ERROR
12xx	OUTPUT DEVICE ERROR
13xx	INPUT/OUTPUT DEVICE ERROR
14xx	LOSS OF ELECTRICAL POWER
15xx	LOSS OF EQUIPMENT COOLING OR HEATING
16xx	SUBSYSTEM FAILURE

Figure 3.5 Sub-groupings of the alert description code points within the HARD-WARE category.

Accepting and Displaying

There are two major ways that a code point can be interpreted and displayed. Consider the example of a node sending the code point X'1201' to describe a printer malfunction. The major category can be displayed, as selected from Figure 3.4, and in this case would be HARDWARE. Or, the focal point can instead attempt to locate the exact code point and its pre-defined text. If this is found, the message displayed as suggested by the architecture would be:

PRINTER ERROR

However, perhaps this is a code point that is missing or has not yet been included at the host. In this case, the sub-category is used by default. This is derived from the high-order byte, and would be:

OUTPUT DEVICE ERROR

This method for displaying code points provides flexibility and support as new IDs are added. It is worth noting that IBM accepts requests for new code points from its customers, based on a demonstrated usefulness. Also, the range X'E000' through X'EFFF' is reserved for customer and vendor applications, and will not be used by IBM.

3.4 Problem Description

An alert is sent in an unsolicited manner to its problem management focal point (i.e., NetView). The most important information conveyed is the exact nature of the problem. The Generic Alert Data subvector contains this information; it is used in both the NMVT and the CP-MSU data structures.

Generic Alert Data Subvector

Figure 3.6 contains a description of the Generic Alert Data subvector. The subvector is always 11 bytes long, with the first two bytes fixed as shown. The flag bytes carry information such as whether:

- An operator directly initiated the alert.
- The alert had been delayed or held, and therefore was not immediately sent.
- The alert was constructed from an SNMP trap.
- The problem resulted in a permanent loss of the resource, as well as other indications of severity.

The Alert Description Code contains the code point which identifies the problem. Finally, the last 4 bytes include the Alert ID Number, which is designed to be a unique for each alert. There is a two-step procedure (documented in the SNA Formats manual) used to create this field which is based on the contents of the entire major vector as well as the application of a CRC algorithm.

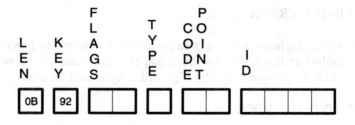

Figure 3.6 An illustration of the Generic Alert Data subvector.

3.5 Use of MS Common Subvectors

The alert major vector uses several of the common subvectors provided with the Management Services architecture. They describe the failing node, its location, as well as the time of the error.

Resource Characteristics

The resource which is sending the alert is described in terms of the hardware and software elements of which it is composed. There are two subvectors that are used together to communicate this information in both the NMVT and the CP-MSU:

- Product Set ID (PSID) subvector
- Product Identifier subvector

The PSID completely describes a single node. It consists of one or more of the Product Identifier subvectors. As its name implies, each Product Identifier subvector is used to identify a single hardware or software product that is part of the node. This subvector is, in turn, composed of one or more subfields. Each of these subfield describes a particular aspect of the product. Figure 3.7 lists the subfields which can be contained in the Product Identifier subvector.

Subfield Key (hexadecimal)	Description
00	Hardware Product Identifier
01	Emulated Product Identifier
02	Software Product Serviceable Component Identifer
04	Software Product Common Level
06	Software Product Common Name
07	Software Product Customization Identifer
08	Software Product Program Number
09	Software Product Customization Date and Time
0B	Microcode EC Level
0E	Hardware Product Common Name
0F	Vendor Identification

Figure 3.7 Subfields that can be included within the Product Identification subvector.

There are two types of PSID subvectors that might be included in the same alert major vector. These include:

■ Alert Sending PSID - identifies the PU sending the alert.
■ Indicated Resource PSID - describes the failing node for which the alert has been created.

If the node sending the alert is the same node which is experiencing the problem, only one PSID is used. The single PSID identifies the sender and the indicated resource. However, there are times when a failing node cannot send an alert on its own, perhaps because it has become disabled. When this happens, a supporting node will send the alert on behalf of the indicated resource. In this case, two PSID subvectors are included in the major vector. The Alert Sending PSID is always first, and describes the alert sender. Immediately following the first PSID is the Indicated Resource PSID subvector. This second PSID identifies the affected resource.

Node Location

An important aspect of responding to alert conditions in the network is understanding the location of each failing node. At the same time, however, identifying a node's location is becoming more difficult as the complexity of networks continues to increase.

There are two subvectors used with the Generic Alert Data subvector to communicate location information. These subvectors describe location in terms of the position of the alert sender and the indicated resource, with respect to the closest SNA control point. Through an analysis of this information, the focal point application can properly determine and display the problem location. The subvectors include:

■ SNA Address List (SAL) subvector
■ Hierarchy-Resource List (HRL) subvector

The SNA Address List subvector is only used with the NMVT envelope; it represents a request to VTAM for a translation from the local address (i.e., boundary function) of the indicated resource to its full SNA address equivalent.

If the alert sender and indicated resource are the same, there is no need for this translation or subvector, because VTAM is already in session with the sending PU. The SNA Address List subvector is only needed when the alert sender and failing resource are different. For example, the alert might be for an LU that the sending PU supports. In this case, the local address would need to be translated.

The Hierarchy-Resource List subvector is a newer and more general approach to conveying location information. Where the SAL represents a request to VTAM for the addressing information, the HRL carries the complete domain hierarchy for the affected resource.

The Hierarchy-Resource List is always used when the alert is packaged within a CP-MSU. With the NMVT, however, it is an optional subvector used when the indicated resource cannot be mapped by VTAM. This can occur, for example, in the case of a down-stream or independent logical unit.

Time of the Problem

The time of the alert is communicated with one of two subvectors:

- Date-Time subvector
- Relative Time subvector

As its name implies, the Date-Time subvector contains the date and time of the failure in binary format. An optional subfield can be used to indicate the difference between the local (e.g., sender's) time and Greenwich Meantime (GMT).

The Relative Time subvector does not specify an exact time. Rather, it indicates when the alert was constructed relative to other records sent by the same node with a time stamp "delta." This subvector is more difficult to use since synchronization of timing becomes an issue.

Because the Date-Time subvector is more direct, it is used where possible by the alert sender instead of the Relative Time subvector.

3.6 Resolution Assistance

There are several subvectors used to assist the problem management focal point in resolving the problem. Figure 3.8 contains a list of these subvectors.

Probable Causes

The Probable Causes subvector is examined first by the host-based focal point application. It is used to isolate the problem to a specific system or component.

Subvector Key (hexadecimal)	Description
93	Probable Causes
94	User Causes
95	Install Causes
96	Failure Causes
97	Cause Undetermined

Figure 3.8 A list of subvectors used in the alert major vector to assist with a problem's resolution.

Multiple code points can be included, beginning with the most relevant in terms of significance. That is, the most probable cause is included first, followed by the second most probable, etc.

Further Classification

Where the Probable Causes code points identified the failing component, the remaining subvectors are used to further identify the exact cause of the error. Each can provide more detail.

The following information is used for these subvectors:

■ User Causes. This is something usually corrected easily, and is presented first. It might include, for example, a shortage of paper in a printer.

- Install Causes. Errors in the configuration and installation of equipment requires further attention.
- Failure Causes. Finally, actual hardware and software failures, which are generally not expected and at the same time not necessarily easy to correct, are conveyed.

The above three subvectors each contain one Specific Causes and one Recommended Actions subfield. There can be multiple code points within each of the subfields.

3.7 Additional Alert Information

The previous sections described and explained the most important structures carried within the alert major vector. There are several other subvectors available which are either optional or must be included under certain circumstances. Figure 3.9 contains a list of these additional subvectors which further augment the alert data.

Text Messages

The Text Message subvector is used to send a simple EBCDIC-coded message; subfields are not used.

The Self-Defining Text Message provides more flexibility in how the same sort of message might be sent. This second subvector uses the following subfields, several of which use a code point style of communication:

- Coded Character Set ID. This field identifies the character coding used for the message.
- National Language ID. The language of the text message is declared.
- Sender ID. This field defines in a general way the nature of the sender (e.g., terminal user).
- Text Message. The actual text message is contained within this subfield.

Event Correlation

Each of the correlation subvectors uses one or more tokens to communicate the information. The MSU Correlation format is used by the alert receiver to correlate MSUs from different senders to the same condition.

Subvector Key (hexadecimal)	Description
00	Text Message
31	Self-Defining Text Message
47	MSU Correlation
48	Supporting Data Correlation
4A	Incidence Identification
51	LAN Link Connection Subsystem Data
52	Link Connection Subsystem (LCS) Configuration Data
8C	Link Station Data

Figure 3.9 The optional or conditionally present subvectors available for use with the alert vector.

The Supporting Data Correlation subvector helps the receiver extract additional information from the alert for display and processing. Finally, the Incident Identification data structure can be used to relate multiple major vectors to a single alert condition.

Hardware Configuration

The LAN Link Connection and the Link Connection Subsystem Configuration Data subvectors contain LAN topology and link configuration data.

The SDLC Link Station Data format is used to report problems with the operation of SDLC link devices. When a link error occurs, this subvector contains the SDLC-specific information that can be used in solving the problem.

4

SystemView

SystemView is an evolving collection of definitions, interfaces, formats, and protocols which forms the basis for a unified approach to the development of enterprise-wide systems management applications. It employs IBM, international, and de facto standards working together to enable a broad application to today's heterogeneous, multivendor networks. The strategy was first announced by IBM in September of 1990 and has been updated and enhanced several times since then, each time adding more clarity, options, and compliant products and services.

The SystemView initiative is important with regard to the NetView product for several reasons. First, much of what constitutes systems management is also found, at least to some extent, within the network management specifications. For example, one can see a clear overlap between the SystemView application disciplines and the major categories of functionality as described within the SNA/MS specifications. Also, at an implementation level, systems management and network management intersect with NetView. That is, the NetView product supports both network management and systems management as specified by SystemView. NetView is the SystemView enterprise network management and automation platform for the System/390 and System/370 environments. The product has been further strengthened by recent improvements in its automation, integration, and user interface.

This chapter provides an introduction to SystemView with a focus on the implications for the NetView product and network management in general.

4.1 Structural Framework

Over the past 10 years, the number and variety of computing and networking solutions has grown rapidly. Where the IBM mainframe was once the only practical choice, the business community has seen the development and availability of several alternatives within the midrange, workstation, and PC arenas. As organizations struggle to absorb and deploy this increased processing power and functionality, these information system resources have become an even more important aspect in their daily business operations.

This situation, characterized by diversity and distribution, creates a major challenge for customers and vendors in several areas. Most notably, the delivery of operational control and systems management functionality has become more important and, at the same time, more complex.

SystemView provides the IBM customer base with a framework for administering their enterprise information systems. The strategy consists of a structure as well as a list of conforming products, and stresses:

- Integration of systems management applications
- Automation of systems management tasks
- Creation of an open structure
- Comprehensive coverage, with respect to platforms and functionality

An SAA Implementation

Systems Application Architecture (SAA) was announced by IBM in March, 1987. It provides the basis for consistent application development across IBM's multiple computing environments. Although the objective of application portability was originally stressed by IBM, SAA also enables the cultivation of a common development skill set and alignment of the various IBM product plans. The major concerns of application developers addressed by SAA are presented in Figure 4.1.

SystemView follows the guidelines specified by SAA, and in this sense can be considered to be an implementation of SAA. At the same time, SystemView and SAA are related at a more fundamental level and consequently influence each other's development. One example of this is IBM's recent commitment to the concept of client-server computing; the SAA framework has been enhanced to support this model. In turn, SystemView now places an emphasis on providing support for the management of distributed resources operating within a client-server computing environment.

It is also important to note, however, that although SAA is a fundamental aspect of IBM's systems management strategy, it is only a part of the overall SystemView framework. The architects of SystemView have had to take into consideration a wider range of technologies in order for it to be of practical value to many corporations today.

Aspect of SAA	Description
Common User Access (CUA)	Defines standards for the construction of user interfaces. CUA 91 replaced CUA 89 with a strong object orientation.
Common Programming Interface (CPI)	Includes a set of programming services which can be accessed from one of several supported languages.
Common Communication Support (CCS)	Attempts to provide consistency for data exchange by identifying which protocols and standards can be used.
Common Applications	This is the result of adhering to the defined set of cross-platform application development standards.

Figure 4.1 Elements of IBM's Systems Application Architecture (SAA).

Functional Disciplines

The SystemView functionality is arranged into three major elements called dimensions. These include:

- End-use dimension. This utilizes the advanced capabilities found at the workstation level, within the SAA/CUA guidelines, to provide a consistent and expandable user interface.
- Application dimension. This dimension is divided into six separate disciplines and identifies the functions to be performed by the SystemView-compliant applications.

■ Data dimension. Through a set of data definitions and structures, the systems management information can be commonly stored and accessed by the applications.

IBM's stated goal is to provide SystemView coverage across all of the SAA platforms, VSE, AIX, as well as other IBM and non-IBM environments. A whole range of environments, from standalone LANs to enterprise-wide networks have been included. The platforms which were initially emphasized include: MVS/ESA, VM/ESA, AS/400, and OS/2. The AIX environment had been included through what IBM described as interoperability with the SystemView applications, primarily with TCP/IP.

However, IBM recently elevated the AIX operating system running on the RS/6000 platform to the list of SystemView management environments. This means that AIX will not only participate in SystemView, it will play an important role in providing management and control features. The use of the AIX environment in this context is a response to user demands for management support of the growing number of non-SNA local networks. The NetView/6000 product has been positioned, within the SystemView framework, to provide a functional equivalent to NetView on the host. However, there are a large number of practical issues that must be addressed before NetView/6000 would be able to completely replace the NetView product on MVS.

Definition of Resources

To be effective, SystemView has been designed to support a complete spectrum of the systems management requirements. This includes the day-to-day operational aspects associated with managing the resources, as well as the higher-level, more strategic, long-term elements of systems management. As such, SystemView is targeted to provide for operating, as well as planning and coordinating, the enterprise-wide information systems.

Another consideration is the nature and definition of the resources to be included for control and management. SystemView identifies five major concentration groups, which are listed in Figure 4.2. Each functional group is broadly considered to be a resource, and spans the six disciplines within the application dimension.

A particular emphasis has been placed on business administration. A group of applications are included to support enterprise-wide business planning, administrative support, and process management, which are stated goals for the overall SystemView framework.

Resource Focus	Description
Host	Includes the role definitions for the platforms involved, including MVS, VM, AS/400, OS/2, and AIX (RS/6000).
Business Administration	Emphasis is placed on the practices and procedures required to operate a business.
Network	The communication and management protocols which support the underlying structure are included.
Storage	The administration, control, and access to storage at several levels of the enterprise are defined.
Database	Provides a consistent user interface and methods for integrating the databases and support tools.

Figure 4.2 Major resource areas identified by SystemView.

Emphasis on International Standards

Support is provided for three major networking architectures within the SystemView framework for communicating management information: SNA, TCP/IP, and OSI. In defining the three dimensions of SystemView, IBM has favored OSI and drawn heavily from its systems management specifications. The OSI network and systems management protocol architecture represents an open, well-defined, and functionally advanced structure. It provides IBM with the solid technological foundation necessary for future development.

The OSI definitions have a strong object orientation. While the SNA/MS architecture has been enhanced and matured, it is less sophisticated and more of a proprietary choice as compared to OSI. And although the SNMP protocols included with TCP/IP are widely utilized, they are even more basic in many respects when compared to SNA and OSI.

One of the major aspects of SystemView which has been extracted from OSI is the concept of a managing system (i.e., manager) and a managed system (i.e., agent). The systems management tasks in the application dimension are arranged according to this model; a platform can be designated to participate as either a manager or an agent. IBM has extended this manager-agent structure to enable communication among the resource managers.

The SystemView applications utilize standards such as:

- Common Management Information Services (CMIS); ISO 9595
- Common Management Information Protocol (CMIP); ISO 9596

Also, the SystemView data model will use the OSI "Guideline for the Definition of Managed Objects" (GDMO - ISO 10165-4), with design work also drawn from:

- OSI Management Information Model; ISO/IEC 10165-1 (X.720).
- OSI Definition of Management Information; ISO/IEC 10165-2 (X.721)
- OSI/Network Management Forum
- The Directory - Overview of Concepts, Model, and Services; ISO/IEC 9594-1 (X.500)

The above listed standards include the ISO document number, as well as the CCITT designation, of the form "X.7nn" (X 700 series).

Also, SystemView embraces the X/Open Management Protocol (XMP), as adopted by OSF for its Distributed Management Environment (DME) standard.

4.2 Delivery of SystemView Products

As with other large-scale, visionary initiatives, there has been a healthy degree of skepticism surrounding SystemView. Customers tend to be leery, and seek the actual products as well as a demonstration of their applicability and usefulness.

IBM has responded in several ways to enable the delivery of the SystemView applications and services. The extreme size and scope of this task has necessitated a plan for gradual implementation and conformance, as well as support by several outside vendors.

Levels of Product Conformance

Due to the wide variety of applications and requirements, it becomes obvious that a migration must in many cases take place. At the same time, customers and vendors need a set of specifications to help guide the development of SystemView products. Therefore, IBM has introduced a structure which identifies a graduated conformance to SystemView integration. While this applies to each product as a whole, the end use aspect has been emphasized in describing the conformance.

There are currently two levels of SystemView conformance defined. They share common attributes - both are required to:

■ Use a programmable workstation running OS/2
■ Conform to the CUA aspect of SAA
■ Use the Presentation Manager, GraphicsView/2, or the EASEL product
■ Create and display icons following IBM standards

A level 1 product must conform to CUA 89 or higher. In addition to OS/2, IBM has recently included the OSF/Motif interface within the AIX RS/6000 environment to its list of level 1 options.

The level 2 product has additional restrictions and options:

■ It must follow the CUA 91 guidelines and use the OS/2 V2.0 workplace shell.
■ In addition to the above named presentation vehicles used under OS/2, the ScreenView or the Graphics Interface Kit/2 display facilities can also be selected.
■ If automation is utilized on the System/370 or System/390 hosts, NetView must be used.

Through the use of a conformance definition, IBM will be able to guide internal and external product development.

Alliance with Software Vendors

To help make SystemView a reality, IBM has enlisted the involvement and support of several prominent independent software vendors. This recognizes not only the size of the effort, but also IBM's diminished clout in mandating standards from on high in this brave new world of heterogeneous computer manufacturers and open systems.

The International Alliance for SystemView consists of a group of outside vendors selected by IBM. These vendors have development partner and marketing agreements with IBM; they include:

- Bachman Information Systems (now withdrawn)
- Candle Corporation
- Information Retrieval Companies
- Legent (previously Goal Systems)
- Platinum Technology

Although Goal Systems, Inc. had a development arrangement with IBM, this was changed to marketing only after they were acquired by Legent. Also, Bachman Information Systems had been among the development partners, but has since withdrawn its participation.

The Development Partnership is particularly focused on the SystemView data model. The model is based on OSI standards; these vendors have the opportunity to influence its design based on their requirements.

Services and Consulting

Within the overall SystemView delivery framework, IBM has included additional services, including consulting. This approach has several benefits, enabling IBM to:

- Accelerate the user community's acceptance of the SystemView strategy
- Gain account control where necessary
- Generate additional revenue

The Problem Management Productivity Service (PMPS) is an offering consisting of automation tools and services to assist with the customer's technical and end-user support groups. It utilizes LAN and expert systems technology.

Failure Analysis and Support Technology (FASTService) is designed to improve the reliability of customer application systems. It has been enhanced several times, and is now available in the MVS, AS/400, AIX (RS/6000), and OS/2 environments. Through the use of probes, software failures can be detected and reported to a central problem management system.

IBM also offers a software packaging service for MVS products called SoftwareXcel MVS Customized Packages, which complements the existing CBIPO and CBPDO offerings.

SiteManager Services is a consulting and operational service designed to assist in the implementation of central monitoring and control facilities. The service is built around NetView automation, and utilizes an existing set of IBM products, including: AOC/MVS, TSCF, and other MVS facilities.

The AIX RS/6000 environment has been recently enhanced with several service and consulting offerings. These include installation, performance analysis, data support, and technical support.

4.3 System Management Dimensions

The SystemView structure is arranged into three major dimensions. Each dimension is designed to provide a necessary aspect of the overall systems management structure. Figure 4.3 provides an illustration of the SystemView dimensions.

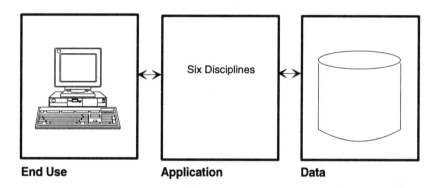

End Use   **Application**   **Data**

Figure 4.3 Three dimensions within the SystemView structure.

End-Use Dimension

The end-use dimension enables a common user interface to be used with all of the systems management applications. It is based on the CUA element within SAA, and is designed primarily for the OS/2 workstation. Recently, the OSF/Motif user interface has been included for use in the AIX RS/6000 environment.

An object-action paradigm is used, where SystemView applications and elements within the data model appear as objects. A set of actions can be performed on each object through a common set of semantics. The appearance, behavior, and terminology used is consistent regardless of the exact application or data element. Such an approach has benefits for the many operators, analysts, and systems programmers using the interface. Among them, productivity can be improved, and the skill level and training costs reduced.

As mentioned above, the SystemView products can have a varied degree of compliance with respect to integration and functional utilization. Concerning the end-use dimension, level 1 specifies conformance to CUA 89 (or later), using OS/2 or Motif under AIX. Level 2 products must adhere to CUA 91 which utilizes the Workplace Shell found in OS/2 version 2.0. Productivity and useability are improved with the more advanced level 2 interface. In this case, the object orientation has been substantially increased.

IBM has included two additional display technologies that can be used with OS/2 when implementing level 2 conforming products. The ScreenView and Graphics Interface Kit/2 are available, in addition to the other facilities also available within level 1.

Application Dimension

The functions required of the systems management applications are divided into six disciplines. The goals of the application dimension include:

- Enhance the implementation flexibility and control of the various enterprise-wide systems management tasks
- Embrace and support open systems standards, such as OSI
- Implement the capability to navigate between the various management functions
- Allow for increased automation of the identified systems management tasks

Each of the five resources which were identified above is supported by the six application disciplines as required. Particular emphasis has been placed on Business Administration, which spans all of the disciplines. Figure 4.4 provides an illustration of how the five resource groupings are supported across the six disciplines of the application dimension.

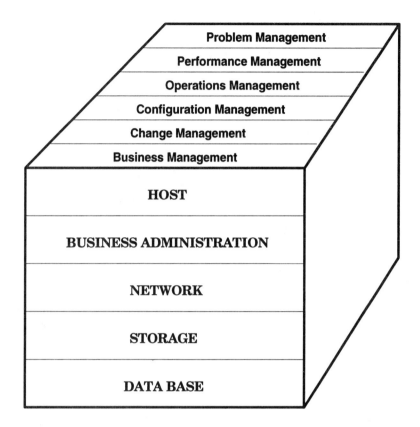

Figure 4.4 The five resource groups supported by the application dimension disciplines.

Data Dimension

The SystemView data dimension defines the format of the data and the APIs used to access it. Like the application dimension, the standards available with OSI have been used in its definition.

The data dimension has been divided into two commonly accessible information repositories:

■ Enterprise Information Base (EIB)
■ Control Information Base (CIB)

The EIB is a repository for data and information required to support the background, higher-level features within SystemView. For example, tasks related to business management or change control would use the EIB.

On the other hand, the CIB is designed to satisfy more immediate operational requirement. It contains an object-oriented representation of each of the resources within the enterprise, including location and status information.

In September, 1991, IBM announced an initiative related to SystemView called the Information Warehouse (IW). This framework provides consistency in access and administration among the database management systems within the enterprise. The DATABASE is considered to be a resource within the SystemView strategy, and is addressed by the IW framework.

The DataHub product family was announced in October, 1992 to be the first IW implementation. Following this, IBM further clarified its strategy in December of 1992 by stating that the DataHub products will use the SystemView data model.

4.4 Network Management Strategy

In September of 1991, IBM clarified its plans with respect to network management within the SystemView framework. An increased emphasis was placed on NetView and its related products for providing the type of integrated, advanced, and comprehensive features and functions required. In fact, this was a turning point for the product, as it became a strategic SystemView platform.

The SystemView network management strategy announcement letter identified four key initiatives that would help define the role of network management within SystemView. This section explains the initiatives with a focus on their general intent and benefits.

Integrated Applications and Services

As the number and complexity of computer systems has grown rapidly in recent years, it becomes more obvious that developing standards for closer integration can speed development and facilitate usage. Consider a simple example of a network resource, such as a terminal or printer. Such a device can be:

- Defined to VTAM on the MVS host: at startup in the initialization dataset and subsequently in the VTAM private area (i.e., as a control block)
- Defined to the NetView status monitor facility through the STATMON preprocessor statement

■ Part of one or more configuration databases, such as the NetView Asset Manager
■ A failed resource, with one or more problems currently outstanding in the Information/Management database

All of the above information is related, but the task of accessing or operating on any of it is different in each case. For example, a VTAM VARY command is used at the MVS console to change the resource's state, while the status monitor user interface can be used within NetView to actively monitor its status. This simple example illustrates a much larger problem which SystemView is meant to address.

Through adherence to the SAA CUA specifications, a common interface can be developed for all of the tasks related to managing and administering each system resource. This interface is specified within the SystemView end use dimension.

Internally, a common data definition and API can also improve access to and operation of the network resources by speeding application development. The SystemView Control Information Base (CIB) is designed to support a common operational view of all the resources in the network.

With a common user interface and data definitions, the development of more powerful systems management applications, with an emphasis on automation, becomes possible.

Open Access

An important element in encouraging the acceptance and usefulness of the SystemView strategy is open access. This is provided through the support of well-documented, international standards, including OSI, TCP/IP, and SNA. The IBM Open Network Management (ONM) initiative, which was initially announced in 1986, was expanded in 1990 with the announcement of SystemView.

From an SNA network management perspective, there are two SNA service points available. Within the network management architecture supported by ONM, these service points (i.e., NetView/PC and AIX Service Point) provide access and support of non-SNA devices by the host NetView.

IBM is also developing plans to support CMIP/CMIS over various transports, such as TCP/IP (CMOT). This demonstrates their commitment to future OSI-based standards, while providing flexible options for existing protocols.

Comprehensive Scope of Coverage

With SystemView, IBM is attempting to extend its reach into the network. This includes support for an end-to-end management capability, and inclusion of voice as well as data management.

The NetView family of products provides a base of functionality which support the SystemView strategy. In addition, IBM will define and implement links between its various products. This can be seen where NetView is already being connected to products such as Information/Management (i.e., NetView Bridge), and with the various automation options.

Delivery of Complete Solutions

As mentioned above in section two, the SystemView strategy has included additional services and consulting. The NetView Extra service has been specifically tailored to assist in implementing NetView and a set of existing, related products. It has two offerings - both consist of consulting, customization, and training. The two offerings within NetView Extra include:

- NetView Graphics and Automation Offering
- NetView Multi-vendor Operations Offering

The graphics and automation offering assists in managing a customer's logical and physical network. The multi-vendor operations offering allows for the management of a hetergeneous network from a single console.

4.5 SystemView's Influence on NetView

The SystemView network management strategy put forth by IBM in September of 1991 defined its position with respect to NetView. With its focus on network management, NetView has been elevated to become the strategic SystemView platform for the System/390 environment.

This section provides a list of the major facilitates of the NetView product that have been influenced by SystemView. While each is discussed only briefly, most of these features are described in more detail later in the book.

In addition to these individual features, the NetView product family in general is being positioned more aggressively to provide systems management functionality. For example, NetView was named by IBM in 1991 as the primary support vehicle for the VSE operating environment. Also, NetView/6000 is finding a more strategic role in the lower end, non-SNA world.

Automation Table

With NetView version 2.2, the automation table was enhanced to support not only message traffic, but also SNA/MS data. The Management Services Unit (MSU), including the Network Management Vector Transport (NMVT), can now be passed through the table. Each IF statement is examined, and will generate a defined action for a match (e.g., command execution).

This enhancement greatly increases the NetView automation capabilities. Data can now flow in from the network in a generic format and take advantage of the NetView automation.

Management Service Transport

Another V2.2 addition is the MS transport facility. There are actually two transports included: the MS transport and the High Performance (HP) transport.

These transports are based on LU type 6.2 connectivity and represented a more comprehensive implementation of the SNA/MS architecture on the host. NetView is now positioned to more directly manage the network resources. Several applications are included by IBM which utilize the transport. One of these is designed to accept MSUs for processing by the automation table.

Resource Object Data Manager

RODM, included with NetView version 2.3, is a direct implementation of the CIB data structure, as defined within the SystemView data dimension. It is an object-oriented, real-time repository for operational information. Each system and network resource can be represented as an object, which is then accessed by the applications on the same host for updates and inquiries.

In the future, RODM will become the foundation for systems automation as more products are updated to support this data structure. For example, the AOC/MVS product has been enhanced to utilize RODM with release 2.

Graphic Monitor Facility

GMF is the strategic user interface for all NetView information. It conforms to level 1 of the SystemView guidelines, and runs on OS/2. Version 2.3 includes some major enhancements, such as a closer integration with the Information/Management problem database.

In May, 1993, IBM shipped the first new RODM application, called the GMF Host Subsystem (HS). GMFHS accepts and interprets data from non-SNA devices and platforms in the network. Utilizing RODM, GMF HS maintains a real-time view of the non-SNA network, which is then displayed using GMF on a workstation.

Bridge to Information/Management

The NetView Bridge provides a link between NetView-based applications and the Information/Management products. The recently announced AutoBridge/MVS product enables the automatic conversion of alerts into problem records.

Automation Options

Recognizing the interdependence of the various systems and applications, IBM introduced the concept of an "automation option." This is a family of products, each of which enables a connection from NetView to a specific subsystem. These options thus extend NetView's reach. For example, the OPC/AO product, part of which runs inside of NetView, allows a connection with IBM's work flow management system, OPC/ESA.

NetView/6000

The NetView/6000 product is based on the OpenView technology licensed from Hewlett Packard. Version 2.1 became available from IBM in June, 1993, and includes significant enhancements.

NetView/6000 is now positioned, together with several related products such as AIX Systems Monitor/6000, to manage the AIX environment. It was recently added to the list of "managing" systems within the SystemView framework. Its OSF/Motif interface now allows for level 1 conformance. Together with NetView on the host, NetView/6000 extends the systems management umbrella.

With the rapid maturity of this product, many users will be faced with the decision of where to center their network management activities. That is, NetView on the host is currently superior in managing SNA networks, and has recently been expanded to handle the heterogeneous, non-SNA devices. Enhancements like RODM and GMFHS are moving the product in this direction. On the other hand, NetView/6000 is primarily an SNMP-based (i.e., TCP/IP networking) system. The new SNA Manager/6000 product from IBM will attempt to add the SNA management component, therefore making NetView/6000 a more complete platform. In fact, both product groups within IBM (i.e., NetView and NetView/6000) seem determined to make their product the ultimate platform for enterprise-wide management.

And of course, the OpenView product, being the foundation for NetView/6000, is also a viable alternative. Of course, there is a loyalty and political factor which might influence "true blue" customers to select the IBM product.

Some of the major factors that will influence the success or failure of each effort include:

- Nature of the network. Are most of the devices SNA or TCP/IP ? If SNA is still the dominate architecture, the use of NetView still makes sense.
- Location of the applications. If the vast majority of the applications are moved off of the mainframe, or a customer gets rid of the mainframe equipment all together, then NetView under MVS (as we know it today) is no longer an appropriate option.
- Features. How well can NetView under MVS manage the non-SNA world ? And what about NetView/6000, and its links to SNA ? One of the early entries in the workstation market was OpenSNA from Peregrine Systems, a product designed to "manage" SNA from the OpenView platform. However, while well publicized and promoted by Peregrine, the first release actually lacked even the most basic information that is already available with NetView running at the host (e.g., displaying alerts, session awareness data, trace data, etc.).
- Success of OSI products. IBM has preferred a strategy of using SNA for the pure IBM world, and OSI in a multiple vendor environment. If OSI begins to take off, then the use of TCP/IP (and its managers) will lose strategic importance.

■ Hardware, software, and operating costs. One of the
often stated reasons for moving to workstation-based
management is the large cost savings. Of course, this
must be balanced against other issues, such as reliability, complexity, and training costs.

So will NetView or NetView/6000 be the ultimate platform of choice
for enterprise network management? Well, that depends. Certainly the
workstation approach is a strong growth area. But in a large shop, with
a commitment to its mainframe technology, both products will likely find
a place.

One probable scenario is that NetView will bequeath some of its
control and management to NetView/6000, which would then help to
manage the LAN world. NetView could use NetView/6000, and other
products such as LAN NetView, to extract information and perform a
subset of the required automation. With this approach, NetView under
MVS would still be the "manager of managers."

TCP/IP and OSI Network Management

IBM has long dominated the computer industry, and with it, network management. The earlier CNM specifications, with the application and service element definitions, were adequate for most host-based networks. And the SNA Management Services protocols gradually expanded and formalized the IBM proprietary approach, concentrating on the data formats and exchanges.

However, as IBM was evolving its SNA/MS structure, other groups outside the IBM world were creating their own techniques for monitoring and managing data networks. The two major network management architectures relevant today for most corporations are part of the Transmission Control Protocol/Internet Protocol (TCP/IP) suite and the Open System Interconnection (OSI) model.

Since their beginnings, they have grown to challenge, and even surpass, the traditional IBM solutions. This trend is most evident in the growing LAN/workstation arena. While an enhancement to the traditional SNA has been put forth in the form of the Advanced Peer-to-Peer Networking (APPN) architecture, its implementation within actual products has been slow. IBM has therefore been forced into a position of accommodating its user community by supporting both of these alternative network management protocols.

This chapter presents an introduction to the Simple Network Management Protocol (SNMP), part of the TCP/IP suite, as well as the OSI network management specifications. The first three sections provide an overview of their evolutionary paths and common characteristics. The last two sections include descriptions of the specific details for each. Of course, these subjects are too vast for a single chapter; the interested reader should refer to the appendix for suggested reading.

Both SNMP and the OSI initiative have affected IBM's strategy with respect to network management, and data communications in general. It is clear that IBM's support for these architectures, through new products and enhancements, will continue to grow in order to mirror the reality of today's enterprise networks. However, IBM has stated its preference of OSI over SNMP, and has pursued a strategy of embracing this more robust framework wherever possible.

5.1 Overview and Development Process

TCP/IP and OSI by nature are not proprietary communication architectures, but rather originated with the intent of widespread usage in an "open" environment. Each was created, has evolved, and is maintained differently. The two frameworks do, however, share several common characteristics.

For example, the protocols for TCP/IP and OSI, like SNA, are arranged in a layered structure; Figure 5.1 contains an example. The TCP/IP specifications are far less detailed and complete than either OSI or SNA. Also, the TCP/IP protocols do not interface strictly with the adjacent layer(s) in the model. Because of this, the representation of TCP/IP according to a layered model has less of a formal meaning, but is still useful for comparison purposes.

TCP/IP and the RFC Mechanism

In 1969, the Advanced Research Projects Agency (ARPA, later changed to DARPA), as sponsored by the Department of Defense, was successful in bringing the first packet switching network on-line. ARPANET, as it was called, was to be used primarily for research and then as a cohesive framework for U.S. military data communication.

As its use began to grow, several inadequacies in the network design became apparent. Outages due to system crashes were more frequent, and it was clear that a new approach would be needed. In the mid-1970's, a proposal was put forth for a new set of networking protocols that would be used in the ARPANET. This architecture, TCP/IP, consisted of a suite of protocols and services, and was named after its two most important operational elements. The communication model was updated and finally stabilized by the end of that decade.

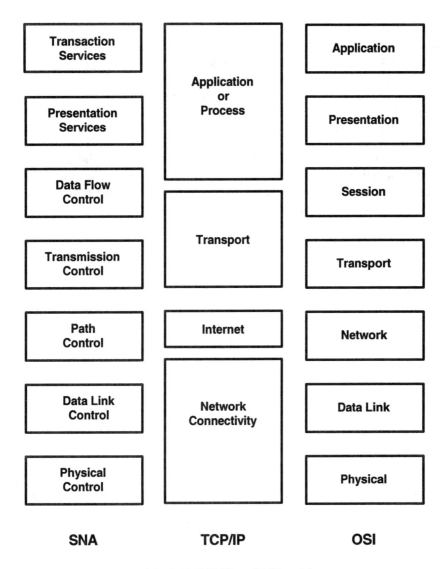

Figure 5.1 Comparison of the SNA, TCP/IP, and OSI models.

The ARPANET was subsequently split into two major parts in 1984:

- ARPANET - for continued research and development
- MILNET - for general (unclassified) military communication

The decade of the 1980's continued to see increased usage, and a rapid formalization of the mechanisms needed to support the expanding

ARPANET architecture. This was especially true beginning in 1983, when two major events took place. First, the Department of Defense adopted TCP/IP as a standard, thus assuring its long-term acceptance and growth. Also, the Berkeley Software Distribution (BSD) version 4.2 UNIX system was designed to include native support for TCP/IP, again through DOD funding.

Gradually the U.S. Internet developed, based on the TCP/IP protocols, and replaced the original ARPANET which was finally eliminated in 1990. The Network Information Center (NIC) of the Defense Data Network (DDN) was put in charge of providing information and other services to users and network administrators. The Internet Architecture Board (IAB), an independent body, was established to oversee the acceptance of new and revised TCP/IP protocols.

A process was created at that time, which is still used today, to permit the orderly evolution of the network specifications. After a new protocol is designed and tested, it is available for a type of group review. A Request For Comment (RFC) document is then created and submitted for circulation to TCP/IP users, vendors, and other interested parties. These submissions usually contain detailed protocol specifications, but can also include information or indices.

Each RFC must go through several phases before becoming a final standard, including:

■ Experimental
■ Proposed
■ Draft
■ Standard

This RFC procedure enables information to be very easily accessed, and therefore provides an "open" approach to the architecture's development. The technique encourages participation in the ongoing process, and also in the construction of actual TCP/IP-compliant products.

One of the early management tools for the TCP/IP network is the PING command. This allows a user to generate a null request to a named system, which under normal conditions will solicit a reply. In this manner, the availability of a resource can be determined.

In 1988, the IAB began to consider several different, and more sophisticated, network management options for TCP/IP. By 1990, several key RFCs were created which established the Simple Network Management Protocol (SNMP) as an acceptable solution.

As its name implies, SNMP is a relatively simple protocol which, in fact, required enhancement soon after its release. The chronology of SNMP updates began with the proposal for a "secure" SNMP. This was followed by a second-generation protocol, initially named the Simple Management Protocol (SMP). SMP was first published outside of the official RFC process, and then later transferred nearly intact as SNMP version 2 (SNMPv2). SNMPv2 is a major step forward, and is intended for use with both TCP/IP as well as OSI networks.

ISO and CCITT Committee Work

In 1977, the International Standards Organization (ISO) embarked on the creation of the OSI model. Its goals included creating a set of standards which would promote interconnection and interoperability among computers, applications, and networking products.

The ISO standardization process operates differently than the TCP/IP's RFC mechanism. Committees and sub-committees, largely consisting of interested vendors and governmental agencies, meet on a regular basis to devise, examine, analyze, review, revise, and approve standards, one part at a time. This has meant a relatively slow, sometimes politically charged, development where all types of issues must be considered up front. Large volumes of detailed specifications are gradually produced for general availability and subsequent implementation.

Standards are described in a document, which proceeds through several stages before acceptance:

■ New item
■ Working draft
■ Draft proposal
■ Draft International Standard
■ International Standard

Each ISO standard is assigned a number, by which the draft can be referenced. One of the criticisms of the ISO process is the relative difficulty (and expense) with which these documents can be retrieved. This of course has the effect of slowing the creation of compliant products.

From early in the OSI project, ISO worked closely with the International Telegraph and Telephone Consultative Committee (CCITT). Many of the standards were jointly developed, and documents will have both an ISO as well as a CCITT designation.

The area of systems management, of which network management is a subset, gained early interest and support within ISO. Figure 5.2 includes a list of the most important ISO standards for systems management within the OSI model.

ISO	CCITT	Description
7498-4	X.700	Management Framework. First document released in 1988; specifies functional components.
10040	X.701	Systems Management Overview. Formalizes manager/agent structure, layers, and functional elements.
9595	X.710	Common Management Information Service (CMIS) definition. Available services for systems management.
9596	X.711	Common Management Information Protocol (CMIP). Defines format of protocol exchanges.
10164-m	X.7nn	Systems Management Functions. Over a dozen common functions supporting five functional components.
10165-1	X.720	Management Information Model. Defines actions performed on certain attributes of named, managed objects.
10165-2	X.721	Definition of Management Information. Defines object classes, and other attributes, for MIB construction.
10165-4	X.722	Guidelines for Definition of Managed Objects. Contains rules and other information for creating MIB structure.

Figure 5.2 Major systems management standards jointly issued by ISO and CCITT.

The first two establish the overall systems management framework, including the concept of a manager and agent. Both CMIS and CMIP have been widely discussed, and provide the services and protocol definitions for executing distributed management. The 10164 series contains a number of different standards for common services available at the participating stations. Some of the services include:

- Object and state management
- Alarm and event reporting
- Security and access control
- Accounting, monitoring, and testing

The final three shown in the figure (i.e., 10165 series) determine the structure and content of the Management Information Base (MIB). The MIB is a database containing multiple data objects, each of which represents a resource or aspect of the network.

The OSI systems management definitions are characterized by functional richness, completeness, and flexibility. For this reason, OSI is the solution which is preferable to either SNMP or SNA. However, because of the rapid rise of SNMP, OSI implementations have been delayed even further.

5.2 Management Framework

Although the TCP/IP and OSI network management structures were developed separately, they share several common characteristics. Figure 5.3 contains an example of the basic framework utilized with each.

Manager-Agent Model

The manager/agent model implies an unbalanced allocation of control. The manager function, located at a central workstation or host, is responsible for monitoring and controlling network resources through remotely distributed agent functions. Each agent acts on behalf of its manager to implement the required network management disciplines.

The manager is actually more complex than shown in the figure. It contains the elements required to collect data from its agents through communication connections. The actual management function is usually implemented as one or more applications, each having access to and control over the data (or some subset).

In addition, the agent can include more sophisticated functionality allowing it to further off-load processing from the manager. For example, it can analyze and report on conditions based on pre-defined thresholds and targets. The agent platform might also include some type of automation which allows it to responsd to minor problems locally.

The manager/agent interaction basically consists of monitoring the network through information gathering as well as taking some type of action, where an agent is directed by the manager. The monitoring function can be further divided into two types of processes:

■ Polling
■ Event reporting

Polling is the mechanism where the manager specifically requests information from the agent. Event/alarm reporting is performed by the agent without any direct request from the manager. For example, an object (and therefore corresponding resource) might change states, thus generating an event report from the agent to the manager. In the SNA/MS architecture, this event is called an alert.

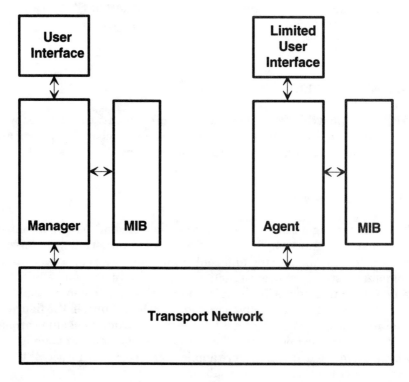

Figure 5.3 Basic network management framework common to SNMP and OSI.

There can potentially be a large number of agents reporting to a single manager. The manager platform must therefore include display technology allowing complex status information from many sources, usually arranged according to topology, to be displayed and easily understood by the network operator.

GUI Display Technology

A user interface is included with the manager in order to display collected data, and direct the operation of the network through the underlying manager/agent links. A display can also be implemented at the agent; it is however generally more restrictive, being limited to the local environment only.

Graphical User Interface (GUI) technology, based on an event-driven windowing approach, is commonly available. This allows updates to be made asynchronously from the information presented to the manager. Different symbols and color encoding schemes are employed to differentiate types of nodes and their respective states (e.g., active, inactive).

GUI display technologies are found on most personal computer and workstation platforms. Examples include Windows, OS/2 Presentation Manager, and the various strains of UNIX where the Open Software Foundation (OSF) Motif style guide is very popular.

Managed Objects

Each of the network resources visible to the manager is represented by an object, which in its basic form is a data structure (i.e., control block). The correspondence between the object and actual resource can be one-to-one, and therefore relatively straightforward. Or, there might be a layer of abstraction involved where, among other things, the object depicts a virtual or composite entity.

The objects are considered to be "managed" because of the control exercised using the manager/agent framework. They are collected into a Management Information Base (MIB), which is a type of network-oriented database. This management information can be thought of as a logical structure spread across all of the participating platforms in the enterprise, but will, at the same time, be implemented as one or more databases.

The MIB at the manager platform contains information for local resources as well as for all of the remote objects that it is aware of through its agents. The MIBs at the agent platforms contain representations of the local resources.

Each of the MIBs in use, as defined by the various standards, can have varying degrees of complexity. To a large extent, the MIB structures are influenced by the content and attributes of the managed objects of which they are comprised. For example, the nature of a MIB structure depends upon the complexity with which objects model the network resources, and how they are assigned names and attributes.

This in turn determines how objects can be accessed (i.e., read from and written to). For example, an object can be directly named, or located through a defined search procedure.

Protocol Exchanges

In order for the manager to properly execute monitoring and control over the managed objects in the network, it must be in communication with the target agents. This communication of course involves the basic transport of data units from one node to another. At the same time, a formally defined protocol must be adhered to. This protocol involves specifying the allowable operations, as well as the formats used in the communication. Both the manager and agent must "speak the same language."

In addition to using the same protocols for management exchanges, the paired manager and agent must also share common MIB definitions. This is obvious, because if a manager requests the status of a named object, the agent must recognize the format of the object name and be able to locate it. To state it more clearly, the MIB definitions are actually reflected in the format of the common data units sent in each direction.

Comparison to SystemView

The IBM SystemView framework is meant to be a comprehensive umbrella for enterprise-wide systems management. It pulls together several elements that can be said to be proprietary to IBM (e.g., SNA and SAA), and others which are part of the collection of open systems standards (e.g., OSI and TCP/IP). In this sense, it is more comprehensive and ambitious than any one of the standards that it consists of.

The manager/agent concept was already a part of SNA, in the sense that Open Network Management (ONM) includes a central focal point with remote entry points which provide information and carry out requests. The SNA/MS specifications can be used to communicate with the management "agents" from the focal point. At the same time, the concepts of a managing system (i.e., manager) and managed system (i.e., agent) have been formally recognized and established in SystemView, and thus allow for growth beyond the ONM structure. Also, SystemView has adopted the ISO standards of CMIS and CMIP, which will be supported within the application dimension.

The SystemView data dimension is consistent with the ISO standards that form the basis of the OSI MIB, such as 10165-1 (Management Information Model) and 10165-4 (Guidelines for the Definition of Managed Objects). The SystemView Control Information Base (CIB) is in fact the MIB containing operational data in the IBM environment. The Resource Object Data Manager (RODM) of NetView version 2.3 is an implementation of the CIB under MVS.

5.3 Abstract Syntax Notation One

The Abstract Syntax Notation One (ASN.1) is a simple, yet powerful type of programming language. It was formally defined by ISO, and is published in the document ISO 8824 (X.208). ASN.1 is used to define the structure and value of data records. In particular, ASN.1 can be used in three major areas to define data with respect to network management:

- View of data for applications (at the application and presentation layers)
- Format of messages exchanged between paired layers and nodes (i.e., data units)
- Format of a Management Information Base, including those used for OSI and SNMP management

Another related standard provides an exact format for the same information as it is encoded for actual transmission, as described below.

Elements of the Language

The main purpose of ASN.1 is to describe the format and structure of data. To do this, each field in a record (i.e., module) must have a specific type specification as well as a value. This allows the receiver to properly interpret the data. For example, a field could be an integer value or a character string. The various types defined by ASN.1 are arranged into four major groups, as shown in Figure 5.4.

Within each of the four groups, each specific type is assigned a unique number or "data tag". For example, UNIVERSAL (1) signifies a boolean value, while UNIVERSAL (2) specifies an integer.

The language statements are arranged sequentially, using assignment and declaration operands, in order to define a specific module. The variable types used with ASN.1 can be simple or complex. Simple variables map exactly to a single type and field value, while complex types can contain more than one specific type, much like an array or structure.

Basic Encoding Rules

While ASN.1 is useful at the upper layers of a communications architecture for defining and accessing data, another standard is needed to transfer the information from one program (or host) to another. The primary encoding syntax used together with ASN.1 is called Basic Encoding Rules (BER). BER, like ASN.1, was developed by ISO, and is contained in ISO 8825 (X.209). In addition, other encoding schemes have recently been proposed.

Type	Description
Universal	General and commonly used types, such as integer and bit strings.
Application	Reserved for specific applications and defined elsewhere (e.g., FTAM).
Context-specific	Also for use with an application, but of a more limited scope.
Private	For private use, not defined by ISO.

Figure 5.4 Four ASN.1 variable classes into which the types are arranged.

Using BER, the exact type and length of each data field is placed before the actual data. Using a common header, the receiving node can then decode the data after it has been transferred.

Figure 5.5 contains a basic presentation of the encoding scheme for a type value. The first two bits identify the major type grouping. The next bit is used to signal either a simple (primitive) or more complex (recursive) variable type. The remaining bits hold the tag number, with a maximum of 32 (5 bits) per class. Following the type declaration, the length of the actual data is provided in one of several different forms.

ASN.1 Macros

Macros can also be used with ASN.1 as well. As with other languages, the macros provide a convenient technique for communicating a particular format that is commonly referenced and repeated. The notation allows new types to be created. Templates can be constructed, which have been included in some of the ISO publications.

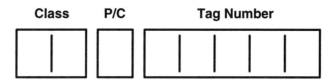

Figure 5.5 An octet (i.e., 8-bit byte) is used to describe the variable which follows.

5.4 Simple Network Management Protocol

The SNMP network management protocol and supporting framework is described in a series of RFCs, and is part of the overall TCP/IP protocol suite. The RFC documents that form the basis for the original functionality include: 1155, 1157, and 1213. In addition, there are perhaps dozens more RFCs, not yet at full standard status, providing further operational details and enhancements.

Major Components

SNMP is an application level protocol in the TCP/IP stack. It requires the implementation of the basic connectionless service enabled by:

- ■ User Datagram Protocol (UDP) - the transport layer protocol which passes packets of information to IP for transmission
- ■ Internet Protocol (IP) - used for routing data through the network
- ■ A network link-level protocol, such as Ethernet, to transport data frames.

The manager-agent model is used, where the agents report to the managing platform. In the case where an agent cannot be provided, a "proxy" agent supports the resources outside of the direct manager connection. A proxy agent is very similar to the SNA service point, as implemented by NetView/PC.

Many agents can be connected to a single manager or, conversely, an agent can report to more than one manager. In administering the management framework, the concept of a community, or user group, is used. This allows for necessary features such as security to be implemented.

A MIB is used to hold the objects representing the network resources. To control the network, a manager can issue requests to its agents in order to read and write MIB data. Also, an agent is able to send an event report to the manager in the form of a trap. There are five basic messages that are generated and flow through the network to carry out the SNMP operations, as shown in Figure 5.6.

SNMP Data Format	Description
Get Request	Used to obtain information from the agent; prepares for further data access.
Get-Next Request	Similar to the get operation, except executes read based on logical position in the MIB structure.
Get Response	Data returned from the two get requests as well as set operation.
Set Request	Used as a write operation to set a MIB data value.
Trap	Provides a method to report conditions in the network.

Figure 5.6 Basic protocol messages available with SNMP.

MIB Definition and Registration

The MIB used with SNMP has evolved, like other aspects of the TCP/IP architecture, in order to meet vendor and user requirements. There are actually two major MIB structures approved for use with SNMP. MIB-2 is a superset of the earlier MIB-1, and can therefore be viewed as a functional replacement. And in fact, MIB-1 is given the designation of historic; MIB-2 should be used instead.

The MIB-2 model is arranged in a hierarchical tree structure. The highest level serves as the root, splitting to form lower, more specifically defined resources.

In defining the MIB, a subset of the ASN.1 language is used. Each object is assigned a unique integer identifier, or object ID. Therefore, a particular object in the structure can be described as a chain of object IDs, proceeding from least to most specific.

The MIB is defined within the broader ISO framework. The ISO registration tree, arranged like a MIB, is used to classify and register a wide range of entities on a world-wide basis. There are three main parents in the registration tree: ISO, CCITT, and joint ISO-CCITT. Under the ISO parent, four major classifications have been established:

- Standards (0)
- Registration authorities (1)
- Member-bodies (2)
- Organizations (3)

The SNMP MIB-2 is defined as a part of the registration tree, under the branch formed by the sequential concatenation of ISO, Organizations (3), then Department of Defense (as an instance under the "organizations" parent), and finally Internet.

Under the Internet, four branches are used to hold the MIB definitions, each used for different purposes in varying degrees of completion. Figure 5.7 includes an illustration of the comprehensive Internet MIB structure.

The directory is reserved for future use with the OSI directory (i.e., X.500). Accepted standards fall under the management (MGMNT) branch. The third classification can be used for experimentation. The final branch is reserved for proprietary use, where vendors might define extensions for their TCP/IP-based products.

The MIB-2 definitions, falling under the management class, are further divided into ten categories of object data. These include:

- System - general overall information regarding the system
- Interfaces - connections from system to the network

■ At - address translation information
■ IP - data supporting execution of the Internet Protocol
■ ICMP - data supporting execution of the Internet Control Message Protocol
■ TCP - data supporting execution of the Transmission Control Protocol
■ UDP - data supporting execution of the User Datagram Protocol
■ EGP - data supporting execution of the External Gateway Protocol
■ Transmission - general information about transmission algorithms and access protocols
■ SNMP - data supporting execution of the Simple Network Management Protocol

This comprehensive MIB format allows instances of object data to be grouped in order to support SNMP.

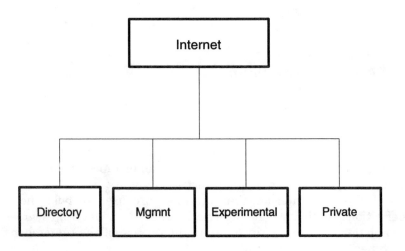

Figure 5.7 SNMP MIB definition structure arranged within the ISO registration tree.

The formally defined Structure of Management Information (SMI) also contributes to the MIB definition by providing a general framework. For example, it identifies data types, and how resources are named. The SNMP MIB uses scalar values, and simple two-dimensional tables. It is much simpler and less robust than the OSI MIB.

Version 2 Enhancements

A major step towards improving the capabilities of SNMP came with the Remote Monitoring (RMON) feature. RMON represents an extension to the MIB-2, defining interfaces and protocols that allow remote network monitors to collect and forward information. While an important addition to the basic SNMP protocols, RMON is not able to solve the larger problems encountered by users when attempting to use SNMP in an enterprise-wide role.

An important revision of the basic protocol arrived with version 2 (SNMPv2). There are 12 major documents associated with this new version. The enhancements can be grouped into four areas, including:

■ Structure of Management Information (SMI)
■ Protocol exchanges
■ Manager-to-manager capability
■ Security

These improvements further extend the usefulness of SNMP. For many organizations, they may be sufficient to adopt the protocol for wider use within the enterprise.

5.5 OSI Systems Management

Although its development has been slow, and its specifications long and complex, the OSI network management framework is richer in the features and functions required to administer today's enterprise networks. In fact, IBM has adopted several OSI standards and has stated its desire to favor OSI over the SNMP architecture. This section presents a basic overview of the OSI standards.

System Management Framework

What is referred to as network management is really a part of the larger systems management structure defined by OSI. There are several documents, jointly released with the CCITT, that form the basic framework.

Also included with the overview are the MIB definitions, descriptions of the CMIS and CMIP protocols, detailed systems management application functions, as well as an intricate description regarding the dispersion of support functionality throughout the layered OSI model.

Functional, there are five major areas which the OSI specifications attempt to address, as shown in Figure 5.8.

Functional Area	Description
Fault Management	Detection, isolation, and correction of network problems.
Accounting Management	Determination of usage, and therefore cost of network operation.
Configuration Management	Collection and management of configuration and change-related data.
Security Management	Protection from unauthorized access and use of system resources.
Performance Management	Ability to monitor, evaluate, and manage performance.

Figure 5.8 Functional areas identified by OSI systems management.

MIB Format

The OSI MIB is a collection of managed objects, arranged according to the defined Structure of Management Information (SMI). The ASN.1 notation is utilized in describing the MIB.

Like SNMP, the ISO registration tree is used as a basis for defining the OSI MIB. However, the attributes, allowable field types, and characteristics of the objects are more complex and varied than those of SNMP. More of the formally recognized object-oriented design technologies are implemented. This includes, for example, encapsulation where data and program logic are associated and stored together. In this case, "active" objects are created. One use of this is the inclusion of notification routines, where events and status changes can notify another application or system.

Also, the concept of inheritance is employed, where class character-istics (e.g., fields) can be passed to child classes and object instances.

CMIS and CMIP Interactions

In support of the desired functional areas, the OSI application layer specifications define a Systems Management Application Entity (SMAE). Each SMAE can be broken down into smaller, related functional parts called Application Service Elements (ASEs). ASEs are general OSI entities allowing certain procedural logic to be defined. There are several ASEs that are specialized and specific to systems management.

CMISE Operational Service	Description
M-GET	Requests information.
M-SET	Updates object in target system.
M-ACTION	Requests that a specific action be carried out.
M-CREATE	Creates an object instance.
M-DELETE	Deletes an object instance.
M-CANCEL-GET	Cancels a previous request.

Figure 5.9 Operational services available through the defined CMISE.

One of these is the Common Management Information Service Element (CMISE), an ASE defined for systems management. Each CMISE supports its local applications by providing logic and a functional interface through which systems management requests can be presented for execution.

The services provided by CMISE allow applications to become associated (i.e., connected), as well as to exchange notification and operational requests. For example, there are six major management-operation (operational) requests, as displayed in Figure 5.9. All rely on a connection to a remote, peer CMISE in order to carry out the operations.

The CMIS elements communicate by exchanging messages. These data units are defined according to the Common Management Information Protocol (CMIP). CMIP defines the format of the messages that are exchanged between CMIS elements, as resulting from the application requests.

NetView Domain Definitions

6

Basic Installation

As with the other IBM mainframe software products, NetView is distributed to the customer as a set of tapes and supporting documentation. The product is first installed on one or more MVS systems, usually by the network systems programmer. Following the installation, a complete configuration and customization can then be performed.

This chapter presents the most basic steps involved in establishing a NetView domain, beginning with the installation procedures. Some of the more important administration steps are also included. This information provides a basis for the rest of the book, where the more advanced definition parameters are described as appropriate.

6.1 Installation Options and Procedures

The implementation of the NetView product under MVS is accomplished by following a set of well-established installation procedures. The product libraries are first loaded from tape to disk where they can then be integrated into the MVS operating system. Following this, the configuration and customization of the NetView domain can take place.

Operational Overview

Figure 6.1 provides an illustration of NetView version 2.3 running under the MVS operating system. The four address spaces currently available are shown.

The first release of NetView represented a combination of several previously existing products into one MVS address space. The NetView application address space includes the individual functional components, such as the Hardware Monitor and Session Monitor.

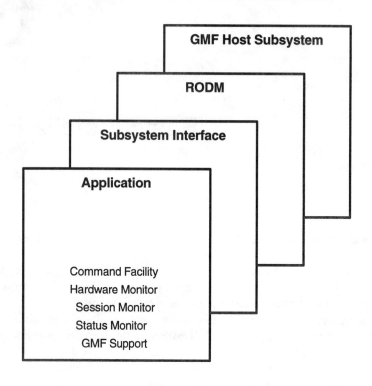

Figure 6.1 NetView product implemented across multiple MVS address spaces.

With release 2, support was introduced for the MVS subsystem interface (SSI), with NetView now defined as a subsystem. The NetView SSI address space connects to this MVS facility on behalf of the NetView applications; messages and commands are buffered here. Release 3 added the program-to-program interface (PPI) communication capability, which also uses the SSI address space. These data buffers are temporarily stored as they flow from a PPI sender to receiver.

Version 2.1 included the Graphic Monitor Facility (GMF), an OS/2-based display facility for NetView, initially focused on the SNA network. With version 2.2, IBM included enhancements which improved NetView's management across a wider array of devices and network resources. The APPC transports, as defined by the SNA Management Services (SNA/MS) architecture, allow NetView and its facilitates (e.g., automation) to be applied in a more consistent manner.

A major turning point in the evolution of NetView came when IBM added the Resource Object Data Manager (RODM) with version 2.3.

RODM is an implementation of one aspect of the SystemView data model, and contains real-time operational information describing the resources within the enterprise network.

The GMF Host Subsystem (GMFHS) address space has also been included with version 2.3. GMFHS is an RODM application which tracks non-SNA resources, providing the GMF user at the OS/2 workstation with a more complete view of the multivendor network.

Purchase Packages

One of the concepts that has been stressed within the IBM network management strategy, and indeed with most of their other major initiatives, is centralization. That is, command and control capabilities are designed to be administered from a central location.

NetView located on the mainframe is used to access and control the devices and resources in the network. Also, multiple NetView domains can be connected in order to communicate such that one domain has ultimate management authority. To accommodate the situation where multiple NetView domains are used, IBM allows for the following licensing options:

- Central system
- Distributed system
- Standalone system

The central system option provides for central control of a network of distributed NetView systems. The standalone system is a special case of the central system option, with support for NetView-to-NetView communication removed.

All of the packages include RODM, a standard set of NetView functions, national language support, and on-line help. In addition, the central system option provides a fully functional operator interface and Graphic Monitor Facility (GMF) capability for the OS/2 platform.

NetView Data Sets

When installing NetView, there are three main types of libraries involved:

- NetView definition files
- NetView VSAM clusters
- MVS system datasets

The NetView definition datasets have a partitioned organization; each member holds configuration information, panels, or other data. The VSAM clusters are allocated for use by NetView during normal operation. For example, the Hardware Monitor uses its VSAM clusters to hold alert information received from the network. The MVS system datasets must be updated during installation in order to fully integrate the product into the operating system.

SMP/E Installation

The customer receives a distribution tape from IBM containing the NetView product libraries and other information needed during the installation. Using release 5 of the System Modification Program Extended (SMP/E) system, the NetView product can be installed and maintained. The NetView version 2.3 products available for MVS include:

- Program number 5685-1111 for MVS/ESA
- Program number 5685-138 for MVS/XA

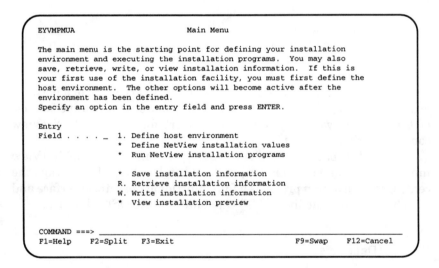

```
EYVMPMUA                        Main Menu

The main menu is the starting point for defining your installation
environment and executing the installation programs.  You may also
save, retrieve, write, or view installation information.  If this is
your first use of the installation facility, you must first define the
host environment.  The other options will become active after the
environment has been defined.
Specify an option in the entry field and press ENTER.

Entry
Field . . . . _   1. Define host environment
                  *  Define NetView installation values
                  *  Run NetView installation programs

                  *  Save installation information
                  R. Retrieve installation information
                  W. Write installation information
                  *  View installation preview


COMMAND ===> _____
F1=Help    F2=Split   F3=Exit                 F9=Swap    F12=Cancel
```

Figure 6.2 Main menu for the NetView Installation Facility running under TSO/ISPF.

During the installation process, the NetView libraries are copied to disk from tape. An installation library (CNMINST) and a samples library (CNMSAMP) contain JCL, code, and other samples which are

useful during the installation and administration of the NetView product. Also, the user has the option of installing the product for the first
time or migrating from a previous release.

NetView Installation Facility

The NetView Installation Facility (NIF) provides an alternative to the
normal installation procedures available with SMP/E. Instead of tailor-
ing and submitting a series of batch jobs, the user utilizes an ISPF
interface to install and configure the product. A set of command lists are
used under the covers.

Figure 6.2 displays the NIF main menu. With its interactive nature,
NIF can provide for a smoother installation as compared to the traditional SMP/E method. However, there have been problems with NIF in
previous releases of NetView, and many systems programmers still
choose to use the traditional method of product installation.

6.2 MVS System Considerations

During the installation process, the NetView product must be integrated
into the MVS environment, which involves changes to the various system
libraries. This section provides a list of the major steps required when
updating the MVS system.

System Parameters

The most important changes are made to the MVS parameter library,
SYS1.PARMLIB. Figure 6.3 includes a list of the members that should
be changed during NetView installation. Like many of the NetView
definitions, these changes take place only after the MVS operating
system is restarted (i.e., IPL'ed).

VTAM-STATMON Interface

The Status Monitor component of NetView provides a status display of
the entire NetView domain to the operator. This information is maintained within the private area of the NetView application address space
as a collection of control blocks.

With the early releases of NetView, unsolicited text messages were
accepted from VTAM and examined. When a resource being monitored

changed status, the appropriate Status Monitor control block was then updated. This in turn caused a change to the terminal user's display screen.

Parameter	Description
SCHEDxx	Use this member to affect the operational characteristics of the NetView application address space; in particular to mark it non-swappable to the dispatcher.
LNKLSTxx	The MVS link list is a group of libraries which are searched by default when a module must be located. The NetView libraries can be added to the list.
LPALSTxx	The SCNMLPA1 dataset, as well as the C and PL/I run-time libraries, should be added to the LPA list; this will improve NetView's performance.
IEAAPFxx	Any datasets which are allocated to the NetView started task, or the LPA list, must be marked as authorized; update this member with their names.
IEFSSNxx	The subsystem name shared by the application and SSI address spaces, as well as the RODM subsystem, must be added to this list.
IEASYSxx	If the VTAM-STAMON interface or SSI address space is being used, update MAXUSER and RSVNONR to prepare for the MVS program call interface.
CONSOLxx	Tasks within the NetView application address space can utilize subsystem allocatable consoles, which must be defined in this member.

Figure 6.3 Updates required to the SYS1.PARMLIB dataset during NetView installation.

As of VTAM version 3.3 and NetView 2.1, IBM has included a more direct method for updating these control blocks used by the Status Monitor, and consequently the user's display. Once the interface is activated, any status change for a VTAM resource causes a direct cross-memory update to the Status Monitor control blocks within NetView. In this way, the inefficient process of examining VTAM messages is by-passed.

The module ISTIECCE is shipped in the NetView library SCNMLNK1. This dataset should be included in the VTAM started task procedure as part of the VTAMLIB concatenation. More information on this interface and its use is presented in the chapter dedicated to the Status Monitor.

6.3 Major Domain Parameters

Once the product has been installed and implemented within MVS, the task of completely defining the NetView domain begins. Figure 6.4 provides a list of the major NetView definition libraries. The DSIPARM dataset is the most heavily utilized, containing a majority of the definitions presented in this book.

NetView Library	Description
CNMSAMP	After installing the product, the samples found in this dataset can be used during customization.
DSIPRF	The profiles for each terminal operator, autotask, and NNT are defined in this file.
DSIPARM	The majority of the product's parameter definitions are found in this dataset.

Figure 6.4 List of the most important datasets used in NetView parameter definition.

Many of the parameters will take effect only after the NetView application address space has been restarted, while some can be changed by recycling only the tasks to which they apply.

The first step in configuring NetView is to update the member DSIDMN within the DSIPARM dataset. This file is read at NetView startup and defines the characteristics of the NetView domain.

NCCFID Parameter

The first statement within DSIDMN is NCCFID; Figure 6.5 provides an example of this parameter.

```
NCCFID    DOMAINID=CNM23,DMNPSW=CNM23,DROP=YES,SUPPCHAR=?
```

Figure 6.5 An example of the NetView domain identification statement.

The DOMAINID can be from 1 to 5 characters long and must be unique throughout the network. Not only does it define the NetView domain id, but it is also the name of the primary VTAM application identifier (APPLID) used for communication by the NetView application region. The other parameters include:

- DMNPSW - the domain password.
- SUPPCHAR - the suppression character which, when included before a command in column one, causes the input to be suppressed from the terminal, hard-copy log, and network log.
- DROP - determines the response to certain error conditions for those terminals in session with NetView; DROP=YES (no recovery) and DROP=NO (attempt recovery) are permitted.

NetView must be recycled for these parameter values to be altered.

Miscellaneous Global Parameters

There are several more parameters included in the DSIDMN member. Rather than presenting all of them here, they have been arranged according to function and described as appropriate throughout the next few chapters.

Some of the DSIDMN parameters are global in nature, including:

- NETVTYPE - indicates the type of NetView being used, based on the package selected: CENTRAL, DISTRIBUTED, STANDALONE.
- NCCFIC - an initial command is named for execution when the NetView application address space is first started.
- TRANSTBL - the translation table determines how the output will be presented to the terminal operator (e.g., EBCDIC).
- MAXABEND - this is the number of times a specific operator or autotask can abnormally terminate and then be reinstated. Once the limit has been reached, the session must be recovered.
- STORPOOL - this parameter determines the amount of storage allocated within NetView. A cell allocation method is used; this value can range from 1 to 7, with 1 a recommended default for most cases.

6.4 Optional Subtask Definition

The NetView application address space includes a number of different subtasks, each designed to perform a specific function. These tasks work together to provide the full range of network management and automation services required.

The optional subtask is a general-purpose task built on top of the underlying command facility; it provides the means to integrate a wide range of functionality in NetView.

Major Subtask Types

Figure 6.6 lists the major types of NetView subtasks. While their functions differ, they have certain attributes in common. Each task is identified by its type, task ID (i.e., name), dispatching priority, module name, and status.

A subtask is defined in one of several methods, depending on its type. For example, the optional task (OPT) is identified with the TASK statement.

NetView Subtask	Description
Main Task (MNT)	The main task initializes the command facility environment and attaches all of the subtasks within the NetView application address space.
Primary POI Task (PPT)	VTAM's primary operator interface (POI) is used to access unsolicited messages. Among other things, the PPT processes messages related to network status.
Optional Task (OPT)	An OPT allows for the development of optional functions or services not provided for by the other subtasks; it is defined with the TASK statement.
Data Services Task (DST)	The DST is a special OPT which provides a set of services, including access to VSAM and CNM data. It serves as a base for several of the NetView components.
Operator Station Task (OST)	Each terminal operator is served by a separate OST subtask, which accepts commands and formats the output according to the attached device.
Autotask (AOST)	An AOST is a special case of the OST, where there is no terminal session. The autotask is used to implement background automation within NetView.
NetView-to-NetView Task (NNT)	A NetView operator connects to another NetView domain with an SNA session; an NNT is created to accept messages and commands in the remote domain.
Hard-copy Task (HCT)	NetView messages can be directed to an HCT, which prints the output on a dedicated output device. This can supplement disk logging by DSILOG.

Figure 6.6 Subtask types used within the NetView application address space.

Task Statement

The TASK statement pre-defines an optional task to NetView. At startup, the DSIDMN member is read, and a Task Vector Block (TVB) control block is reserved for each of these tasks. Most of these are shipped by IBM with the NetView product. However, a vendor or customer can develop a task and define it in this way.

```
TASK     MOD=DSIZDST,TSKID=ALIASAPL,MEM=DSIALATD,PRI=5,INIT=N
```

Figure 6.7 An example of a DST definition, which is a special case of the optional task.

Figure 6.7 provides an example of how the TASK parameter is used to define an optional task. The following parameters are used in the example:

- MOD - this is the name of the load module which the task will use; it is named on the ATTACH macro by NetView when the task is created.
- TSKID - each subtask must be uniquely defined by name within the application address space.
- MEM - a subtask has access to an initialization member in the DSIPARM dataset; the content depends upon the task.
- PRI - the dispatching priority of each OPT can range between 1 (high) and 9 (low).
- INIT - a task can be activated automatically at NetView startup (Y), or defined to be initially inactive (N). The START and STOP commands are used to control the individual subtasks.

A DST is a special type of optional task, described below. The other subtasks defined to NetView do not use the TASK statement.

6.5 Data Services Task

NetView includes a special type of OPT called the Data Services Task (DST). The DST provides a set of services that are commonly required by the tasks within NetView. This type of OPT therefore provides a platform enabling a more rapid development of functionality.

DST Exits	Description
BNJPALEX	Screen 4700 loop alerts.
XITBN	BSAM file is empty.
XITBO	Output record to BSAM file.
XITCI	CNM input data received.
XITCM	GMF command support exit.
XITCO	CNM output data request.
XITDI	DST initialization.
XITST	Resource Status Manager.
XITVI	VSAM record input.
XITVN	VSAM file is empty.
XITVO	VSAM record output.
XITXL	External logging record.

Figure 6.8 Exits that can be included for a Data Services Task.

A DST is defined like the other optional tasks, with certain restrictions. For example, the module DSIZDST must be named for use. Also, there are standards guiding the format of the initialization member.

Access to Services

The operation of a DST is similar to the other subtasks, in that the task waits for messages on its input queues. The work is scheduled and executed as it arrives in the form of data services command processors (DSCPs); section 6.7 provides a more complete explanation of the DSCP.

Within the command processors running on a DST, macro instructions are used to access the two major DST services:

- CNM interface (DSIZCSMS).
- VSAM access (DSIZVSMS).

DSTs are frequently used as background subtasks, maintaining control over one or more resources.

DST Exits

Figure 6.8 provides a list of the exits which can be included for a DST. These exits are optional, although a few of the important ones are commonly included.

Each DST within NetView can define its own set of exits. If an exit is shared among DSTs, it must be designed and link edited to be reentrant.

Also, multiple exits can be concatenated; that is, for each exit point, up to ten modules can be named. In this case, the routines are called under the DST sequentially. For a specific event, this process continues until the last exit has been invoked or until one of the routines provides a return code equivalent to USERDROP (4).

Initialization Statement

The initialization member named on the TASK statement contains parameters controlling the operation of the DST. The statement DSTINIT, one per line, is used to communicate parameters. These include:

- Which, if any, of the DST-specific services will be used
  by the task.

- Information related to the configuration of VSAM, such as DD names and passwords.
- The name of a command processor to be scheduled when CNM data arrives unsolicited at the task.
- The number of control blocks reserved to handle solicited and unsolicited requests (DSRBs)
- Module names to be used for the various DST exits.

The initialization exit (XITDI) can be a powerful way to control DST startup. After the DSTINIT defining the name of an XITDI exit has been read by NetView, this exit is then invoked for each of the subsequent lines in the configuration deck. Calling the initialization exit for each statement allows non-standard parameters, specific to the particular task, to be included and processed.

Data Services Request Blocks

The DSRB control block is used to hold information relating to a single active DST request (e.g., a VSAM write operation). These control blocks are pre-allocated by NetView at DST startup. Since the function and utilization of each subtask is different, there must be a way to tailor the size of this pool.

```
DSRBS  Data Services Request Block Usage for AAUTSKLP  11:21:58   Page 1 of 2

Unsolicited DSRBs:     5   Used:    0                      Free:    5
   Solicited DSRBs:   10   Used:    0  VSAM Redrive:   0   Free:   10
        TOTAL DSRBs:  15   Used:    0  VSAM Redrive:   0   Free:   15


Current DSRB Usage

No.  DSRB  Status  Taskname  Type  Request  Redrive  Serial No.  Step No.
001  UNSL  INACT
002  UNSL  INACT
003  UNSL  INACT
004  UNSL  INACT
005  UNSL  INACT
006  SOLI  INACT
007  SOLI  INACT
008  SOLI  INACT
009  SOLI  INACT
010  SOLI  INACT
011  SOLI  INACT
012  SOLI  INACT

ENTER= Refresh          PF2= End  PF3= Return          PF8= Forward
```

Figure 6.9 Example of the DSRBS command which can monitor control block usage.

There are two parameters, specified on the DSTINIT statement, which directly influence the allocation of the DSRBs. DSRBU sets aside a specific number for unsolicited CNM data. The DSRBO parameter allocates DSRBs for concurrent, solicited requests; these are used for solicited CNM as well as VSAM requests.

The proper specification of these two values can affect the performance of a DST, as well as NetView in general. To help monitor this aspect of NetView's operation, IBM includes a display command. Figure 6.9 lists the output of the DSRBS command, used in this case to examine the DSRBs in use by the Session Monitor.

6.6 Operators

Each operator is known by a unique name; these logon names are defined and shared by three types of NetView tasks:

- Terminal operators (OST).
- Autotasks (AOST).
- NetView-to-NetView tasks (NNT).

This section explains the important parameters used to support the subtasks listed above, with an emphasis on terminal operators; the autotasks and NNTs are discussed at the end.

Enabling Terminal Logons

There are several global parameter statements defined within the DSIDMN member affecting terminal operators.

The POS and POSPOOL statements together determine the number of operators that can be logged on at any given time. The POS parameter reserves a task-related control block for each VTAM terminal identified (i.e., LU name), effectively guaranteeing that an operator will always be able to logon from the named terminal. This parameter might be used for key systems programmers and operators. POSPOOL, on the other hand, defines the size of a general pool of available logon slots. These control blocks are pre-allocated, but not assigned to any particular user; they are available for any terminal other than those defined with the POS statement.

The MAXLOGON parameter specifies the maximum number of times an operator can attempt to logon using an incorrect password. Once this limit has been reached, the session terminates. This parameter has a secondary meaning at a focal point or intermediate focal point host. In this case, when data forwarding is being used (alert, message, or status), the value also represents the maximum number of forward operators at the host where it is defined.

The RRD statement names other NetView domains with which operators can establish sessions; it can be included multiple times. This parameter applies to an operator based on other values described below.

MAXSPAN is used to define the maximum number of span names that will be used. NetView reserves storage based on this number.

Finally, if any of the operators use a dedicated hardcopy printer, the device(s) must be defined in DSIDMN using the HARDCOPY statement. Each printer, as it is known to VTAM (i.e., LU name), is named. The devices can be shared and are assigned to operators based on the profile being used.

Defining Operators

The NetView operators, including AOSTs and NNTs, are defined in the DSIOPF member of the DSIPARM dataset. There are two statements used:

- OPERATOR - this statement defines the operator name and password.
- PROFILEN - immediately following the OPERATOR definition, this parameter specifies the name of a profile for the operator.

The PROFILEN statement can contain more than one profile name. In this case, an operator is able to chose a profile at logon. If one is not selected, the first profile is used by default.

Profiles

The profiles named on the PROFILEN statements are defined in the DSIPRF dataset; each profile is contained in a separate member.

Every profile begins with the PROFILE parameter, which has two optional parameters:

- HCL. A hardcopy printer can be started and dedi- cated to the session. This allows all terminal activity to be printed as it occurs, as opposed to the back- ground disk recording available with the network log task (see Chapter 8).

■ IC. This parameter names an initialization command
to be executed immediately after logon.

Some of the other statements applying to a profile are presented
below.

Security Options

There are three major areas of customization related to operator security: span of control, scope of command, and domain access. The
OPTIONS statement in DSIDMN, with the single VERIFY parameter,
must first be defined properly. Once defined, it applies to all operators.
The three security options include:

■ MINIMAL - only checks if an operator is defined and
not already logged on.
■ NORMAL - an operator's password and all logon
parameters are examined; the three security mechanisms mentioned above are enabled.
■ MAXIMUM - an external security system (e.g., RACF)
is used.

Span of control and scope of command are defined below.

Span of Control

Span of control (SOC) is a method for controlling which network resources an operator has access to (i.e., can activate and inactivate). In
defining SOC, there is a close relation to the option of controlling access
to other domains.

Assuming that the NetView security mechanisms have been enabled with OPTIONS, the next parameter affecting SOC implementation for a given operator is the AUTH statement in the profile. If
GLOBAL is selected, then span of control is not used and the operator can
connect to the domains listed with the RRD statement with NNT
sessions. If SPECIFIC is defined instead, then SOC is enabled and the
operator can establish sessions according to the DOMAINS definition,
immediately following AUTH.

ISPAN and SPAN are used in the profile to list span list names for
the operator. The names used are matched with a SPANLST name in the
DSISPN member.

Scope of Command

Another parameter used in the profile is OPCLASS. Each operator is said to have access to certain NetView commands by class; an integer number identifies each class.

An operator is authorized for a finite number of classes, which are checked against the command definitions in the DSICMD member. This is presented in the next section.

Automation Tasks

An autotask is a special type of OST without a terminal session. It is used for background automation processing, and can be dedicated to a particular use. A particular MVS console can be optionally assigned to an autotask, allowing NetView commands to be entered from the console for processing.

Once defined, an autotask is started with the AUTOTASK command. Also, the newer RMTCMD is used to route a command to a remote domain; it activates an autotask to execute the command.

NNT Tasks

A NetView-to-NetView task is created in a remote domain by an operator who issues the START DOMAIN command. The DSIDMN statement CDRMSESS is used to define the maximum number of cross-domain sessions that can be started with the local NetView domain.

6.7 Command Procedures

A NetView command procedure is basically a transaction program which is scheduled, executed, and then terminated on a single subtask. There are two main categories of command procedures:

- Command processor - this is an MVS load module which has been assembled or compiled, and then link edited.
- Command list (CLIST) - a CLIST, written in either the Restructured Extended Executor (REXX) or NetView CLIST language, is easy to construct but relatively inefficient because it is usually read and interpreted one line at a time.

Both types of procedures are considered to be commands, and are used interchangeably throughout the book.

Command Types

There are basically only three types of commands that can be defined to NetView. These include:

- Regular - this type of command runs as part of the NetView mainline code under a task; it does not run asychronously. A regular command can be interrupted by other commands as well as NetView and VTAM exit routines.
- Immediate - an immediate command runs in an asynchronous fashion, and can interrupt a regular command.
- Data Services - a DSCP is designed to execute under a DST.

In addition, there are several other variations of these basic types of commands. They include the long running and presentation services command, both of which are discussed later in the book.

Command Definition

Every command processor that will be used in NetView must be defined in the DSICMD member of the DSIPARM dataset. An example of a command is presented in Figure 6.10.

```
AUTOTBL     CMDMDL    MOD=DSIAMP,TYPE=R,CTL=N,RES=N,ECHO=Y,PARSE=Y
            CMDSYN    AUTOMSG
            CMDCLASS  5
```

Figure 6.10 An example of command definition in NetView.

The CMDMDL statement identifies the command with the following parameters:

- MOD - this is the load module to be scheduled.
- TYPE - the command runs as a regular (R); immediate (I); DST (D); either regular or immediate (B); regular or DST (RD).

- CTL - defines the command as normal (N) or special (S); special commands are used to handle PF keys and other terminal input control.
- RES - the command can be pre-loaded and resident (Y), or loaded on demand (N).
- ECHO - this determines if the command input is echo back at the terminal (Y) or not (N).
- PARSE - the command line can be parsed as a service to the command (Y) or not (N).

CMDSYN is used to declare a synonym for the command. This can be done for an individual keyword as well, using the PARMSYN statement.

Command Security

In defining operator profiles, the OPCLASS parameter is used to associate the operator with one or more scope classes. In this case, every command entered by the operator is checked for authorization.

At least one of the CMDCLASS and OPCLASS values must match for the command to be valid. Individual keywords can also be restricted in the same manner using the KEYCLASS and VALCLASS parameters.

Another method for implementing security is to take advantage of the global exits that are scheduled after a command is entered but before it is executed. Refer to Chapter 9 for information on the NetView global exits.

CLIST Definition

A CLIST can also be defined in DSICMD. In this case, the module named is always DSICCP. Once scheduled, this routine searches the DSICLD dataset. If a CLIST is not defined in DSICMD, NetView will still search DSICLD. Including the CLIST in DSICMD improves NetView's performance.

6.8 Starting the NetView Application

The NetView application address space can be started as an MVS started task (STC) or a batch job. There can be two programs named on the EXEC card, depending on the function desired.

The program DSIMNT is the main NetView task driver which attaches the other optional subtasks at startup. Alternatively, the module BNJLINTB can be used when local error data from the LOGREC facility is required for the hardware monitor. If this module is named, DSIMNT is then attached.

Relation to SSI Address Space

The MVS subsystem name defined for use by NetView can be up to four characters long. The application and SSI address spaces for a single NetView domain are paired together based on this subsystem name; each address space name must begin with the MVS subsystem name selected for use.

7

Interfaces and Communication

The subtasks within NetView are driven by the flow of messages coming in from the network, as well as from other applications on the same host. In order to understand the features available with NetView, it is first important to appreciate how this data is accessed.

This chapter presents the basic connections and interfaces available to the programs running within NetView. These communication facilities are used as a basis for the individual components and for creating the more advanced functionality, such as network and system automation, which is described later in the book.

7.1 MVS Subsystem Interface

Support for the MVS subsystem interface (SSI) was added with release 2 of NetView. This was a natural step in the product's evolution. The SSI implementation gives NetView-based applications access to a wider range of information regarding system and application activity on the host.

This section describes the basic MVS message and command interfaces which were originally provided with the product. While still available for use, some of the subsystem connectivity has been superseded by the newer MVS extended multiple console support (MCS) facility, described in the next section.

SSI Overview

The subsystem interface provides a means to establish communication between well-defined subsystems, each identified with a unique four-character name. Information, carried as discrete events, can be sent to a specific subsystem or broadcast to all active subsystems. Every subsystem provides a routine to handle one or more of the events, depending on the type of data it needs to access.

The Subsystem Control Vector Table (SSCVT) control block anchors a specific subsystem. The event-handling routines included with the subsystem are identified in the Subsystem Vector Table (SSVT). Figure 7.1 provides a list of the MVS subsystem events that NetView supports through its SSI implementation. The NetView SSI address space provides the connection to the subsystem interface on behalf of the NetView applications.

SSI Event	Description
End of Task	NetView is notified when each task (TCB) in the system terminates.
End of Address Space	Each address space, or memory, termination is presented to NetView.
WTO Message	Write-to-operator (WTO) messages resulting from the SVC 35 instruction can be processed.
WTO Message (command)	Console commands, issued using SVC 34, are intercepted and examined for the prefix character.
Delete Operator Message	DOM messages complement the WTO support.

Figure 7.1 List of the MVS subsystem events supported by NetView.

Write-to-Operator Messages

An important feature of NetView's SSI support is the access to Write-to-Operator (WTO) messages. These messages can be solicited, in that they are responses to MVS commands issued from within the NetView application address space. Or they can be unsolicited, describing unexpected changes in the system.

In either case, the process starts when a task on the host issues the WTO macro resulting in an SVC 35 instruction. The WTO buffer is first passed through the MVS Message Processing Facility (MPF); the definitions governing its operation are stored in the SYS1.PARMLIB dataset. MPF provides control over the characteristics of each message for display and automation. After examination by MPF, a WTO is either marked for or excluded from NetView automation with a flag in the message header. The MPF AUTO parameter is set to YES (automate the message, pass to NetView) or NO for each message. This is done either explicitly or by default.

The message is then passed through the MVS Multiple Console Support (MCS) facility, where it is broadcast to the active subsystems. The NetView subsystem tests each message, accepting and buffering those which have been marked for automation by MPF. The NetView SSI address space temporarily holds each message, both unsolicited and those solicited WTOs destined to be forwarded to waiting NetView subtasks.

The messages are extracted from the SSI address space by the subsystem receiver task (CNMCSSIR) in the NetView application address space. The WTOs are then delivered, as appropriate, and passed through the NetView automation table.

MVS Commands

Subtasks within the application address space can issue MVS operator commands and receive the corresponding replies. Each command must be prefixed with 'MVS', which is really the name of a NetView command processor. This NetView-supplied program prepares the local environment and issues the actual command.

When processing the command, the MVS command processor first makes sure that the SSI address space is active. Then a subsystem allocatable console is selected for use from the pool of available consoles. These MCS subsystem consoles are defined at IPL time in the CONSOLxx member of SYS1.PARMLIB. If the subtask already has a console reserved, a new one is not required. With such a console allocated, the command replies can then be directed back to the sender. The number of subsystem consoles that can be used by NetView is limited to 99.

After an MCS subsystem console has been acquired, the SVC 34 instruction is used to send the command to MVS. Any resulting WTO reply messages flow back through the SSI address space to the command sender.

NetView Commands

It is possible for commands to flow in a reverse direction as well. That is, NetView commands can be issued by an MVS console operator. In this case, a background automation subtask within NetView is dedicated to each active MVS console.

The NetView AUTOTASK command is used to start the autotask, and in the process is associated with a specific console. The console operator can then issue a NetView command, prefixed by the special character defined with the SSI address space start procedure JCL. Each MVS command is examined for the NetView prefix character; those destined for NetView then flow through the SSI address space to the dedicated autotask where they can be interpreted and processed.

7.2 Extended MCS Console Support

The extended MCS console feature was first introduced with version 4.1 of MVS/ESA. It has several advantages over the previous console support. NetView can use this new facility when running on an MVS version 4.2.2 (or later) system, thereby augmenting and improving its automation capabilities.

More Direct Flow

The extended MCS consoles enable a more direct connection from NetView to the operating system, where the MVS subsystem interface is effectively bypassed. The MVS messages, instead of passing back through the SSI address space, are sent directly to the destination task within NetView. Through an extension to the MCS component of MVS, applications can operate so as to more closely resemble actual console devices.

Acquiring an Extended Console

Consoles are acquired by NetView subtasks either implicitly through the MVS command processor, or explicitly with the GETCONID command. Either way, NetView attempts to allocate a console on behalf of the requesting program. The console is then reserved for the subtask until it is released with the RELCONID command or the task terminates.

The extended MCS consoles do not have to be pre-defined in the CONSOLxx member like the subsystem allocatable consoles. Instead, they are dynamically defined with the MCSOPER macro. Each console is given a name by which it is known; NetView attempts to use the subtask name for which the console is being acquired. And unlike the older console support, there is no limit to the number of extended consoles that can be defined within the NetView application address space.

Automation Processing

Use of the extended MCS consoles enhances NetView automation facilities. For example, autotasks can be dedicated to monitor and control specific system resources. Unsolicited system messages can be received over the extended consoles as well.

As with the earlier MVS console support, the CNMCSSIR subtask still accepts and processes the unsolicited messages. When an extended console is allocated by CNMCSSIR, it is assigned the name of CNMCSSIR and given the automation attribute via the MSCOPE parameter of the MCSOPER macro. This causes the eligible unsolicited messages to be passed to the subtask. Actually, any task which uses the load module named CNMCSSIR (i.e., on the TASK statement) can access the messages in this manner.

WTO messages which are assigned the characteristic of AUTO(YES) or AUTO(token) by MPF can be automated by NetView. Both variations have the same effect, where "token" is an optional parameter that, when specified, is passed along with each message.

The Message Data Block (MDB), an MVS structure supported by NetView, carries more information than was possible with the SSI connection. Many of the MDB variables can be accessed by NetView programs when processing a message.

7.3 Program-to-Program Interface

The NetView PPI provides a method for any two programs on the same host to communicate. Generally, the PPI facilitates better integration among the host subsystems. In particular, it enables NetView-based applications to gain a wider access to information through a standard programming interface. Since it was introduced with release 3 as a small programming enhancement (SPE), the PPI has grown to become an integral part of NetView processing.

Store and Forward Flow

The flow of PPI data through the NetView SSI address space is accomplished with a relatively simple store-and-forward mechanism. During a single exchange, one program is the sender while the other is the receiver. Full-duplex communication is possible when both sides are defined as receivers.

A send operation results in the data being copied to the SSI address space where it is temporarily stored. Each receiver has a private queue designed to hold its data, with the maximum number of available buffers defined at registration time.

When a buffer is queued for a receiver, the waiting subtask is notified via the MVS POST service. The buffered data can be accepted by the receiver, and is then deleted from the SSI address space.

Application Development Considerations

Before the PPI can be used, the NetView SSI address space must be active. Then any program executing with the following characteristics can access the PPI:

- Task Control Block (TCB) mode.
- 31-bit addressing mode.
- Primary address space mode.

The application makes specific requests of the PPI by invoking the NetView load module CNMCNETV (alias CNMNETV). This module can be loaded when needed, or linked with the calling program. At entry, register one must hold the address of a fullword which, in turn, points to a Request Parameter Block (RPB).

The RPB identifies the request type and contains additional information depending on the exact operation. CNMNETV performs the function by utilizing cross-memory techniques, as necessary, to access the SSI address space. Upon return, the status of the request is returned in the RPB.

PPI Request Types

Figure 7.2 provides a list of requests that can be made to the PPI. For each request, an RPB must be formatted and passed to NetView. Although the PPI does not use an SNA session, and is relatively simple, there is still a protocol that is followed when a sender and receiver interact.

Uses for the PPI

There is a large and growing list of IBM and non-IBM products which utilize the PPI. Some of the major users include:

- NetView Bridge
- NetView Performance Monitor (NPM)
- OPC/ESA
- CICS Automation Option
- Resource Object Data Manager
- NetView alert receiver subtask

In the future, this list will undoubtedly continue to expand.

7.4 SSI Address Space Definitions

The configuration and operation of the NetView console, message, and PPI facilities can be controlled by the user. These parameters are found in two main places:

- NetView SSI address space JCL
- MVSPARM parameter in DSIDMN of the DSIPARM dataset

Figure 7.3 provides a list of the parameters defined as part of the NetView SSI started task. CBUF, MBUF, and REG control the allocation of virtual storage in the SSI address space. The DSIG parameter identifies the prefix character that will be recognized by the NetView subsystem address space when accepting commands from MVS consoles. MSGIFAC determines which console facility will be used: subsystem or extended.

MSGIFAC and MVSPARM work together, and should be defined so as to be compatible. The level of MVS being used also has an effect on the

PPI Request	Description
Type 1	Query the NetView subsystem status; this request should be used first.
Type 2	Query the status of a named PPI receiver.
Type 3	Obtain the ASCB and TCB addresses which must be provided with several of the other request types.
Type 4	Define and initialize a receiver, with its status set to active.
Type 9	Deactivate a receiver, which is the final request used.
Type 12	Send an NMVT or CP-MSU formatted alert to NetView.
Type 14	Send a data buffer to a named receiver program.
Type 22	Receive one data buffer from queue; caller does not wait if there is no data available.
Type 24	Wait for data to arrive for the receiver; request type 22 must then be issued.

Figure 7.2 Types of requests for the NetView PPI running under MVS.

SSI Parameter	Description
CBUF	The number of 256-byte buffers used to hold NetView commands entered from an MVS console.
DSIG	Identifies the NetView subsystem designator which precedes all commands entered from an MVS console (e.g., "%").
MBUF	The number of 256-byte buffers used to hold WTO and DOM requests for processing by NetView.
MSGIFAC	Determines use of the extended MCS console facility (if available) versus the MVS subsystem; must be compatible with MVSPARM.
PPIOPT	Specifies whether the PPI is activated and utilized, or not initialized. There can be only one NetView SSI address space with an active PPI.
REG	This parameter specifies the size of the SSI address space in kilobytes.

Figure 7.3 Parameter definitions included with the NetView subsystem address space.

operation of these parameters. The major choices in defining the message and command support include:

■ Allow the level of the operating system to determine whether extended MCS consoles will be used - NetView supports them with MVS/ESA version 4.2.2 and above.

■ Force MVS messages to flow through the SSI address
space, regardless of the MVS level. This option is
useful when controlling migration to extended consoles.

■ Disable the SSI support so that neither MVS messages nor NetView commands flow through the SSI
address space. Unsolicited messages can still be
forwarded for automation if extended consoles are
available.

In all cases where the SSI has not been disabled, NetView commands from MVS consoles flow through the SSI address space.

Multiple NetView Address Spaces

The basic NetView domain consists of an application and subsystem
address space. The names of the two address spaces must begin with the
name of the MVS subsystem name being used. For example, in the
samples shipped with NetView a subsystem of CNMP is assumed for the
two address spaces named CNMPROC (application) and CNMPSSI
(subsystem).

It is possible to have more than one NetView domain active on a
host. This can be done to separate function among NetView domains or
to provide a certain level of backup capability. For example, it is not
uncommon to have a NetView for problem determination (i.e., manage
alerts for the hardware monitor) and automation. The address spaces
must be coordinated so there is no conflict with the domain and subsystem names.

In the case of multiple active subsystem address spaces, there
should be only one serving PPI requests. These address spaces can be
individually controlled with the MVS start and stop commands.

7.5 Network Definitions

VTAM is widely used to support the features and components within
NetView, providing access to network-related data. There are obvious
examples, such as when a terminal operator logs on to the product. In
addition, many of the components (e.g., hardware monitor) utilize VTAM
on behalf of the user to transfer information throughout the network.

This section presents the major areas for definition and configuration for the commonly used network communication capabilities. Additional communication customization is required for the individual
NetView components, which is described later in the book.

Main Domain APPLID

The NetView domain identifier (domain ID) is defined on the NCCFID statement of the DSIDMN member, as described in Chapter 6. The same parameter defines the name of the VTAM application identifier (APPLID) for the main task in the application address space. That is, the NetView domain ID and APPLID are the same. The samples shipped with NetView use the five-character domain ID CNM01.

The main APPLID has several uses. For example, an operator first logs on to this APPLID. The terminal session is then passed off to another APPLID. Also, LU type 6.2 communication can flow through the main APPLID. An example is the Graphic Monitor Facility (GMF) running on the OS/2 workstation which connects to NetView in this manner.

Figure 7.4 provides an example of the main NetView APPLID statement defined to VTAM. If LU 6.2 (including a connection to the GMF server) is not used, then the definition is slightly different.

```
CNM23     APPL   AUTH=(NVPACE,ACQ,PASS),PRTCT=CNM01,                    X
                 MODETAB=AMODETAB,DLOGMOD=DSIL6MOD,                     X
                 APPC=YES,PARSESS=YES,                                  X
                 DMINWNL=4,DMINWNR=4,DSESLIM=8,                         X
                 AUTOSES=2
*                STATOPT='NETVIEW'
```

Figure 7.4   An example of the VTAM APPLID defined for NetView's main task.

Primary Program Operator Interface Task

The PPT was originally designed to accept unsolicited messages from VTAM using the primary Program Operator Interface (POI). These messages reflect status changes in the network and can be used to update the status monitor data areas and drive automation tasks as required. The PPT also anchors system-related features, such as timing requests, that are initiated by other tasks within NetView.

The usefulness of this VTAM interface has been superseded by the new VTAM-Statmon interface, which is described in Chapter 13. With the proper level of NetView and VTAM, the status monitor control blocks are updated directly by VTAM using MVS cross-memory techniques. Note that if the PPT is not configured to accept VTAM messages, they will flow over the subsystem interface.

There is a single APPLID which must be defined for the PPT, giving the task authority to become a primary program operator. There can be only one such APPLID active within an SNA domain at a time.

Operator APPLIDs

After an operator initially logs on to NetView, the session is passed over to another APPLID selected from a pool of available applications. In this way, each operator is serviced by an individual APPLID. Each of the defined application IDs begin with the NetView domain id and are numbered sequentially (e.g., CNM23001, CNM23002).

Terminal Access Facility

The TAF functionality included with NetView provides the means for applications and operators to connect to other applications (outside of NetView) through SNA sessions. There are two types of TAF connections possible:

- Operator-control (LU type 1) - this is a line mode connection used to pass commands and other data; the messages can be automated by NetView.
- Full-screen (LU type 2) - while not automated by NetView, these sessions provide a convenient way to connect and toggle between sessions.

Two sets of APPLIDs must be defined to enable TAF support. The facility is then accessed through the commands provided with NetView. Figure 7.5 lists the available TAF commands.

7.6 CNM Interface

The Communication Network Management (CNM) interface was described in Chapter 1; it provides access to the physical resources of the network with an indirect connection through VTAM. That is, the SSCP maintains a session with each of the physical units in its domain. The NetView-based applications (i.e., LUs) communication with the SSCP to access the PU, and other, data.

Information can be transferred across the CNM interface in basically two ways:

- Unsolicited - flows arrive at the host indicating unexpected problems or other events.
- Solicited - response messages to specific requests made by the host-based applications.

CNM data can be accessed by the DST-based code through a macro interface (for assembler) or a documented API call (for high-level language). When defining a DST, a command processor is named to receive control for unsolicited CNM data.

NetView Command	Description
BFSESS	Starts a full-screen (LU 2) session with another VTAM application.
BGNSESS	Starts or resumes a session.
BOSESS	Starts an operator-controlled (LU 0) session with another application.
ENDSESS	Terminates a TAF session.
LISTSESS	Obtains and displays information regarding a user's TAF sessions.
RSESS	Returns to a disconnected session.
SENDSESS	Used to forward commands and data over a TAF session.

Figure 7.5 Command procedures used to access TAF services.

CNM Router

The CNM routing table has been a part of VTAM since the network management products which preceded NetView. Each unsolicited request is examined for its type, and then routed based on an entry in the table.

With release 1.2, the CNM Router task was added to NetView as a central point for receiving unsolicited traffic. This task accepts all of the messages and then forwards them within NetView as required. The DSICRTR task must be defined with an APPLID; its session with VTAM is needed in order to receive the CNM data.

7.7 Alias Facility

The SNA Network Interconnection (SNI) is supported by the VTAM and NCP software. It provides a method for connecting multiple SNA networks, each with a unique network identifier, through session establishment assistance and network address translation.

When establishing cross-network connections, there can often be duplication of network names and addresses among the networks involved. The address translation is carried out within the communication controller by the NCP software. Translation of the resource names is an optional function which can be implemented by using the NetView alias facility.

Alias Definitions

The alias function requires both a TASK and APPLID definition; additional definitions are stored in the DSIPARM dataset. When a cross-network connection is in the process of being established by the gateway SSCP, a request for translation is generated. The message is passed to through the CNM routing task to the alias subtask.

There are three names that can be translated with the parameters available:

- LU name
- Class-of-Service (COS) entry name
- Mode table entry name

Figure 7.6 presents an example of the alias definitions. In each case, the variables to be updated by the user are shown in small letters.

```
        ORIGNET USCORP1


[label]  LU   real_name,owner_network,alias_name,[sscp_owner]

[label]  COS  adjacent_name,adjacent_network,local_name

[label]  MODE destination_name,destination_network,local_name
```

Figure 7.6 Example of definitions used with the Alias translation facility.

8

Data Recording and Archival

NetView utilizes several different logs in order to record information regarding its operation and the network in general. This chapter presents the common NetView logs that are shared by subtasks within the application address space. Other databases and log files, specific to the individual components, are presented later in the book.

The Resource Object Data Manager (RODM) feature, included with version 2.3, also has its own log facility. Refer to Chapter 18 for more information regarding the RODM log.

8.1 Basic Operation and Definition

Each of the NetView logs is controlled and accessed by a single dedicated DST task. The initialization member named on the TASK definition statement contains parameters affecting the log's configuration and operation.

Each log usually consists of one or two actual datasets which are allocated in the started task JCL with data definition (DD) statements. When two datasets are used, one is designated as primary while the other is secondary. Only one dataset can be active (i.e., being written to) at a time.

The DST initialization member consists of multiple DSTINIT statements, each using one of the several different keyword parameters per line. The type of information conveyed with the DSTINIT parameters, affecting the log, includes:

■ Whether or not VSAM support is enabled.

- Primary and secondary DD names for the VSAM clusters.
- Primary and secondary DD names for the sequential log files (non-VSAM).
- Passwords for the VSAM clusters.
- DST initialization exit, which receives control for each line read from the initialization member.
- One or more DST exit routines which receive control during file processing, such as at open, input, output, and file empty time.
- For VSAM, whether or not the local shared resources and deferred write performance options are used.

Following the DSTINIT statements, there can be additional configuration parameters. For example, the LOGINIT parameter is available for the network, sequential, and trace logs and determines how the task handles a log full situation.

```
*
*    INITIALIZATION PARAMETERS FOR NETVIEW TRACE.
*
*
*    DSTINIT PARAMETERS:
*
*        PDDNM   - VSAM PRIMARY DD NAME.
*        SDDNM   - VSAM SECONDARY DD NAME.
*        XITVN   - DST EXIT CALLED WHEN AN EMPTY
*                  VSAM FILE IS OPENED FOR PROCESSING.
*        FUNCT   - VSAM SUPPORT IS ENABLED.
*        DSRBO   - NUMBER OF DSRBS ALLOCATED.
*        MACRF   - DETERMINES IF VSAM LSR AND DEFERRED
*                  WRITE (DFR) IS USED.
*
     DSTINIT PDDNM=DSITRCP
     DSTINIT SDDNM=DSITRCS
     DSTINIT XITVN=DSIWLMED
     DSTINIT FUNCT=VSAM
     DSTINIT DSRBO=1
     DSTINIT MACRF=LSR
     LOGINIT AUTOFLIP=YES,RESUME=YES
```

Figure 8.1 Example of log configuration using the DSTINIT statement.

Figure 8.1 contains an example of log definition parameters, in this case for the network log. Recording begins with the primary file, and then switches to the secondary file. LOGINIT determines what happens when the secondary becomes full. In this case, the task will switch back to the primary file and resume recording following the last entry.

Queuing Log Messages

In order to write data to the various logs, messages must be sent from the originating task to the dedicated recording task. This process involves an intertask queuing technique within the NetView address space.

Applications can use the write log services macro (DSIWLS) to record to the following logs:

- Network log
- Hardcopy log
- External log
- Sequential log
- MVS system log

The message queuing service macro (DSIMQS) is also available to send message buffers between tasks, but is usually reserved for commands.

8.2 VSAM Definitions

The Virtual Storage Access Method (VSAM) is used for the majority of the log datasets and databases, and is therefore an important aspect of NetView's processing and overall performance. Figure 8.2 contains a list of the VSAM files used by NetView.

Local Shared Resources Pools

The Local Shared Resources (LSR) facility is available when using VSAM files on the MVS host. NetView provides support for LSR which the user can define and enable on a task-by-task basis.

LSR improves VSAM performance by allowing certain VSAM data areas, such as Input/Output (I/O) control blocks, buffers, and channel programs, to be shared among several clusters in the same address space. Also, both the LSR and deferred write (DFR) options reduce the number of disk input and output operations.

The BLDVRP macro instruction describes a set of one or more pools, each of which contains multiple fixed-length buffers. Each BLDVRP is uniquely identified by a shared pool number. There can be up to 16 shared pools (BLDVRP macros) defined within a single address space.

Facility	Number of Clusters	Description
Network Log	2	The network log is used to record text messages generated or processed by NetView.
Trace Log	2	The NetView trace provides the means to capture and record internal activity.
Save/Restore Dataset	1	Global variables and timers can be saved to disk, then accessed when NetView is restarted.
Online Help	1	Contains on-line help and messages displayed to the terminal operator.
Hardware Monitor	2	Alerts, events, and statistics are processed and recorded by the Hardware Monitor.
Session Monitor	2	The Session Monitor records session-related and response time information.
Central Site Control Facility	1	CSCF is used to remotely control 3172 and 3174 control units.
4700 Support	2	NetView can optionally provide support for the 4700 financial series of devices.
RODM Clusters	6	There are two log files and four checkpoint datasets which support RODM.

Figure 8.2 List of VSAM datasets allocated to NetView.

When an ACB is opened with the LSR option, a shared pool number is supplied which, in effect, points to the definitions of a particular BLDVRP macro. The cluster can then utilize one or more of the buffer pools based on its own particular allocation characteristics.

The VSAM control interval (CI) is the actual physical record read from and written to disk for the cluster; it can contain multiple data records which are individually accessed through the programming API. The data and index components of the cluster each have separately defined CI sizes and storage allocations.

When a cluster is opened with LSR enabled, a buffer pool is selected from the appropriate BLDVRP definitions (shared pool) for both the data and index components. In each case, the buffer size used is based on the CI size. If a pool's buffer size matches the CI size, that pool is used. Otherwise, the next largest buffer pool is selected.

DFR extends LSR processing by deferring write operations as long as possible so that I/O operations can be reduced. For example, when multiple records are changed in the same CI, the data is updated first in virtual storage. In this case, the I/O operations are reduced because the multiple records are "blocked" together for one I/O operation.

Defining LSR and DFR Support

Activating the basic LSR and DFR support is relatively simple. Additional customization is possible based on installation requirements.

```
DSIZVLSR CSECT
         BLDVRP KEYLEN=255,STRNO=30,TYPE=LSR,MF=L,              *
                LOC=ANY,SHRPOOL=0,                              *
                BUFFERS=(2048(23),4096(33),8192(30)))
         END
```

Figure 8.3 Shared pool definitions supplied with NetView using the VSAM BLDVRP macro.

The statement VSAMLSR in member DSIDMN names a non-executable load module which contains the BLDVRP macro. This parameter enables LSR support by establishing the buffer pool definitions for the address space.

The module DSIZVLSR is shipped with the product, providing default values which are adequate for most installations. The module can be updated and reassembled, or entirely replaced, as required.

Figure 8.3 shows the LSR definitions supplied with NetView. Note that there is only one shared pool (i.e., SHRPOOL) defined; this macro defines multiple buffer pools.

After the base LSR support is available within the NetView address space, each task can then be configured to use it if desired. The MACRF parameter of the DSTINIT statement, if included, specifies LSR or DFR (which includes LSR). When activated, the buffer pools are assigned to each cluster as described above.

Monitoring Performance

In a heavily utilized NetView environment, VSAM processing can have a significant impact on overall performance. For this reason, it is important to monitor and tune VSAM where possible.

The LSR and DFR options should be utilized, as recommended by IBM. LSR allows storage to be shared, and can reduce read I/O operations by first searching the appropriate buffer pool. DFR also reduces I/O by updating the CIs in storage on write operations, and then flushing them to disk only when necessary (e.g., for a buffer shortage).

Performance of the VSAM clusters and LSR pools can be monitored with two NetView operator commands. In Figure 8.4, the LISTCAT command provides information similar to the Access Method Services utility, except activity is displayed for open clusters. This is done by directly examining the VSAM data areas in virtual storage.

```
LISTCAT    Listcat of Active VSAM Data Base for BNJDSERV    17:17:14  Page 1 of 1

    VSAM ACB Options: LSR, ADR, KEY, SEQ, DIR, OUT
    Cluster Information:
        DDNAME: BNJLGPR        KEYLEN: .........76      RKP: ..........0
        BSTRNO: ..........0    STRNO: .........11       STRMAX: ..........1
        BUFSP: ..........0
    DATA Component Information:
        LRECL: ........4086    CINV: ........4096
        BUFND: .........12     BUFNO: ..........0
        NEXT: ..........1      FS: .........28
        NCIS: ..........0      NSSS: ..........0
        NEXCP: .........24     NLOGR: ..........2      NRETR: ..........3
        NINSR: ..........0     NUPDR: ..........3      NDELR: ..........0
        AVSPAC: .....1716224   ENDRBA: ......573440    HALCRBA: .....1720320
    INDEX Component Information:
        LRECL: ........4089    CINV: ........4096
        BUFNI: ..........0     BUFNO: ..........0
        NEXT: ..........2      NIXL: ..........1
        NEXCP: ..........9     NLOGR: ..........1
        AVSPAC: .......49152   ENDRBA: .......45056    HALCRBA: .......53248


    ENTER= Refresh  PF1= Help  PF2= End  PF3= Return
```

Figure 8.4 Example of output from the LISTCAT command.

Figure 8.5 presents output from VSAMPOOL, which is used to monitor all LSR buffer pools or only those in use by a named subtask.

```
NCCF                    N E T V I E W    CNM23 OPER1    08/02/93 15:07:31
* CNM23    VSAMPOOL AAUTSKLP
' CNM23
CNM260I VSAM LSR/DFR RESOURCE POOL STATISTICS FOR AAUTSKLP
CNM261I   CINV   BUFNO    BFRFND    BUFRDS      NUIW       UIW      EXCPS
CNM261I   2048     23      1510       12         0          8       851
CNM261I   8192     30       506      219        189        28      13477
CNM262I END OF DISPLAY
-----------------------------------------------------------------------------



???
```

Figure 8.5 Example of output from the VSAMPOOL command.

8.3 Network Log

The network log is the most visible and immediately useful of the NetView logs. It consists of two VSAM files, and is designed to record activity (e.g., all OSTs) within NetView, including text messages and commands.

As a general rule, all of the text messages generated within or processed by NetView are written to the log. This includes operator commands, NetView messages, MVS messages and commands, as well as cross-domain messages.

The network log can be useful in analyzing and debugging NetView's operation and performance. For example, the output from performance monitoring commands, such as VSAMPOOL, is written to the log. Once recorded, this data can be extracted and viewed.

There are two subtasks associated with the network log:

■ DSILOG - the main log task accepts data buffers and writes them to the active cluster.
■ CNM01BRW - this task is used by an operator to read from, or browse, either of the log datasets; it is defined as a part of the status monitor.

Because of the potentially large volume of data, use of the network log can have an impact on performance. NetView's performance can be improved by limiting the number of unnecessary or unwanted messages sent to the network log. This can be done by restricting the flow of messages into the NetView address space, or by filtering messages within NetView from going to the log through automation table statements.

Browsing

There are several commands available for viewing the network log, and controlling its operation, from an operator terminal. The currently active or inactive log can be selected, as well as either the primary or secondary (regardless of their states). To summarize, the parameters used with the BROWSE command include:

- NETLOGA - active log
- NETLOGI - inactive log
- NETLOGP - primary log file
- NETLOGS - secondary log file

In addition, there is flexibility in which data records are selected for display. For example, a date/time range can be specified to qualify the search.

Figure 8.6 contains a display of the active file as viewed from an operator terminal. Note that the log is really a part of the status monitor, which must be active before the network log can be browsed. This is discussed in Chapter 13.

Printing

Many times it can be useful to analyze the network log in a background, or batch, manner. The log datasets can be printed, either to hardcopy or a sequential disk file. In order to accomplish this, the NetView samples library includes JCL to print a log cluster.

In addition to text message data, each record contains other fields including:

- Date and time
- Message type
- Operator name
- LU name
- Domain ID

Through an analysis of the log data, important events or general trends can be detected.

```
STATMON.BROWSE      ACTS  NETWORK LOG FOR 08/02/93 (93214) COLS 017 094  13:00
HOST: HOST02             *1*   *2*   *3*   *4*  SEARCH MAX:           SCROLL: CSR
 ---2----+----3----+----4----+----5----+----6----+----7----+----8----+----9----
 CNM23      12:59:04  $HASP628 LINE1       SNA ACTIVE
 CNM23      12:59:04  $HASP628 LINE2       SNA ACTIVE
 CNM23      12:59:04  $HASP628 LINE3       SNA ACTIVE    (USMHSE2C)
 CNM23      12:59:04  $HASP628 LINE4       SNA ACTIVE    (MVSPS1)
 CNM23      12:59:11 3 DSI064A OPENACB FAILED, ACBOFLG = X'02', ACBERROR = X'58',
 CNM23    % 12:59:11  CNM039I AN IMPORTANT MESSAGE HAS BEEN LOGGED - PLEASE BROW
 CNM23      12:59:16  $HASP250 RSCS4218 IS PURGED
 CNM23      12:59:38  CCX001 TRANFER COMPLETED
 CNM23      12:59:38  IEC070I CATALOG.UCAT.MAIN
 CNM23      12:59:38  K2VSAMIO01 REQUEST=PUT  , RETURN CODE=08, FDBK=1C
 CNM23      12:59:38  DBF0023I INTEGRATION STARTING WITH RECORD =    21
 CNM23      12:59:38  DBF0161I COMPARE OF KEYS ENCOUNTERS ERROR
 CNM23      12:59:40  DBF0210E TERMINATION IN PROGRESS
 CNM23      12:59:40  CCX002 REQUEST RECEIVED FROM USER = OPER2
 CNM23      12:59:41  PDX0020 DEBUG MODE ENTERED
 CNM23      12:59:41  IEC070I CATALOG.UCAT.MAIN
 CNM23      12:59:41  K2VSAMIO01 REQUEST=PUT  , RETURN CODE=08, FDBK=1C
 CNM23      13:00:11 3 DSI064A OPENACB FAILED, ACBOFLG = X'02', ACBERROR = X'58',

CMD==>
1=HLP 2=END 3=RET 4=TOP 5=BOT 6=ROL 7=BCK 8=FWD 9=RPF 10=LFT 11=RGT 12=ALL
```

Figure 8.6 Sample output from the network log viewed from an operator terminal.

8.4 External Log

The external log is slightly more complex than the other logs. Once data is queued to the DSIELTSK subtask, it can then be written to a disk dataset or to the System Management Facility (SMF) log.

The external log is used primarily by the two NetView components:

- Hardware monitor
- Session monitor

Information sent to the external log by these components is basically the same as recorded to their own individual databases, consisting of text and binary numeric values. Evident in its name, the external log provides a way to record data "externally," where it can then be accessed and analyzed. For example, the records can be used to verify service level goals or to implement network accounting procedures.

Recording to SMF or External File

Once queued to the external log, records are written to SMF or the disk file allocated to the NetView address space. This recording capability is implemented through the use of command processors and DST exits.

Dataset recording is provided as part of DST exit processing. A default exit is shipped with NetView, which can be updated, replaced, or augmented.

The default support includes writing to the SMF log. The SYS1.PARMLIB dataset should be updated so as to enable the recording of SMF records 37 (hardware monitor) and 39 (session monitor).

8.5 Sequential Log

The sequential log supports the recording of data in variable-length blocked (VB) format. While not used by the major NetView components, it provides an option for recording data for user or vendor-developed systems.

Unlike the other NetView logs, multiple sequential logs can be active, each serviced by a separate subtask. Each subtask can have a primary and secondary file. The initialization member contains DSTINIT statements which are used to define the log datasets and their processing options.

8.6 NetView Trace Facility

Like most of the IBM subsystem products, NetView includes a trace facility which records internal processing activity. The trace is used to debug NetView-based applications, as well as problems with the NetView product itself.

Each of the trace records is defined and documented by NetView. The type of data written to the trace log includes parameters, addresses, and return codes. This trace data can be recorded in two different manners:

- Internal (INT) mode - a wraparound table, allocated in virtual storage, holds the trace entries.
- External (EXT) mode - the records are written to the primary and secondary disk datasets; the DSITRACE subtask must be defined and active.

The operation of the NetView trace can have an impact on performance. It is recommended that the trace be active at all times with the

INT mode; however, access to and use of the EXT mode should be carefully restricted.

Controlling Trace Operation

Figure 8.7 contains an example of the TRACE command, which is utilized to control the operation of the NetView trace. Here, all trace options are captured and recorded in the internal table, the size of which is defined to be 100 pages. Also, only activity for the Operator Station Tasks (OSTs) is monitored.

```
TRACE   ON,OPTION=ALL,MODE=INT,SIZE=100,TASK=OST
```

Figure 8.7 An example of the command used to control operation of the NetView trace.

Many times, it is not necessary to collect all types of trace records. In this case, the operator can specify a subset to be recorded. Figure 8.8 describes the types of trace data that can be captured using the OPTION parameter.

As mentioned above, the DSITRACE subtask accepts and records trace data from other tasks when the trace is activated with external mode recording.

Trace Analysis

All of the trace records are defined and described in complete detail in the IBM Problem Determination and Diagnosis manual. Refer to the appendix for a summary of the types of records included.

Each record typically begins with a header, which includes an EBCDIC record identifier. For example, when an LUC session is allocated, the corresponding trace record will start with "LUCA".

Data written to the internal table is more difficult to access and view than the external mode data. One exception to this is the situation where NetView abends for some reason, and the trace table is printed with the dump.

Trace Option	Description of Trace Data
QUE	Intertask queuing of buffers with the NetView macro DSIMQS.
PSS	Presentation services, including terminal input and output using the macro DSIPSS.
DISP	Dispatching activity, including wait (DSIWAT), post (DSIPOS), and dispatch from wait.
STOR	Storage allocation, both getting and freeing.
UEXIT	Calls to the user exit routines, both global and DST.
MOD	Entry to and exit from a subset of NetView modules.

Figure 8.8 A description of the options available with the NetView trace.

The internal trace table is anchored by a header, which is pointed to from the Main Vector Table (MVT) at offset x'AA8'. The information in the table is used to manage the trace operation. The fields include:

- Eye-catcher "NIT"
- Length of table
- Time stamps for most recent entry placed in the table, and most recent wrap
- Address of the next available slot and the end of the table

When debugging a specific problem, it is considerably easier to use external mode recording. Here, the trace datasets can be printed and examined off-line.

8.7 Global Variable Recording

The variables used by the NetView-based applications are dynamic in nature and can be lost when the NetView application address space terminates. This can create a problem, or at least require additional CPU resources, when attempting to recreate the data.

With version 2 of NetView, support was added to record this type of data to a log dataset so that it can be easily recovered when NetView is restarted.

Save/Restore Function Task

The DSISVRT subtask can be used to save and then restore the NetView operational environment; it allocates one primary dataset. The types of information which can be saved from within NetView includes:

- Automation timers
- Global variables
- Programmable Network Access (PNA) registrations
- Focal point information

This NetView feature is particularly useful as NetView is more heavily utilized, with a number of complex and interrelated applications.

Figure 8.9 includes an example of a simple command used to restore the automation timers that are currently in the save/restore database. These include timers previously established with the commands AT, AFTER, and EVERY. Refer to Chapter 14 for more information on these and other automation services.

```
                          RESTORE    TIMER
```

Figure 8.9 An example of command used to restore internal timers.

9

Application Development

NetView offers a rich set of facilities and services for creating powerful network and automation related applications. The developer has several options in terms of the scope, complexity, and language which can be used. This chapter presents the basic elements of application design and coding which are part of the NetView product.

9.1 Types of User-written Code

There are three major types of user-written code that can run within the NetView application address space. Figure 9.1 provides a list and explanation of these areas for development. Both assembler and a high-level language (HLL) can be used when writing a command processor. Command List (CLIST) programs can utilize either the Restructured Extended Executor (REXX) or original the NetView CLIST language.

In a general sense, the command procedures and exits can be considered to be transactions. Each is scheduled, runs, and then terminates. They are event-driven, responding to specific conditions within NetView and the network in general. Communication of these events is accomplished through messages carried within buffers. For example, when an operator types the name of a command procedure and presses the ENTER key, several different global exits are called, followed by the scheduling of the actual command module itself.

The optional subtask (OPT) can have a larger scope, but also requires more careful planning and design. If a DST is selected for use, it functions as a dedicated engine for running Data Service Command Processors (DSCP). Developing a complete OPT is an even larger effort in that more of the underlying subtask services must be written by the user. For example, NetView provides message queues which must be examined when one of the specified ECBs is posted.

Development Plan

The user has several different options to consider when developing and implementing a NetView-based system. For example, what is the reason for, and purpose of, the system ? What specific business problems does the application address ? How does it align with the strategic goals of the corporation, and what type of commitment will it have ? What is the skill set and experience level of the staff ? What will be the estimated cost ? Will the system involve multiple domains and alternative platforms ?

Development Option	Description
Command Procedures	This is a broad term which includes both the command processor and command list (CLIST).
Exits	The global exits are scheduled on several different subtasks and must be reentrant.
Optional Subtasks	Each OPT implements a specific function. The DST is a special type of OPT.

Figure 9.1 Major types of user-written code that can be implemented within the NetView application address space.

After these (and other) major issues are resolved, then some of the high-level design decisions can be made. For example, the type of user-written code and language must be decided upon. These choices can affect many aspects of a project's development process, as well as the operation and performance of the system itself.

9.2 Available Services

The command procedures, exits, and optional subtasks all have access to services that are necessary when building many types of applications. The assembler code usually makes use of macro instructions, while high-level languages call service routines. The REXX language also has its own set of functions that can be utilized.

There are differences in the availability and access to these services, depending on both the type of program and language used. Based on the system being created and the goals of the developer, an appropriate environment and tool set can be selected.

Major Categories

Figure 9.2 provides a list of the major categories of services available. They are generally provided in each language, however, there are several differences and restrictions. For example, creation of and access to the named storage areas is not possible with the REXX language.

Global Data

Many times, a NetView application consists of multiple units of work, perhaps running on several different subtasks. In this case, information must be stored and communicated through commonly addressable storage. These areas are available to pass data between transactions on the same or different subtasks. There are three major structures used to store information in this manner:

- Task global variables.
- Common global variables.
- Named storage.

The task and common global variables are available in all three of the languages: CLIST, HLL, and assembler. Each variable is accessed by name after it has been defined. Data can be written into and read from the variable. Also, the save/restore function, described in Chapter 8, can be used to save variables in a disk log file.

Named storage is accessed from assembler or a HLL. Each area of storage is allocated and given a name. In this case, larger areas of virtual storage can be allocated, containing a wider range of information. Like the task global variables, named storage is unique per task and can only be accessed by the task which created it.

NetView Service	Description
Data Access and Recording	Access to a wide range of system and network data is available; reading disk files; recording to one of the logs.
Subtask Environment	The local environment can be controlled, including storage allocation, variable content, and module loading.
Presentation	Several options including construction of 3270 datastreams, line-mode output, parsing, PAUSE/GO, and VIEW.
Authorization	The command scope data, as discussed in Chapter 6, can be accessed and verified.
Command Execution	Different types of commands can be scheduled for execution.
Automation	Messages, including MSUs, can be passed through the automation table; a task can wait for and trap messages.

Figure 9.2 A general description of the services available to NetView-based code.

9.3 Selecting a Language

An important aspect of system design is the selection of a language. Each has different characteristics which should be considered before beginning on a major development effort.

Different Characteristics

As mentioned in the first part of the chapter, the application developer can select from several different languages, including CLIST (REXX or the native language), assembler, C, or PL/I. Four of the major determining factors in choosing one language over another include ease of use (i.e., creating and maintaining), performance, range of services, and available skill set.

Basically, CLISTs are quicker to develop and require less skill, but can use significant system resources. The use of a HLL or assembler requires a higher degree of skill and more development time, but can result in lower overhead. Also, not all of the NetView services are available in each language.

If a CLIST language is used, REXX is the recommended choice because it:

- Is a structured language, generally resulting in higher-quality code.
- Is easier to learn than the native CLIST language.
- Enjoys widespread usage across the various IBM platforms as the SAA procedural language.
- Contains a rich set of functions and facilities.

Assembler language allows a greater degree of flexibility and application complexity, as well as improved performance. The underlying NetView control blocks can be examined and updated (where necessary). Certain operations, such as access to the actual 3270 data stream used for terminal presentation, are only available from assembler. Also, the entire range of MVS systems services can be utilized.

Resolving HLL External References

When a HLL is used, the NetView systems programmer responsible for product installation must ensure that the required run-time libraries are available. The NetView samples library includes a job which link edits the run-time routines for a C or PL/I program. If the library CNMLINK has been placed in the linklist concatenation, the MVS linklist lookaside (LLA) must be refreshed after running the job.

9.4 Assembler Data Structures

There are a large number of control blocks allocated within the NetView address space, many of which are addressable by the assembler language programmer. These data structures can be mapped and accessed through data sections (DSECTs), provided in macro form.

The DSECTs in many cases must be included with each assembler language program, regardless of whether the application code directly uses them or not. This is because the NetView macro expansions resulting from the various NetView service requests reference the individual control block fields.

From the application developer's perspective, there are two types of NetView control blocks:

■ System-wide and task-related areas, which are generally fixed across the life of an individual transaction.
■ Transaction-oriented areas relating to the dispatch of a specific unit of work, such as a command processor.

The majority of the NetView data areas begin with a common header described in the macro DSICBH. Some of the more important control blocks are discussed below, with further explanations provided in Chapter 10. Also, refer to the appendix for a more complete list of these control blocks.

Task-Related Control Blocks

There is one Main Vector Table (MVT) per NetView application address space. It contains global information and anchors the various queues required in defining and managing the local task environments.

Each subtask within NetView is described with a Task Vector Block (TVB). A queue of TVBs is pre-allocated at NetView startup, one for each of the tasks defined DSIDMN. These include the optional tasks (i.e., TASK statement), operators, NNTs, and hardcopy tasks. In addition, TVBs can be dynamically added to the end of the chain when an autotask is started.

In addition to the TVB, each subtask also includes a Task Information Block (TIB). The TIB is pointed to from the TVB, but is only allocated when a subtask becomes active.

Application Development Structures

Figure 9.3 presents the most important data areas accessible from assembler language. Each is designed for a specific purpose, as described in the figure. During program execution, these areas can be addressed as necessary. For example, the CWB contains a workarea which is designed for use by the program as a temporary storage area.

NetView Control Block	Description
BUFHDR	The message and command buffers are prefixed by a buffer header, which includes the buffer's type and length.
CWB	A Command Work Block (CWB) anchors the execution of a command, including parameters, savearea, and workarea.
DSRB	The Data Services Request Block (DSRB) is an extension to the CWB and is used by commands running under a DST.
IFR	An Internal Function Request (IFR) provides a more precisely formatted structure which is used during inter-task queuing with DSIMQS.
PDB	Input command data can be parsed by NetView for the application; the Parse Descriptor Block (PDB) carries this data.
SCE	Internal information regarding a command is stored in a System Command Entry (SCE) control block by NetView.
SVT	NetView routines are anchored from the Service Vector List (SVL) and accessed on behalf of the user-written application.
SWB	The Service Work Block (SWB) contains parameters and is used by most types of NetView macros and user-written code.
USE	The Installation Exit Parameter List (USE) anchors all relevant data areas for each instance of a global or DST exit.

Figure 9.3 Major NetView control blocks used by applications written in assembler.

Entry Conditions

NetView precisely defines the conditions at entry to each type of user-written code. The application is passed the address of a control block; from this the other data areas can be located. A command processor is provided with the address of a CWB, an exit receives the USE, and an OPT subtask is initialized with a TVB. Also, a REXX user function is passed the address of an evaluation control block (EVALBLOK).

Figure 9.4 illustrates the environment at entry to a regular command processor. The Parse Descriptor Block (PDB) is provided when the command is defined with the parameter PARSE=Y in the DSICMD file.

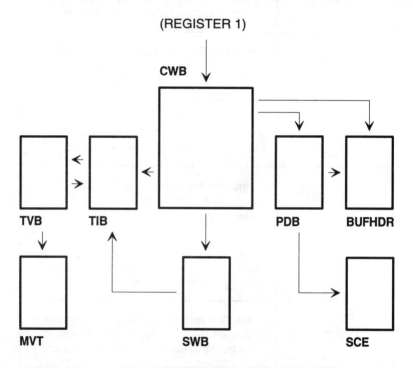

Figure 9.4 Control block structure at entry to a regular command processor.

9.5 Command Processors

A command processor is assembled or compiled, and then link edited. The load module must be made accessible to the address space so that a LOAD operation can be successfully performed on behalf of the user. Placing the module in an authorized library, as part of the STEPLIB or linklist concatenation, is done before NetView startup.

Definition and Inquiry

As mentioned in Chapter 6, commands are defined in the DSICMD file. These modules can be loaded by NetView at startup, or as needed, depending on the parameters used.

```
DSICES   SWB=(R2),BFR=(R3),PDB=(R4),MODNAME=MYMOD1,SCTADDR=STORHERE
```

Figure 9.5 Macro used to invoke the NetView Command Entry Services routine.

Once a command has been brought into virtual storage, NetView makes a record of the load module and its location. The macro DSICES, shown in Figure 9.5, can be used by a program to locate the entry point for a named command. Under certain circumstances, a command can be directly branched to by another command; in this case the entry point must be known.

Regular versus Immediate Commands

There are differences among the several types of command processors. Two types of command processors which run under the OST and NNT subtasks are of particular interest to the assembler developer.

The major difference between the two is in how they are dispatched by the MVS operating system. A regular command is called by NetView under its mainline code, and is therefore said to run in a synchronous fashion. The immediate command, on the other hand, executes asynchronously and can interrupt any work that is currently active on the subtask (e.g., regular command).

Immediate commands provide an option for rapid scheduling and execution of transactions under a subtask. For example, when an operator enters a command, it might be executed right away, perhaps suspending other work. Because VTAM processing takes place under an exit for a subtask, the immediate command can be branch entered before control is returned to the mainline processing.

Commands defined to NetView can be designated as being both a regular and immediate command, whichever is most convenient given the nature of the transaction and the current processing environment. For these "dual role" processes, as well as some of the NetView user exits, the application developer should first test the TVB control block. When a transaction is dispatched asynchronously, the TVBINXIT flag is set. In this case, certain restrictions apply to the process.

9.6 Command Lists

A CLIST is a type of interpretive program; that is, each line of the program is read, interpreted, and then processed. As mentioned above, there are two languages currently available for NetView users: REXX and the original NetView CLIST language.

CLISTs, while easy to create and use, can be a source of poor performance for the following major reasons:

■ Interpretive nature - programs that are compiled have intrinsically better performance.
■ Excessive disk I/O - with the original design of NetView, each task reads its own copy of the same CLIST, a process which is repeated every time the CLIST is executed.

IBM has made some performance improvements in NetView CLIST processing which are discussed below.

CLIST Definition

An individual CLIST program is stored in the DSICLD dataset within a separate member.   Internally it is known as a command; or more precisely every CLIST is known as the same command, a NetView module which reads and processes the CLIST text.

In addition to placing the actual program in DSCLD, a CLIST can also be identified within the DSICMD member. The name of the CLIST is placed on the left of the CMDMDL statement, with a module always defined to be DSICCP. Including a CLIST as a command in this manner improves performance.

When a command processor or CLIST is issued, NetView first searches its command definitions in virtual storage. If found, the module is loaded (if necessary) and then called. In the case of a CLIST, DSICCP processes the program. If a command entry cannot be found, NetView then searches the DSICLD library. An error results if the CLIST is then not found.

REXX Language

REXX is a powerful tool that can be used to quickly develop applications; it is also the designated SAA procedural language. In order to use the REXX language in a NetView environment under MVS, the TSO/E version 2 product must first be installed.

A REXX CLIST is initiated like any other command. Once started, an environment is created for its execution under the subtask where processing takes place. This environment can be retained for later use, but cannot be shared by another CLIST at the same time. Several different CLIST environments can be allocated concurrently; they are stacked together, although only one is active at one time.

A REXX CLIST program can be identified because the first line includes a comment statement. A comment in REXX begins with /* and ends with */. The statements are EBCDIC encoded text, where each line is 80 bytes long. Columns 73 through 80 can include sequence numbers, if desired.

Processing generally proceeds in a sequential manner, although nesting and internal routines can be used therefore allowing flexibility in logic specification. External functions, some of which are provided by IBM, can be used to add more power and features to a program.

REXX user functions can be developed in assembler langauge, and then called by a REXX CLIST. The EVALBLOK data area passed at entry to the function is used to return the results of the function. This information is then used during the interpretation of the complete statement.

Finally, a REXX compiler is available for use that can help to eliminate performance problems which are otherwise part of using an interpretive language. In addition to TSO/E, the C runtime libraries must also be available when using the REXX compiler.

Preloading CLISTs

In addition to using the REXX compiler where possible, another performance improvement can be realized by pre-loading CLIST programs. In this way, disk I/O is reduced because the CLISTs are already in virtual storage and available to all eligible subtasks in the address space.

NetView includes three commands which help to manage the CLIST environment:

- LOADCL is used to load a named CLIST.
- MAPCL provides a display of the CLISTs currently in storage.
- DROPCL provides the ability to remove a CLIST from storage.

Figure 9.6 includes an example of the MAPCL command, showing the CLISTs that are currently loaded. Among other things, the display includes the size of each CLIST, when it was loaded, and how many times it has been called.

```
NCCF                      N E T V I E W    CNM23 OPER1      08/02/93 13:14:44
* CNM23    MAPCL
' CNM23
CNM429I MAPCL DISPLAY
NAME        USAGE    RECORDS    BYTES    DATE       TIME       DP  R/C
--------    --------  --------  --------  --------   --------   --  ---
TEST1         2         2       1104     08/02/93   13:14:01        R
DBFX          2         2       1104     08/02/93   13:13:55        R
ECHOLAKE      1         2       1104     08/02/93   13:13:49        R
COM2          7         2       1104     08/02/93   13:13:40        R
--------    --------  --------  --------  --------   --------   --  ---
4            12         8       4416     --TOTALS--
---------------------------------------------------------------------------


???
```

Figure 9.6 Example of output from the MAPCL command showing the CLISTs currently loaded.

9.7 Global Exits

Global exits are different from the DST exit routines, as described earlier, in several ways. There can be multiple DST exits defined for each entry point per DST, and each of these can be unique to the individual subtask. This simplifies program design, because the exits do not have to be shared.

Global exits are more complex and have the following characteristics:

■ Multiple exit points are defined by NetView (e.g., command entry).
■ Only one exit can be identified per entry point.
■ The load module used for each exit has a strictly defined name.
■ They are scheduled under several different types of subtasks.
■ Must be designed to be shared for concurrent use (i.e., reentrant).

A list of the available global exits is provided in Figures 9.7 and 9.8.

Global Exit	Description
DSIEX01	Input from local (OST) or cross-domain (NNT) operator.
DSIEX02A	As part of standard display output, before automation table processing.
DSIEX03	Called before a regular command is processed.
DSIEX04	Log output, not called if DSIEX02A or DSIEX16 dropped the message.
DSIEX05	VTAM command invocation, before it is passed over the POI.
DSIEX06	Solicited VTAM message output.
DSIEX07	Called before commands are sent cross-domain to an NNT.
DSIEX09	Output to the system console using the DSIWCS macro.
DSIEX10	Input from the system console.

Figure 9.7   List of the common NetView global exits (Part 1 of 2).

Global Exit	Description
DSIEX11	Unsolicited VTAM message received over the POI interface.
DSIEX12	Logon validation can be used to implement additional security.
DSIEX13	Certain messages received on a OST or NNT from DSIMQS.
DSIEX14	Logoff processing for the OST and NNT subtasks.
DSIEX16	Post Automation table processing for messages.
DSIEX16B	Post automation table processing for MSUs.
DSIEX17	Receipt of MVS messages and DOMs.
DSIEX18	Network log browse exit, called before records are displayed.

Figure 9.8 List of the common NetView global exits (Part 2 of 2).

9.8 User Subtasks

An optional subtask can be utilized in order to isolate a function and resources. One or more of these background tasks can act as servers to the active terminal operators using NetView. The application designer is strongly advised to first consider using the DST facilities. For the ambitious, a complete optional task can be developed.

The DST removes most of the complexities associated with implementing a subtask within NetView. It acts as a dedicated engine for scheduling command processors and requires minimal customization. The actual development work is done by creating one or more Data Services Command Processors (DSCPs). Each DSCP appears as a transaction, which is processing the specific request. Both VSAM and CNM services are available to the code running on a DST.

Developing an OPT can be significantly more difficult, but also allows for a wider range of functionality and flexibility.

OPT Development

An optional task is installed by including a TASK statement in the DSIDMN member. The subtask must initialize its environment, process requests as received by other NetView tasks, and then terminate.

Initialization usually involves reading a named parameter member, allocating storage, and opening communication interfaces.

During normal processing, the OPT is designed to execute in a loop responding to incoming work requests. There are several input message queues, each with its own ECB which is posted to alert the task. Message buffers are sent to the OPT with the DSIMQS macro. Each carries a request, which the subtask processes before resuming its wait state.

When the termination ECB is posted, the subtask must free any allocated storage and release other resources that were acquired. A flag in the TVB indicates whether it is a normal or abnormal (ABEND) termination.

Major Functional Components

10

Command Facility

The NetView command facility is derived from the original Network Communication Control Facility (NCCF) product. It forms a foundation for the execution and operation of the subtasks defined within NetView.

Several basic services are available to each subtask, many of which can be accessed directly by the application developer. Providing a common subtask base in this manner has enabled IBM to establish both operating system and access method independence for the product. Because of this, NetView runs on several different platforms.

10.1 Basic Services

The command facility provides a basis for the implementation and integration of the IBM-supplied components and user applications within NetView. There are two major categories of services available, as described below. In addition, presentation support, which can be viewed as an extension to the basic SNA communication services, is presented later in the chapter.

Subtask Management

The most basic aspect of the command facility is management of the local subtask environment. This includes the creation, support, and termination of each task. The main task (MNT) within the application address space is the driver responsible for implementing this management function.

At startup, the Main Vector Table (MVT) control block and queue of Task Vector Blocks (TVBs) are allocated, as described in the previous chapter. The main task then attaches the PPT subtask, as well as the tasks that have been defined within the domain definition member (i.e., DSIDMN) for initial activation.

During the course of normal operation, the MNT can receive and process subtask creation requests. In each case, a TVB is located (or allocated, as with an automation task) and a separate MVS Task Control Block (TCB) is created. The main task is also notified of subtask termination, and assists during the cleanup process.

SNA Session Support

Another important feature of the command facility is its underlying support for SNA communication. The most visible example is when an operator logs on to the NetView application address space. But there are other implementations as well.

For example, the NetView-to-NetView (NNT) subtasks are created in a remote domain by the local operator. Commands and messages are routed between the two systems using an LU type 0 session. Also, the Terminal Access Facility (TAF) can be used to logon to other applications in the network over LU 1 or LU 2 sessions.

LU type 6.2 is finding a wider usage across the IBM product line, including NetView. It forms the basis for the Management Services (MS) transport, and is also used by the Graphic Monitor Facility (GMF) feature when displaying data on an OS/2 workstation. The LUC facility is a special, undocumented communication vehicle used by some of the NetView components to exchange data with their counterparts in other domains. It uses LU type 0 protocols, implementing a pseudo-conversation similar to LU 6.2.

10.2 Internals Considerations

In order to understand NetView's operation, it is first necessary to appreciate certain aspects and characteristics of its internal processing.

MVS Exit Routines

The NetView product has been integrated into the MVS environment, and therefore utilizes several of the major operating system facilities and exits.

The Extended Specify Task Abnormal Exit (ESTAE) recovery mechanism allows abends and other errors to be trapped and corrected (if possible), thereby responding to subtask termination. The ESTAE macro is issued to establish a recovery routine which receives control when necessary. The routine is presented with information about an abend, and can supply the address of a retry routine. ESTAE-based recovery is used for each of the NetView subtasks.

The end-of-task exit (ETXR), as specified on the MVS ATTACH macro, is scheduled when a subtask terminates. For normal termination, scheduling of the exit results in all of the task-related storage being freed, as well as detachment of the subtask. During an abnormal termination condition, the task can be reattached for further processing, subject to certain restrictions and limitations.

VTAM Exit Routines

Because of its reliance on SNA communication, NetView makes a wide usage of the various VTAM exit routines. Figure 10.1 provides a list of the major exits used by NetView.

Storage Management

NetView includes its own storage management facility which is used on behalf of the NetView-based applications. It is also possible to directly access these virtual storage operations from assembler code using the macro instructions DSIGET and DSIFRE.

There is a cell pool storage management facility within NetView which is used based on the size of the storage requested and the subpool number specified. Cell pool processing can help to improve performance by avoiding the overhead associated with the MVS GETMAIN service.

Also, storage is assigned to each subtask, when acquired, as either queued or non-queued. With queued storage, each allocation includes a header control block so that the segments can be anchored to a task, allowing for orderly cleanup during task termination.

Message Queuing Service

The messages that flow through the NetView address space from all sources drive the subtask processing. These message buffers are sent from one task to another with the message queuing service, a facility accessed through the DSIMQS macro.

VTAM Exit	Description
LOGON	This exit accepts both terminal and cross-domain logon requests.
LOSTERM	The lost terminal exit provides coverage for session interruption during the logon process.
TPEND	This exit receives control when VTAM is terminated with the HALT command issued by an operator.
NSEXIT	The network services routine is called when procedural errors occur.
RPL	Request Parameter List exits are utilized in several instances with the individual API operations.

Figure 10.1 Major VTAM exit routines used by NetView.

The TVB of each subtask has three "public" queues available that can be used to receive message buffers; each has a corresponding ECB. These queues are arranged in a priority scheme: low, medium (or normal), and high. The normal queue is always active, while use of the high and low priority queues is optional.

The major parameters on the DSIMQS macro specify:

■ Destination subtask(s) to receive the message
■ The message buffer being queued
■ Whether ownership of the buffer is passed to the receiving task or retained by the sender
■ Message priority, which determines the queue on which the message is placed

When a message is sent, the queuing service anchors the message to the target TVB and posts the appropriate ECB. If the priority is not handled by the receiver, the message is placed on the normal queue by default.

The basic design of each NetView subtask is that of a loop, always waiting for incoming messages and other events (e.g., termination request). When a message is received (often a command request), it is moved by the task from the public to a private queue for processing.

After processing a message, the subtask code checks its message queues for more work and then waits again. The priority arrangement allows certain requests to be honored before others.

Long Running Commands

A Long Running Command (LRC) is a special type of composite command structure which is used by many of the subtasks within the address space. It provides the ability to break up a command into several long-running pieces. One command processor is designated to remain resident on a given task, while still allowing for interruptions and the execution of new work requests. The incoming requests that are queued to the task are processed and terminated, after which the active LRC can be rescheduled (i.e., resumed). Note that while there can be multiple LRCs created per task, only one is active at a time.

NetView supplies the DSIPUSH macro to establish an LRC; DSIPOP is used to remove it. Each push operation creates a new LRC element. A major LRC creates an independent environment, while the minor LRC is part of an existing group of long running commands.

DSIPUSH is used to specify three exits, which are actually the names of command processors. These routines comprise the LRC environment, and include:

- ABEND - to handle an ABEND
- LOGOFF - for normal subtask termination
- RESUME - scheduled by NetView for the task when it is percolated to the top of the LRC stack

Each of the exits is scheduled by NetView, as mentioned. The ABEND command is called after a processing error for the subtask; it can determine whether or not to retain the LRC. The logoff command is scheduled before subtask termination to allow for an orderly cleanup and shutdown.

The resume command is the most important of the three exits in that it defines the essence of the LRC. After a push operation, the named resume routine is on the top of the stack and can be repeatedly scheduled when no other work is queued for the task.

The exact logic of the resume command processor depends on the designer, but it usually prepares to receive the reply from a previous request issued to a local or remove subtask.

When a resume command exits, NetView checks for any queued requests and processes them as required. When the task is idle, the latest (i.e., top) resume command is again scheduled for the task.

The order of the stacked LRCs can be changed with the ROLL command processor as discussed later in the chapter. This command moves the active LRC group to the bottom of the queue while the second in line is migrated to the top (active) position.

10.3 Message Format

Each message, whether it is passed into NetView or generated from within the product, is packaged in a common structure. The buffer header (BUFHDR) control block begins each message, and describes its contents.

Buffer Header

The BUFHDR structure is included within the DSITIB member of product's macro library, which also contains the TIB control block. The major fields in the BUFHDR include:

- Length of the buffer
- Message type
- Sender's characteristics, including the domain and subtask names
- Time it was sent
- Presentation extensions

There are a large number of different message types that can be used, each identified by a unique 1-byte field. Refer to the appendix for a list of the major buffer types.

10.4 Presentation Services

The NetView product supports the display of data on 3270 terminals. From the basic command facility, messages appear to roll down the screen, and then start again at the top, in what is called "line mode." It is also possible to implement a full-screen interface. Access to and customization of these presentation options is presented below.

TYPE Parameter	Description
OUTPUT	Used to send normal message text to an OST or NNT, subject to automation.
FLASH	Messages not suppressed by normal automation, or logged; used for high-priority messages.
IMMED	Invoked to direct a message to the immediate message area at the bottom of the terminal screen.
XSEND	Used to send data to another domain after the required NNT session has already been started.
SCRSIZE	Provides a method for determining the screen size (row-column).
WINDOW	Many terminals have two screen sizes; this option requires MIN/MAX sizes, as well as the current size in use.

Figure 10.2 Options for the TYPE parameter on the DSIPSS macro (Part 1 of 2).

DSIPSS Macro

The DSIPSS assembler macro is used as the basis for managing the NetView 3270-based presentation. It can control the display for both a terminal operator and a cross-domain NNT (i.e., remote command execution).

Display to a terminal operator has been designed to be integrated into the normal line mode operation. That is, the developer constructs a buffer with a text message and invokes the macro service to display the message. It is also possible to write at a lower level by building the actual 3270 data stream panels using what have been called full-screen command processors.

The macro includes the TYPE parameter which is used to specify one of the several different PSS services. Figures 10.2 and 10.3 include a list of the values that can be used on the TYPE parameter.

TYPE Parameter	Description
ASYPANEL	The user routine controls the terminal by sending actual 3270 datastreams.
PANEL	Supported for compatibility with earlier releases of NetView.
CANCEL	Used to cancel a previous full-screen request that is still pending.
PSSWAIT	Can be used to wait for a list of events, including screen input.
TESTWAIT	Used to test for the completion of a specified event.

Figure 10.3 Options for the TYPE parameter on the DSIPSS macro (Part 2 of 2).

The basic parameters available with the macro for interacting with a terminal operator allow messages to be sent and received by the caller. To summarize, the major operations available include:

- Send a line of output to the terminal. There is an option as to where the one-line message is displayed and processed (e.g., the immediate message area - refer to section 10.6).
- Extract the terminal characteristics, including screen size.
- Transmit and receive terminal data in raw 3270 format.
- Wait for and accept input as it arrives for the task.

A basic presentation in line mode, equivalent to DSIPSS although with less flexibility, is also available from a HLL. When using a HLL, however, the developer should consider VIEW command, described below.

VIEW Command

The VIEW facility provides the means to build applications which can interact with the terminal user. It allows user-written programs to display full-screen panels that are defined and stored separately from the application code. Each panel includes output text and input fields that can be customized with respect to color and highlighting.

VIEW is defined as a regular command processor which can be called from a CLIST or HLL program. It accesses one or more panels, each of which describes a single screen image. The panel definitions consist of text characters as well as the names of variables which VIEW first interprets and then displays. It is possible for messages queued to the task, or other subtasks, to update the panel variables. This will therefore cause a user's on-line display to change.

Refer to the appendix for a brief tutorial on the VIEW command.

10.5 Operator Logon

In order to use the product, an operator must first log on to NetView from a 3270 terminal connected to the host. From the VTAM logon (Unformatted System Services message 10) screen, the user can type:

LOGON APPLID(CNM23)

A session is first temporarily established with the main task, which locates a TVB and then attaches an OST subtask to service the terminal. When the OST has completed initialization, it notifies the MNT, which then issues a CLSDST macro to transfer the SNA session to the new subtask. The OST then uses its own VTAM APPLID when communicating with the terminal.

If the session establishment and transfer has been completed successfully, the NetView logon screen will be sent from the new subtask to the terminal, as shown in Figure 10.4. The user must key in a valid userid and password, which is verified depending on how system security has been configured. The operator also has the option, as discussed in Chapter 6, of specifying a profile and hardcopy printer.

```
NN     NN                      VV          VV
NNN    NN    EEEEEE  TTTTTTTT  VV          VV    II   EEEEEE  WW           WW  TM
NNNN   NN    EE         TT     VV      VV  VV    II   EE      WW    W      WW
NN NN NN     EEEE       TT     VV      VV  VV    II   EEEE    WW   WWW    WW
NN   NNNN    EE         TT      VV VV           II   EE      WWWW  WWWW
NN    NNN    EEEEEE     TT       VVV            II   EEEEEE   WW    WW
NN     NN                         V

                (C) COPYRIGHT IBM CORP. 1992 - ALL RIGHTS RESERVED
        US GOVERNMENT USERS RESTRICTED RIGHTS - USE, DUPLICATION OR DISCLOSURE
              RESTRICTED BY GSA ADP SCHEDULE CONTRACT WITH IBM CORPORATION
                     LICENSED MATERIAL  - PROPERTY OF IBM
                           DOMAIN = CNM23

             OPERATOR ID ==>  OPER1      (OR LOGOFF)
                PASSWORD ==>              (LEAVE BLANK TO CHANGE PASSWORD)
                 PROFILE ==>              (PROFILE NAME, BLANK=DEFAULT)
            HARDCOPY LOG ==>              (DEVICE NAME, BLANK=DEFAULT, OR NO)
     RUN INITIAL COMMAND ==>              (YES OR NO, DEFAULT=YES)


          ENTER LOGON INFORMATION OR PF3 TO LOGOFF
```

Figure 10.4 NetView operator logon screen.

A successful logon will allow the operator to access the NetView command facility. The product's main menu can then be displayed using the MAINMENU command. The initial command (IC) for the active profile can be configured to issue the command and display this screen for the user. Figure 10.5 contains the main menu screen.

10.6 Entering Commands

Several different types of commands can be entered from an operator terminal, including:

■ MVS operating system

■ VTAM
■ General NetView product
■ NetView component-specific

Most of the time, these commands result in a reply which is routed to the operator's terminal as one or more text messages. Figure 10.6 shows the typical output from a NetView LIST command. In this case, the status of the subtask implementing the session monitor component is displayed.

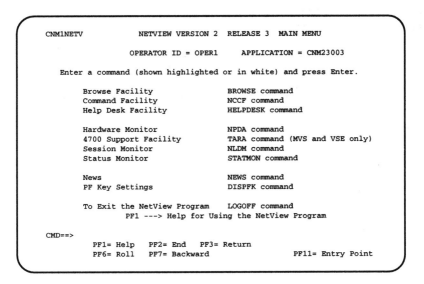

```
   CNM1NETV            NETVIEW VERSION 2  RELEASE 3  MAIN MENU

                   OPERATOR ID = OPER1      APPLICATION = CNM23003

       Enter a command (shown highlighted or in white) and press Enter.

            Browse Facility             BROWSE command
            Command Facility            NCCF command
            Help Desk Facility          HELPDESK command

            Hardware Monitor            NPDA command
            4700 Support Facility       TARA command (MVS and VSE only)
            Session Monitor             NLDM command
            Status Monitor              STATMON command

            News                        NEWS command
            PF Key Settings             DISPFK command

            To Exit the NetView Program    LOGOFF command
                    PF1 ---> Help for Using the NetView Program

   CMD==>
            PF1= Help    PF2= End    PF3= Return
            PF6= Roll    PF7= Backward               PF11= Entry Point
```

Figure 10.5 Main menu which lists NetView's components and services.

Command Facility Display Customization

The command facility screen is divided into several major areas. Some of these include:

■ Title area at the top of the display screen
■ Normal text messages
■ Held/action messages
■ Immediate message area (one line)
■ Command area (one line)

As of version 2.3, it is possible for the systems programmer to have even more control over the characteristics of text displayed in these and other parts of the command facility screen.

When a message passes through the system, there are several points at which its characteristics can be affected. In particular, its color, highlighting, and intensity can be changed.

If a message originates from the WTO macro service, then the MPF definitions take effect first. This is only true, however, if the extended MCS console facility is being utilized. Once presented to NetView, the DSIEX17 and DSIEX02A global exits can examine and change the messages.

Following this, the message is passed through the automation table. With the proper customization, the table definitions can detect and change the message. After this, the DSIEX16 post-automation global exit has access to the message.

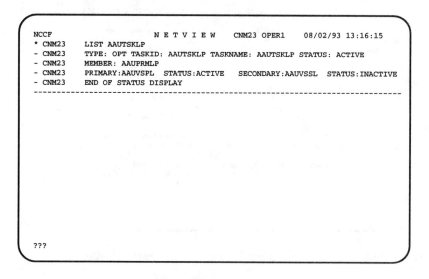

```
NCCF                    N E T V I E W    CNM23 OPER1    08/02/93 13:16:15
* CNM23    LIST AAUTSKLP
- CNM23    TYPE: OPT TASKID: AAUTSKLP TASKNAME: AAUTSKLP STATUS: ACTIVE
- CNM23    MEMBER: AAUPRMLP
- CNM23    PRIMARY:AAUVSPL  STATUS:ACTIVE    SECONDARY:AAUVSSL  STATUS:INACTIVE
- CNM23    END OF STATUS DISPLAY
---------------------------------------------------------------------------



???
```

Figure 10.6 Output from a NetView LIST command.

Finally, if the color of the message has not already been determined by previous processing, the screen format (SCRNFMT) definitions for the target operator then control the characteristics of the message. These parameter values are stored within a member in the DSIPARM dataset, and are set by the OVERRIDE or DEFAULTS command.

The characteristics of a message that has been set multiple times will generally be determined by the last, or most recent, update. The SCRNFMT control mechanism will only be used for a message that was otherwise unchanged.

10.7 Access to NetView Components

After getting through an initial logon and perhaps entering a few simple commands, the terminal operator may want to use one or more of the NetView components. At this point, a command token must be keyed in to gain access to a component. For example, the hardware monitor menu can be displayed by using the NPDA command. Figure 10.7 includes the commands utilized for the major NetView components.

Command Token	Description
NCCF	Displays the basic command facility screen.
NPDA	Provides access to the hardware monitor component.
NLDM	Displays the session monitor component.
STATMON	Provides access to the status monitor component.

Figure 10.7 Tokens used to gain access to the NetView components.

Presentation Services Command Processor

Many times an operator needs to access data which has been collected and archived by one of the NetView components. This creates a problem because the subtasks comprising the component run in the background and are not directly connected to any specific operator. A processing model has been developed to deal with this situation where the OST passes a command processor request to the appropriate DST to access the required information. This situation resembles a client/server arrangement where the DST server can support multiple OST clients. After receiving the request, a reply is then queued back to the operator, with the display managed by a Presentation Services Command Processor (PSCP). An example of this interaction is shown in Figure 10.8.

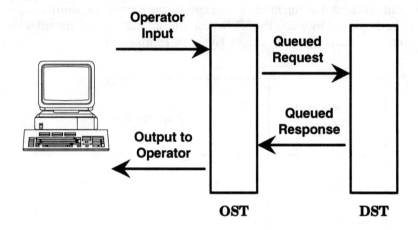

Figure 10.8 A simple interaction between an operator and background DST.

This OST-DST cooperative processing structure is used throughout NetView as a way to share access to the background subtasks.

Rolling through the NetView Components

When an operator first logs on to NetView, the basic command facility is first presented. After this, multiple NetView components can be established as described above. In this case, the component interfaces are logically stacked on the OST; the operator must "roll" through them, allowing access in a serial fashion.

The ROLL command is used to step through the components. It is defined as an immediate command processor, and uses the module DSIROLL. When invoked, the command simply rearranges an internal task-oriented queue, moving the top LRC to the bottom. The second long running command is then moved to the top. After this, the resume routine of the newly activated LRC is scheduled and the (new) component's menu displayed.

10.8 Support Functions

There are other services and subtasks which operate in a support role. For example, the log tasks discussed in Chapter 8 are used to record and archive data. Several other features, which are useful to terminal operators, are described below.

Browse

The browse facility allows the operator to scan the network log, as described in Chapter 8.

In addition, the same command can be used to display the members from certain NetView datasets. When the BROWSE command is issued, a CLIST is invoked which searches a pre-defined list of datasets for the named member. The search order includes:

■ DSIPARM - main parameter dataset
■ CNMPNL1 - panel library
■ DSIPRF - operator profiles
■ DSICLD - CLIST library
■ DSIVTAM - VTAMLST dataset
■ CNMMSGF - messages
■ CNMCMDF - command help panels

This feature utilizes the VIEW command to display the text data; an example is provided in Figure 10.9.

```
NETVIEW.BRWS ------ BROWSE DSIDMN    (DSIPARM ) --- LINE 00233 TO 00251 OF 00292
                                                               SCROLL ==> CSR
         TASK      MOD=DSIZDST,TSKID=BNJDSE36,MEM=BNJ36DST,PRI=6,INIT=N
*****************************************************************
* CAUTION: THE FIRST FIVE CHARACTERS OF EACH OF THE NEXT       *
*          THREE TSKID STATEMENTS HAVE TO BE CHANGED TO        *
*          MATCH THE "NCCFID" OF THE NCCFID DOMAINID           *
*          STATEMENT FOUND ABOVE.                              *
*****************************************************************
         TASK      MOD=DSIZDST,TSKID=NV236LUC,MEM=DSILUCTD,PRI=7,INIT=N
         TASK      MOD=CNMTARCA,TSKID=NV236VMT,PRI=5,INIT=N
         TASK      MOD=CNMTGBRW,TSKID=NV236BRW,PRI=5,INIT=N
*****************************************************************
*  NOTE: THE FOLLOWING TASK STATEMENT IS NECESSARY FOR CSCF    *
*****************************************************************
         TASK      MOD=DSIZDST,TSKID=DSIKREM,MEM=DSIKINIT,PRI=5,INIT=N
*****************************************************************
*  NOTE: THE FOLLOWING TASK STATEMENT IS NECESSARY FOR         *
*        REMOTE OPERATIONS OVER LU 6.2 (RMTCMD/ENDTASK).       *
*****************************************************************
         TASK      MOD=DSIZDST,TSKID=DSIUDST,MEM=DSIUINIT,PRI=5,INIT=N

CMD==>
1=HELP   2=END   3=RET   4=TOP   5=BOT   6=ROLL   7=BACK   8=FWD   9=RPTFND   12=CURSOR
```

Figure 10.9 An example of how the BROWSE command can be used.

Helpdesk and Help Facility

The HELPDESK command represents an attempt by the IBM developers to assist help desk and operations personnel. This CLIST provides advice and assistance. The main menu, displayed by using the HELPDESK command, is shown in Figure 10.10.

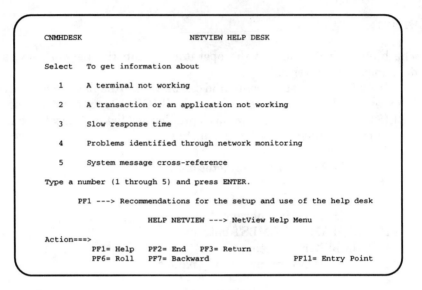

```
CNMHDESK                      NETVIEW HELP DESK


Select    To get information about

    1       A terminal not working

    2       A transaction or an application not working

    3       Slow response time

    4       Problems identified through network monitoring

    5       System message cross-reference

Type a number (1 through 5) and press ENTER.

          PF1 ---> Recommendations for the setup and use of the help desk

                      HELP NETVIEW ---> NetView Help Menu

Action===>
          PF1= Help    PF2= End    PF3= Return
          PF6= Roll    PF7= Backward              PF11= Entry Point
```

Figure 10.10 The main menu for the HELPDESK facility.

The HELP command processor can run in either regular or immediate mode. It provides on-line help for the terminal user. Both HELP and HELPDESK use the VIEW display facility.

LUC Communication

Much of the communication between like NetView components in different domains is accomplished using the LUC sessions, although the forwarding of alerts that have been converted to text over OST-to-NNT sessions is still possible.

The LUC communication vehicle is still being heavily utilized today. At a low level, LUC is based on the SNA LU type 0. However, its designers added support for a pseudo-conversational framework, similar to the LU type 6.2. In fact, LUC was a predecessor to the now strategic Advanced Program-to-Program Communication (APPC).

The four major LUC transactions include:

- Conversation allocate
- Conversation deallocate
- Send data
- Receive data

There is a subtask dedicated to providing LUC support. Its name is CNM01LUC, where the last three characters must be "LUC" and the first five are reserved for the domain ID. LUC was first used by the session monitor to allow cross-domain access to data, but is now used by other components such as the hardware monitor. This topic is covered in more depth in the chapter Multiple Domain Access.

10.9 Subtask Performance

A typical NetView application address space has dozens of active subtasks, all of which are competing for system resources. For many installations, NetView can consume a significant amount of the processor in terms of both CPU and virtual storage. It therefore becomes important to monitor and tune NetView's operation where possible.

```
NCCF                      N E T V I E W    CNM23 OPER1    08/02/93 13:04:31
 * CNM23     RESOURCE
 ' CNM23
DSI386I NETVIEW RESOURCE UTILIZATION 13:04:32
            TOTAL CPU %              =        10.18
            CNM2PROC CPU %           =         0.65
            CNM2PROC CPU TIME USED   =        18.96 SEC.
            REAL STORAGE IN USE      =         4428K
            PRIVATE ALLOCATED < 16M  =          840K
            PRIVATE ALLOCATED > 16M  =         8360K
END OF DISPLAY
----------------------------------------------------------------------------



 ???
```

Figure 10.11 The RESOURCE command shows the current address space performance.

The RESOURCE command, shown in Figure 10.11, is a basic tool which gives a quick sample of how the address space as a whole is performing.

Figure 10.12 shows the output from TASKUTIL, a system which was originally developed within IBM marketing support, and was then absorbed into the product. This command is more sophisticated than RESOURCE, illustrating the performance of the individual subtasks.

```
NCCF                     N E T V I E W    CNM23 OPER1    08/02/93 13:05:04
* CNM23     TASKUTIL
' CNM23
DWO022I
TASKNAME TYPE DPR   CPU-TIME N-CPU% S-CPU% MESSAGEQ STORAGE-K CMDLIST
-------- ---- ---   -------- ------ ------ -------- --------- --------
CNM23PPT PPT  255    2.24   41.35   0.07      0        31   **NONE**
OPER1    OST  251    1.56   29.68   0.05      0        64   **NONE**
CNM23VMT OPT  250    0.68   11.47   0.02      0        28     N/A
DSICRTR  DST  249    0.15    0.00   0.00      0        29     N/A
DSITRACE DST  254    0.29    0.00   0.00      0        19     N/A
CNMCSSIR OPT  250    1.27    0.00   0.00      0        14     N/A
CNMCALRT OPT  249    0.01    0.00   0.00      0         0     N/A
DSISVRT  DST  253    0.16    0.00   0.00      0       104     N/A
DSIROVS  DST  251    0.14    0.00   0.00      0        15     N/A
DSIGDS   DST  254    0.03    0.00   0.00      0        37     N/A
DSIELTSK DST  253    0.01    0.00   0.00      0        13     N/A
AAUTSKLP DST  247    2.79    0.00   0.00      0      1325     N/A
AAUTCNMI DST  249    0.09    0.00   0.00      0       162     N/A
DSIAMLUT DST  248    0.17    0.00   0.00      0        24     N/A
BNJDSERV DST  249    0.32    0.00   0.00      0        64     N/A
BNJMNPDA OPT  254    0.00    0.00   0.00      0        24     N/A
??? ***
```

Figure 10.12 TASKUTIL provides more insight into NetView subtask performance.

11

Hardware Monitor

The hardware monitor is based on the original Network Problem Determination Application (NPDA) product. Although its name (i.e., hardware monitor) implies management of the physical network, this component supports the more general function of problem determination. Indeed, it can be considered to be a manager of alerts, where the errors and problem notifications flow in from both hardware and software sources.

As a fundamental part of daily system and network operations, the hardware monitor is a core feature provided by NetView. It receives solicited and unsolicited information which can be recorded and displayed by the terminal operator.

11.1 Environmental Characteristics

The hardware monitor functionality is distributed across three main subtasks within NetView. Several different interfaces are used to gather the problem determination data, which can then be recorded in a dedicated database and viewed by the terminal operator as required. This section presents the overall structure of hardware monitor.

Subtask Definitions

Figure 11.1 contains a list of the hardware monitor subtasks. Each must be defined with a TASK statement in the DSIDMN member of the DSIPARM dataset.

The main subtask is a DST named BNJDSERV, which accepts the incoming problem management information from the various sources. This data is processed and recorded in the database depending on how the component has been configured by the systems programmer.

BNJMNPDA is an optional task which serves as an interface between the local operating system (i.e., MVS) and the hardware monitor. It provides a means to gather the local error records. In the case of MVS, this LOGREC data is intercepted from the SVC 76 service.

Subtask	Description
BNJDSERV	Main DST used to process and record the problem determination data received from the network.
BNJMNPDA	An optional subtask which assists in processing the local error data (e.g., LOGREC) when enabled.
BNJDSE36	Provides support for the 4700 financial series of processors; formerly known as TARA.

Figure 11.1 Subtasks used to implement the hardware monitor component.

The 4700 Support Facility provides access to the data generated by the 3600 and 4700 Finance Communication Systems. It is available in the MVS and VSE environments, and was formerly known as Threshold Analysis and Remote Access (TARA).

Finally, the OST subtask for each terminal operator is involved when interacting with the hardware monitor and displaying the collected data. The PSCP-to-DSCP presentation mechanism, as described earlier in Chapter 10, is used to access the data.

Types of Data

There are three major categories of messages received and processed. Each has a set of characteristics defined by the hardware monitor:

- Statistics - information regarding the transmission of data and recoverable error counts for a specific line.
- Events - notification of an unusual occurrence in the network.
- Alerts - an event which is considered to be critical enough to require some type of action or operator intervention.

An alert is actually an event which requires an immediate response of some type. While most alerts within the SNA architecture are also hardware monitor alerts, the two are not necessarily the same. A statistics record can also become an event, and an alert, depending on the number of retransmission errors. Section 11.3 provides an additional description of this data, along with its role in forming the structure of the database.

Basic Definitions

The majority of the operational parameters are stored in the member in the DSIPARM dataset, usually named BNJMBDST. Figure 11.2 shows the major parameters that are used when customizing the main hardware monitor DST.

Operator Access

In order to access the alerts and other data available with this component, the operator must first log on to the NetView product. Then using the NPDA command, the hardware monitor main menu can be displayed; Figure 11.3 contains an example. The dates at the bottom indicate when the entire database, or the individual sections, were last initialized or purged.

The panel-driven interface, which is implemented as a rollable interface within the command facility, can be utilized to access the data. As a complement and alternative, a set of line mode commands is also available.

Parameter Statement	Description
ALT_ALERT	Controls one field displayed on each line of the alert list panels, such as ALD, ALS, and ALH.
AUTORATE	Allows alerts that are blocked by the RATE statement to still be processed by automation.
CTL	Indicates the number of wrap counters and ratio statements to immediately follow in the member.
DBFULL	Used to set the maximum number of times message BNJ022I is issued when the database is full.
RATIO	Allows error-to-traffic ratio to be set for a resource; controls creation of performance events.
RATE	Establishes a maximum rate at which events can be logged by the hardware monitor.
REPORTS	Controls whether reports are sent to the external log facility for recording and later use.
WRAP	Determines at what point the entries in the database wrap, with the oldest entries deleted and replaced.

Figure 11.2 Main parameters used to initialize the hardware monitor.

11.2 Message Sources

NetView maintains several interfaces which can be utilized by the hardware monitor. The major sources of data available within a single domain are presented below; access to additional information in a multiple NetView domain environment is discussed in Chapter 17.

```
N E T V I E W           SESSION DOMAIN: CNM23    OPER1      08/02/93 07:40:24
NPDA-01A                      * MENU *                      HOST DOMAIN: CNM23



SEL#    PRODUCES:
( 1)     ALERTS-DYNAMIC DISPLAY
( 2)     TOTAL EVENTS DISPLAY
( 3)     TOTAL STATISTICAL DATA DISPLAY
( 4)     HELP MENU DISPLAY


         REQUEST DATA FROM NETWORK RESOURCES:
( 5)     SNA CONTROLLERS (CTRL)
( 6)     MODEMS AND ASSOCIATED LINKS (TEST)


                         DATA TYPES INITIALIZED/PURGED
         AL..... (08/02/93)      EV..... (08/02/93)     ST..... (08/02/93)

ENTER SEL#

???
CMD==>
```

Figure 11.3 Hardware monitor main menu accessed with the NPDA command.

LOGREC Data

The MVS LOGREC facility archives errors detected in the local operating system environment. These records include, for example:

- Channel check handler (CCH)
- Machine check handler (MCH)
- Subchannel logout handler (SLF)
- Outboard recorder (OBR)

The hardware monitor can access this information by intercepting the SVC 76 service path. The NetView procedure must first be started using the load module BNJLINTX. This program initializes the mapping structure between MVS and NetView, and then attaches the command facility main task.

After the environment has been prepared, the optional subtask BNJMNPDA processes the LOGREC data, acting as an interface to the SVC 76 facility. These records, once placed in a standard format, are then passed over to the main hardware monitor DST, BNJDSERV.

If this local event data is not required, then the NetView procedure can be started to use the main task by naming module DSIMNT. Also, the BNJMNPDA subtask is not needed in this case either.

CNM Interface and Router

The CNM interface facility is used to accept both solicited and unsolicited data in the following forms:

- Network Management Vector Transport (NMVT)
- Record Maintenance Statistics (RECMS)
- Record Formatted Maintenance Statistics (RECFMS)

Some of the IBM control units keep counters of information that are only transferred to the host as solicited information. In this case, NetView includes several commands that can be utilized (e.g., REQMS and CTRL).

Unsolicited data first flows into NetView to the CNM router (DSICRTR) subtask, where it can be distributed appropriately. There can only be one DSICRTR task per VTAM domain.

NetView PPI

The NetView program-to-program interface (PPI), as described in Chapter 7, is a general interface used by programs on the same host to exchange data. It can also allow problem management data to be sent into NetView. The NMVT and Control Point Management Services Unit (CP-MSU) are both used for this purpose.

The DSICRTR subtask and subsystem address space must both be activated first. Then the alert receiver optional subtask (CNMCALRT) can be started. CNMCALRT waits for PPI data, and then forwards it over to the DSICRTR task for routing to the hardware monitor.

NetView version 2.3 includes an enhancement where it is now possible to have multiple alert receiver tasks active per host. This is useful, of course, when multiple NetView address spaces are running. In this case, the alert data is sent to each receiver.

Management Service Transport

The APPC transports are discussed more fully in Chapter 16. One of the transports carries management services data. The ALERT_NETOP application, which is registered and active under the BNJDSERV subtask using the MS transport, receives the Multiple Domain Support Message Unit (MDS-MU). This structure can hold alert as well as other data, which is processed and recorded by the hardware monitor.

GENALERT Command

The GENALERT command can be used under an OST or autotask to create an alert. The data structure is queued to the DSICRTR subtask, and then forwarded to the hardware monitor. This mechanism operates even when VTAM is down.

The following forms of GENALERT are supported:

■ Generic
■ Non-generic
■ RECMS

The GENALERT command provides a convenient method for creating alerts, without the need to deal with the complexities of data formatting.

11.3 Database Structure and Processing

The hardware monitor, as with many of the other components, has a database actually consisting of two VSAM clusters: primary and secondary. Only one cluster is active (i.e., being written to) at a time, which can be switched by the operator. There are several parameters available to control the processing of data with respect to the database.

Format of Database

The physical database consists of three logical sections, one for each type of entry: statistics, events, and alerts. These records are permanently stored in the VSAM file. The key identifies the database section, as well as other characteristics of each record.

The hardware monitor write three types of records to the database:

- History - information which has been accumulated for a specific resource.
- Detail - describes a single event or other incident.
- Cross-reference - allows resources to be correlated with their hierarchy, therefore describing their place in the network.

The events and statistics databases include multiple detail records, and a history record for each resource. The alerts database contains a subset of the events database detail records, with only one history record.

There is also a temporary area in the database. It contains a block of records, allocated for each operator using the hardware monitor. The information tracks their use of the component and location in the panel-driven hierarchy.

Resource Hierarchy

The physical resources in the network are viewed, from the perspective of the hardware monitor, in a hierarchy arrangement in terms of function and control. At each level, the resource involved can be named. The hierarchy basically moves from most complex (general) to least complex (specific), and includes the following:

- CPU or communication controller (e.g., 3745)
- Link or line
- Control unit (e.g., 3174)

The first level (e.g., CPU) is only used once per event, but the last two resource types can be combined and repeated as required in describing the complete network configuration.

This hierarchy structure is evident in the display of a single event, where a pictorial view is constructed at the top of the screen. Also, in accessing the total events and total statistics, the user must first navigate through a hierarchy in order to arrive at the desired detail records for a specific resource.

The hardware monitor database entries use this hierarchy structure in recording and accessing data. The VSAM key can include up to five resource names which describe the location of the named resource.

Collection and Processing

Information arrives from several sources, as described in the previous section. The data is first prepared for further processing; for example, a CP-MSU with multiple vectors is split up. Statistics records are examined against the ratio (R) definitions to determine if an event should be created.

The filtering options in effect at the time determine the initial setting for each record; see the following section for an explanation of filters. A subset of the MSUs (e.g., alerts) are then passed through the automation table. The records can be written to the database, depending on their final characteristics.

Each resource in the logical database can be defined to have a wrap definition; this parameter determines how many records will be kept. When the wrap count is reached, the database wraps around and the oldest record is deleted.

The RATE statement can be used to restrict the flow of events into the database. A major outage can cause NetView to be flooded, and the alerts-dynamic screen to become unusable. When a single resource sends in the same event, the time it is received is compared to the oldest record being wrapped from the database. If the difference is less than the RATE value, the event is blocked and not recorded. The AUTORATE parameter can be used, however, to allow these blocked events to still be processed by the automation table.

Controlling Database Contents

There are several operator commands available for controlling the contents of the database. These include:

- PURGE - deletes events and statistics records for a named resource, or all resources in the database.
- PRGATT - deletes events and statistics records for a named resource and all of the attached resources.
- RESETDB - clears the named VSAM file while the NetView address space is still active.

Of course, the databases can be cleared or reorganized during regular scheduled maintenance when NetView is inactive.

11.4 Recording and Viewing Filters

A very important aspect of the hardware monitor processing involves its use of filters. This allows certain data to be excluded from recording and display. A set of default options can be used or overridden as required.

The filters can be set at NetView startup and then displayed or changed dynamically as needed during the course of normal operation. There are three NetView commands related to filtering:

- SRFILTER (SRF) - set recording filter
- SVFILTER (SVF) - set viewing filter
- DFILTER (DF) - display filter

The recording filters are used by the main DST, and determine its operation with respect to data recording. The viewing filters apply to each individual operator using the hardware monitor.

Setting these filters properly requires some experimentation. A minimal amount of data can be filtered at first, so as to give a complete access to the incoming data. From this, it can be determined what information should then be excluded. The SRFILTER and SVFILTER commands can be entered multiple times. Each filter entry contributes to the cumulative recording or viewing filters that are in effect.

Flow into the Database

The purpose of the recording filters is to capture and save only the information which will be of use to the NetView operations staff. Also, the space consumed by the database can be minimized.

Figure 11.4 contains a description of the flow of problem determination data into NetView. Each area of the diagram is controlled by one aspect of the SRFILTER command.

A message is first tested based on the ESREC options to determine if it should be recorded as an event or statistic. If so, the data is archived and is then passed through the AREC options. At this point, it is possible for the event to also become an alert.

If the record passes the AREC filters, it is recorded in the alerts database and then passed through the remaining options. These include:

- ROUTE - determines if the alert is forwarded to another domain.
- COLOR - can set color and highlighting.

■ OPER - determines if the text message BNJ146I describing the alert is generated.

All of these options are set by the SRFILTER command.

Each Operator's View

The set viewing filter (SVFILTER) command can be used for each operator to determine what data is displayed on the alerts-dynamic screen. After an alert is created, it is passed through the route, color, and oper options as described above. After this, each alerts-dynamic list for the operators using the hardware monitor is updated.

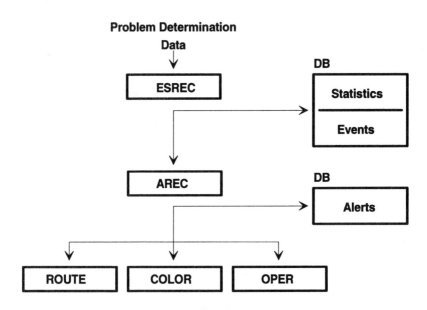

Figure 11.4 An illustration of the flow of data through the recording filters.

However, before the alert is added to the list, it must pass the viewing filters in effect. These definitions can be set individually for each operator. Using the SVFILTER command allows an operator's view of the incoming alerts to be more usable.

11.5 Problem Identification

Identifying and displaying events in the network is the first step towards managing their resolution. The hardware monitor provides several ways to access and display the event information.

Alerts-Dynamic Display

Alerts are actually events that have been given a special significance. The hardware monitor provides access to this alert information, including a list of the most recently received.

```
N E T V I E W          SESSION DOMAIN: CNM23     OPER1      08/02/93 08:05:01
NPDA-30A                      * ALERTS-DYNAMIC *

    DOMAIN RESNAME  TYPE TIME   ALERT DESCRIPTION:PROBABLE CAUSE
    CNM23  K06NJ016 LDEV 08:04  DEVICE ATTACHMENT ERROR:ATTACHMENT MEDIA/DEVICE
    CNM23  3708PU   DEV  08:01  LOST CARRIER DETECT:DEVICE DISCONNECTED/COMMUN.
    CNM23  K06NJ001 LDEV 07:41  DEVICE ATTACHMENT ERROR:ATTACHMENT MEDIA/DEVICE
    CNM23  K06NJ016 LDEV 07:29  DEVICE ATTACHMENT ERROR:ATTACHMENT MEDIA/DEVICE
    CNM23  K06NJ016 LDEV 06:53  DEVICE ATTACHMENT ERROR:ATTACHMENT MEDIA/DEVICE
    CNM23  N1201NJ  LCTL 13:31  CHANNEL DISC:DEACTIVATION/ADJACENT PROGRAM
    CNM23  K1103015 DEV  13:20  INTERVEN. REQ:DEVICE NOT READY/PAPER/COVER OPEN




    DEPRESS ENTER KEY TO VIEW ALERTS-STATIC

  ???
CMD==>
```

Figure 11.5 An example of the alerts-dynamic screen.

The alerts-dynamic screen (ALD) can be displayed from the NPDA main menu; an example is provided in Figure 11.5. This list is dynamically updated as new alerts are received by NetView. Because each of the operators using this facility has their screen updated, there is a search done by the hardware monitor, after receiving an alert, to determine which OSTs are currently using the ALD panel. Of course, limiting the number of operators displaying the alerts-dynamic data can help to reduce NetView's resource consumption.

In order to examine any of the alerts, the user must "freeze" the dynamic screen. Pressing the ENTER key will cause a static version of the same list to be presented. Figure 11.6 contains an example of the alerts-static display (ALS). This panel does not dynamically change, but remains fixed so that each alert can be selected by the appropriate number on the left. The operations available for each alert include:

- Recommended action
- List of most recent events for the resource
- Problem entry into the Information/Management database
- Delete the alert entry

The recommended action panel assists the operator in problem resolution for the specific alert, while the most recent events list provides some perspective, based on recent activity, for the resource. Entering a problem into the Information/Management database is enabled through the NetView bridge connection.

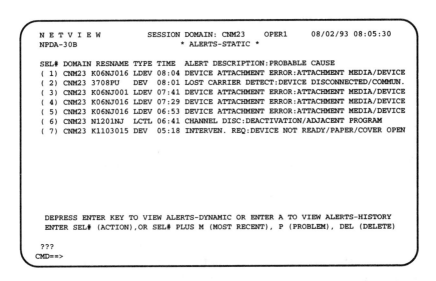

```
 N E T V I E W          SESSION DOMAIN: CNM23    OPER1      08/02/93 08:05:30
 NPDA-30B                     * ALERTS-STATIC *

 SEL# DOMAIN RESNAME TYPE TIME  ALERT DESCRIPTION:PROBABLE CAUSE
 ( 1) CNM23 K06NJ016 LDEV 08:04 DEVICE ATTACHMENT ERROR:ATTACHMENT MEDIA/DEVICE
 ( 2) CNM23 3708PU   DEV  08:01 LOST CARRIER DETECT:DEVICE DISCONNECTED/COMMUN.
 ( 3) CNM23 K06NJ001 LDEV 07:41 DEVICE ATTACHMENT ERROR:ATTACHMENT MEDIA/DEVICE
 ( 4) CNM23 K06NJ016 LDEV 07:29 DEVICE ATTACHMENT ERROR:ATTACHMENT MEDIA/DEVICE
 ( 5) CNM23 K06NJ016 LDEV 06:53 DEVICE ATTACHMENT ERROR:ATTACHMENT MEDIA/DEVICE
 ( 6) CNM23 N1201NJ  LCTL 06:41 CHANNEL DISC:DEACTIVATION/ADJACENT PROGRAM
 ( 7) CNM23 K1103015 DEV  05:18 INTERVEN. REQ:DEVICE NOT READY/PAPER/COVER OPEN




 DEPRESS ENTER KEY TO VIEW ALERTS-DYNAMIC OR ENTER A TO VIEW ALERTS-HISTORY
 ENTER SEL# (ACTION),OR SEL# PLUS M (MOST RECENT), P (PROBLEM), DEL (DELETE)

 ???
 CMD==>
```

Figure 11.6 An example of the alerts-static screen.

Alerts-History

Where the ALD screen provides a list of recent alerts, the alerts-history command (ALH) can be used to display the alerts over a longer range of time. The same type of data and operations included with the alerts-static display are available from the ALH panel. The difference is that a larger set of alerts is provided.

Events Display

In addition to alert data, the most recent events can also be displayed. This is done for a specifically named resource, or through a navigation path where all the events from the database are available.

When the total events option is accessed from the main menu, a hierarchy is utilized in arranging the resources. This necessitates a navigation from a very high level resource down to the lowest level.

```
N E T V I E W          SESSION DOMAIN: CNM23     OPER1     08/12/93 12:04:32
NPDA-41A                    * MOST RECENT EVENTS *              PAGE   1 OF   1

  CNM23      NCP011    L1103      N110300      K1103001
           +---------+           +---------+  +---------+
  DOMAIN   |  COMC   |----LINE----|  CTRL   |---|  DEV    |
           +---------+           +---------+  +---------+
SEL#  DATE/TIME  EVENT DESCRIPTION:PROBABLE CAUSE                  ETYP
( 1)  08/07 13:20  INTERVEN. REQ:DEVICE NOT READY/PAPER/COVER OPEN  PERM
( 2)  08/07 13:20  INTERVEN. REQ:DEVICE NOT READY/PAPER/COVER OPEN  PERM
( 3)  08/07 12:27  DEVICE ATTACHMENT ERROR:ATTACHMENT MEDIA/DEVICE  PERF




    ENTER ST (STAT), SEL# (ACTION), OR SEL# PLUS D (EVENT DETAIL)

    ???
CMD==>
```

Figure 11.7 A list of the most recent events for a particular resource.

Once the hierarchy has been followed downward to the desired resource, a list of the recent events for the device can be displayed; Figure 11.7 provides an example of this events list.

Statistics Display

Statistics are usually generated during the normal course of operation by devices in the network. Or the data can be requested by the NetView operator.

For example, the 3745 running the NCP generates statistics based on the SRT parameter. The operation of the network devices producing statistics records can also be controlled with the NetView TRHESH command.

Figure 11.8 provides a sample display of the statistics data for a network device.

```
 N E T V I E W             SESSION DOMAIN: CNM23     OPER1      08/12/93 12:09:04
 NPDA-51A       * MOST RECENT TRAFFIC STATS FOR SDLC STATION *      PAGE   1 OF   3

   CNM23        NCP012     L1202      N120200
                +--------+            +--------+
   DOMAIN       |  COMC  |----LINE----|  CTRL  |
                +--------+            +--------+

                STAT     TOTAL    TOTAL   E/T RATIO   TRANSMISSIONS        RECEIVES
   DATE/TIME    TYPE     TRAFFIC  TEMPS   SET  CALC   TRAFFIC   TEMPS   TRAFFIC   TEMPS
   08/09 23:28  TRAF-1   49299      0     3.0  0.0    32814       0     16485       0
   08/09 22:33  TRAF-1   49311      0     3.0  0.0    32815       0     16496       0
   08/09 21:38  TRAF-1   49298      0     3.0  0.0    32816       0     16482       0
   08/09 20:44  TRAF-1   49301      0     3.0  0.0    32810       0     16491       0
   08/09 19:49  TRAF-1   49300      0     3.0  0.0    32811       0     16489       0
   08/09 18:54  TRAF-1   49299      0     3.0  0.0    32810       0     16489       0
   08/09 18:00  TRAF-1   49308      0     3.0  0.0    32815       0     16493       0
   08/09 17:05  TRAF-1   49297      0     3.0  0.0    32812       0     16485       0
   08/09 16:10  TRAF-1   49298      0     3.0  0.0    32809       0     16489       0
   08/09 15:15  TRAF-1   49302      0     3.0  0.0    32813       0     16489       0
   ENTER EV (EVENT)

   ???
 CMD==>
```

Figure 11.8 An example of statistics data for a network resource.

11.6 Analysis and Resolution

Once a problem has been identify, the operator will want to examine its characteristics, causes, and possible resolution.

Recommended Action

From the alerts-static, alerts-history, or most recent events list, a particular entry can be selected for analysis. Figure 11.9 presents an example of the recommended action panel. This information is available first in order to help present a possible solution to the operator. Each of the possible actions begins with an action number (e.g., D173). The ACTION line command can be used to obtain further information regarding a specific action, such as:

ACTION D173

This results in a pre-defined panel being displayed, providing more data on the recommended action.

```
N E T V I E W              SESSION DOMAIN: CNM23    OPER1    08/02/93 07:43:22
NPDA-BNI0484C          * RECOMMENDED ACTION FOR SELECTED EVENT *      PAGE 1 OF 1
  CNM23       SA06            CH0C        N06NJ0       K06NJ001
             +--------+                +--------+   +--------+
  DOMAIN     |  CPU   |----CHAN----|  LCTL  |---|  LDEV  |
             +--------+                +--------+   +--------+
USER    CAUSED - NONE

INSTALL CAUSED - NONE

FAILURE CAUSED - LINE
                 REMOTE DEVICE
                 CONTROL UNIT
         ACTIONS - D011 - REVIEW EVENT DETAIL DISPLAY: ERROR CODE, PORT
                   D173 - PERFORM TRANSMISSION LINE PROBLEM DETERMINATION
                     PROCEDURES
                   D005 - CONTACT APPROPRIATE SERVICE REPRESENTATIVE



  ENTER ST (MOST RECENT STATISTICS), DM (DETAIL MENU), OR D (EVENT DETAIL)

  ???
CMD==>
```

Figure 11.9 Recommended action display for a hardware monitor alert.

Details of an Event

From the action panel, more information can be accessed regarding the nature of the alert. Figure 11.10 shows a menu, available for most of the events recorded by NetView, from which one of several choices can be made.

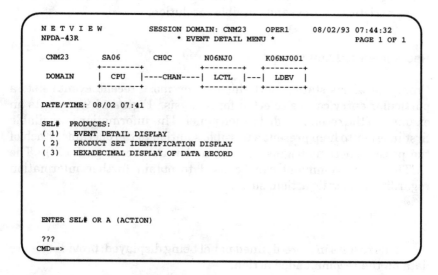

```
N E T V I E W              SESSION DOMAIN: CNM23    OPER1    08/02/93 07:44:32
NPDA-43R                   * EVENT DETAIL MENU *              PAGE 1 OF 1

  CNM23       SA06            CH0C        N06NJ0       K06NJ001
             +--------+                +--------+   +--------+
  DOMAIN     |  CPU   |----CHAN----|  LCTL  |---|  LDEV  |
             +--------+                +--------+   +--------+

DATE/TIME: 08/02 07:41

SEL#   PRODUCES:
( 1)    EVENT DETAIL DISPLAY
( 2)    PRODUCT SET IDENTIFICATION DISPLAY
( 3)    HEXADECIMAL DISPLAY OF DATA RECORD




  ENTER SEL# OR A (ACTION)

  ???
CMD==>
```

Figure 11.10 Detail menu for specific alert.

Figure 11.11 provides more of the event details, and Figure 11.12 shows the actual incoming NMVT record.

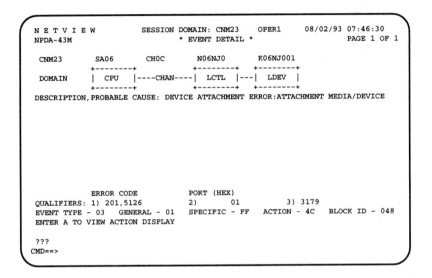

```
N E T V I E W          SESSION DOMAIN: CNM23     OPER1      08/02/93 07:46:30
NPDA-43M                      * EVENT DETAIL *                   PAGE 1 OF 1

 CNM23       SA06       CH0C        N06NJ0       K06NJ001
             +--------+             +--------+   +--------+
 DOMAIN      |  CPU   |----CHAN----|  LCTL  |---|  LDEV  |
             +--------+             +--------+   +--------+
 DESCRIPTION,PROBABLE CAUSE: DEVICE ATTACHMENT ERROR:ATTACHMENT MEDIA/DEVICE




                ERROR CODE         PORT (HEX)
 QUALIFIERS: 1) 201,5126           2)      01         3) 3179
 EVENT TYPE - 03    GENERAL - 01   SPECIFIC - FF   ACTION - 4C   BLOCK ID - 048
 ENTER A TO VIEW ACTION DISPLAY

 ???
 CMD==>
```

Figure 11.11   Display of details of alert.

11.7 Display Customization

The user interface for the hardware monitor can be customized in order to allow for better clarity and improved operator efficiency. The major areas for customization include:

- Update the recommended action and event detail screens, as well as the alert message description, for nongeneric alerts.
- Implement recommended action numbers for generic alerts.
- Include support for user-defined generic code points.
- Control aspects of the display, such as color and highlighting.

Rather than attempt to describe the procedure involved for each, one of the listed techniques is briefly presented below. The reader should refer to the appropriate NetView documentation as needed.

Recommended Action and Event Detail Panels

Each nongeneric alert has a five-digit code number associated with it. The first three digits represent the product ID, or block ID, which identifies the product or resource from the NetView perspective (e.g., "ppp"). The lower two digits determine the panel used for the specific event (e.g., "nn").

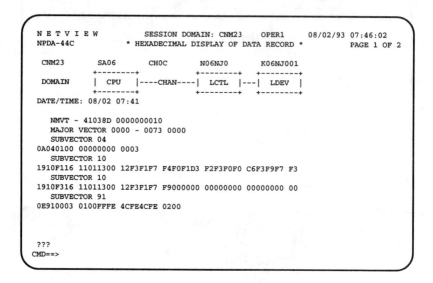

```
N E T V I E W            SESSION DOMAIN: CNM23   OPER1    08/02/93 07:46:02
NPDA-44C               * HEXADECIMAL DISPLAY OF DATA RECORD *        PAGE 1 OF 2

  CNM23        SA06        CH0C        N06NJ0         K06NJ001
            +--------+              +--------+   +--------+
  DOMAIN    |  CPU   |----CHAN----|  LCTL  |---|  LDEV  |
            +--------+              +--------+   +--------+
DATE/TIME: 08/02 07:41

   NMVT - 41038D 0000000010
   MAJOR VECTOR 0000 - 0073 0000
     SUBVECTOR 04
0A040100 00000000 0003
     SUBVECTOR 10
1910F116 11011300 12F3F1F7 F4F0F1D3 F2F3F0F0 C6F3F9F7 F3
     SUBVECTOR 10
1910F316 11011300 12F3F1F7 F9000000 00000000 00000000 00
     SUBVECTOR 91
0E910003 0100FFFE 4CFE4CFE 0200



   ???
CMD==>
```

Figure 11.12   Display of actual NMVT alert record.

From the ALS, ALH, or most recent events screen, an alert can be selected by number along with the letter C (e.g., "1 C"). If the message BNJ378I, or a product ID and alert ID, is displayed then the alert is generic. Otherwise message BNJ962I is used to provide the five-digit code for the nongeneric alert (e.g., "pppnn"). This number is used in determining which of the panels stored at the NetView host can be modified.

The members in the library BNJPNL1 should be edited as follows, where 'pppnn' is the code number:

- BNIpppnn - recommended action panel
- BNKpppnn - event detail panel

Updating these panels is one of the ways that the display of nongeneric alert information can be customized.

12

Session Monitor

The session monitor collects and records data regarding same-domain, cross-domain, and cross-network SNA sessions. It therefore provides a view of the logical, as compared to the physical, aspects of the network.

Based on the older Network Logical Data Manager (NLDM) product, this NetView component is useful for problem solving, availability and performance measurement, as well as capacity planning.

12.1 Subtask Environment

The session monitor gathers and displays several different types of information regarding the operation and performance of the network. This data falls into one of the following categories:

- Session Awareness (SAW)
- Session trace
- Response Time Monitor (RTM)
- Virtual and explicit routes
- Network availability

In order to support the collection and recording of this information, several subtasks are supplied within the NetView application address space. Figure 12.1 includes a list of these tasks, along with a brief description for each.

The LUC subtask is traditionally associated with the session monitor because of its original use in accessing cross-domain NLDM data.

However, this task now supports several different functions and is therefore grouped with the other multiple domain features as described in Chapter 17.

Subtask	Description
AAUTSKLP	The main session monitor subtask which accepts, processes, and archives session information.
AAUTCNMI	The CNM interface task interacts with VTAM in order to control the collection of SAW and trace data
DSIAMLUT	The access method LU task creates a CDRM-to-NCCFID table for cross-domain access; SAW and trace data is also accepted from VTAM.

Figure 12.1 A list of the core subtasks for the session monitor.

AAUTSKLP Definitions

The main DST subtask is configured by the systems programmer to collect and store the session-related data in the session monitor database. As with the other components, two VSAM clusters are utilized, with only one being active at a time.

The DSIPARM dataset member AAUPRMLP is usually named on the TASK definition as the file containing the session monitor definitions. The INITMOD statement is used multiple times, each with one of several different parameters. These configuration options define global characteristics of the SAW, trace, and RTM data collection. Additional files in the DSIPARM dataset are named in AAUPRMLP in order to provide further details of the configuration.

CNM Interface Definitions

The subtask AAUTCNMI is also a DST. It provides a connection to the VTAM CNM interface, through which the flow of SAW and trace data can be controlled.

The access method LU task (DSIAMLUT) accepts the actual SAW and trace data from VTAM. These messages flow over a set of parallel LU-to-LU sessions established with the ISTPDCLU APPLID owned by the VTAM address space. With MVS/ESA, two dataspaces are used instead of the LU sessions to pass the data to the session monitor.

DSIAMLUT also builds a table which allows for the resolution between VTAM Cross-Domain Resource Manager (CDRM) names and NetView domain IDs. This allows operators to access session monitor data in other domains. The member named on the TASK statement, usually DSIAMLTD, contains one or more CDRMDEF statements; each line defines a CDRM-NCCFID pair.

Operator Access

The main menu for the session monitor is displayed when the operator accesses the component using the NLDM command. Figure 12.2 contains an example of the screen.

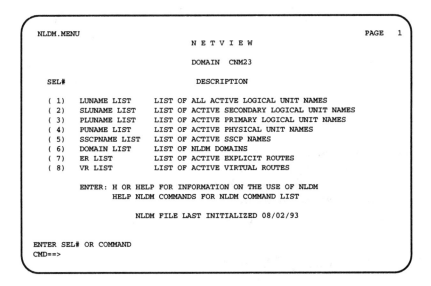

```
NLDM.MENU                                                    PAGE   1
                                N E T V I E W

                              DOMAIN   CNM23

     SEL#                              DESCRIPTION

     ( 1)   LUNAME LIST     LIST OF ALL ACTIVE LOGICAL UNIT NAMES
     ( 2)   SLUNAME LIST    LIST OF ACTIVE SECONDARY LOGICAL UNIT NAMES
     ( 3)   PLUNAME LIST    LIST OF ACTIVE PRIMARY LOGICAL UNIT NAMES
     ( 4)   PUNAME LIST     LIST OF ACTIVE PHYSICAL UNIT NAMES
     ( 5)   SSCPNAME LIST   LIST OF ACTIVE SSCP NAMES
     ( 6)   DOMAIN LIST     LIST OF NLDM DOMAINS
     ( 7)   ER LIST         LIST OF ACTIVE EXPLICIT ROUTES
     ( 8)   VR LIST         LIST OF ACTIVE VIRTUAL ROUTES

             ENTER: H OR HELP FOR INFORMATION ON THE USE OF NLDM
                    HELP NLDM COMMANDS FOR NLDM COMMAND LIST

                    NLDM FILE LAST INITIALIZED 08/02/93


ENTER SEL# OR COMMAND
CMD==>
```

Figure 12.2 An example of the session monitor's main menu.

The component features a panel-driven user interface, as well as several line-mode commands.

Monitoring Performance

The RESOURCE and TASKUTIL commands described in Chapter 10 can of course be helpful in identifying excess resource consumption by the component. In addition, the SESSMDIS command provides more information, which is specific to operation of the session monitor.

```
SESSMDIS  Session Monitor Session and Storage Information 11:20:32  Page 1 of 1

Options in Effect       SAW: YES   LU Trace: NO    SSCP Trace: NO    Acct: NO

Session Counts   SSCP-SSCP      SSCP-PU       SSCP-LU        LU-LU      Filtered
       Current:        2           11           573            68           0
       Maximum:        2           11           576            69           0

Session Monitor Storage Usage
     Resources:      84K        Sessions:     176K  Session Parms:      0K
     PIU Trace:       0K      Accounting:       0K            RTM:      0K
         Total:     260K

VSAM Record Queue
       Current:        8
       Maximum:       26

Session Monitor Workload since 08/02/93 06:27:50
                   SAW       Session   Session    PIU         PIUs    Sessions
                 Buffers     Starts     Ends     Buffers              Recorded
    4 seconds:       4          4         4         0           0          1
        Total:    7471       7851      7196         0           0       7188

ENTER= Refresh            PF2= End  PF3= Return
```

Figure 12.3 An example of the SESSMDIS command.

In tracking and recording SNA session information, the session monitor can potentially use large amounts of virtual storage. SESSMDIS provides a method for displaying the number of sessions being monitored and the storage allocated, as well as other aspects of its performance. Figure 12.3 provides an example of the command.

12.2 Defining Keep Classes

The session awareness data provided by VTAM forms the basis for the other information provided by the session monitor. SAW data collection must be enabled before the trace and RTM data is available.

When a session is started, the session monitor is notified with a SAW message. The session is then mapped into a specific keep class based on its characteristics.

Each class contains its own set of operational parameters which determine, among other things, how the data for the session is processed. The keep class definitions act as a filter, allowing session data to be either retained or discarded.

Global Parameters

In establishing the keep classes, certain global definitions are first specified in AAUPRMLP. These include:

- SAW - the default is to collect SAW data, although it can be disabled as well. The ENABLE command can be used to start data collection.
- SAW buffers - number and size of buffers for SAW data.
- Trace buffers - number and size of buffers for session trace data.
- KEEPPIU - defines the number of trace PIUs to be kept in virtual storage for all sessions. This value can be overridden by the individual keep class as described below.
- KEEPDISC - the number of discarded trace PIUs to be kept in virtual storage.
- KEEPSESS - this parameter controls DASD wrapping for the sessions processed.
- KEEPRTM - the number of RTM collection periods that are kept in virtual storage for each session.

These parameters define global values, which in many cases can be overridden by the operands for each specific session.

Establishing Keep Class Definitions

A keep class is just what its name implies - a set of filtering characteristics which determine how data is processed and kept. There are two parameter statements used in establishing the session monitor keep classes:

- KCLASS - several parameter values are specified which apply to all sessions mapped into the class.
- MAPSESS - a type of template that determines which SNA sessions fall into the named keep class.

The DSIPARM member named with the KEEPMEM parameter in AAUPRMLP holds these definition parameters. Once updated, the session monitor must be restarted for them to take effect. Or, the RELOAD command can be used to refresh the class definitions.

KCLASS Parameter Values

The keep class definitions are specified first, followed by the MAPSESS statements. Figure 12.4 provides an example of how a keep class is established.

```
SPECLU1   KCLASS SAW=YES,+
                 KEEPPIU=10,+
                 DASD=YES,+
                 KEEPSESS=10,+
                 DGROUP=TSO
```

Figure 12.4 Example of parameters used to create a keep class.

Most of the operand values are self-evident. SAW data is collected for the sessions mapped into the class, which retains sessions on disk and PIUs in virtual storage as specified. The DASD keyword parameter can be used to select what sessions are recorded based on the type of data collected. The sessions can be differentiated based on characteristics such as those with trace data, RTM data, abnormal termination, and initiation / bind failures.

The DGROUP parameter allows the sessions mapped into the keep class to be grouped together in one of several ways for archival and reporting purposes.

Mapping the Sessions

The MAPSESS statement provides the method for mapping sessions into a particular keep class. The same parameter, as described below, is also used to map sessions to determine the characteristics of their RTM data collection and recording.

Figure 12.5 illustrates the definition used to map sessions into the keep class SPECLU1. Note that a wildcarding and pattern matching technique can be used with the '*' and '?' characters. Also, the selection process can be further narrowed based on a session's virtual route, explicit route, and transmission priority.

12.3 Session Access

The basic element available for examination and analysis by the session monitor operator is the SNA session. A specific session can be accessed in one of several different ways. The SAW data forwarded by VTAM enables the session monitor to construct the various lists.

```
MAP05     MAPSESS KCLASS=SPECLU1,PRI=TSO*,SEC=A??T????
```

Figure 12.5 Statement used to map sessions into a keep class.

Perhaps the most widely utilized technique for displaying sessions is by logical unit name. That is, the operator can select a particular LU from a list, and then display the session activity.

Logical Unit Access

The session monitor tracks the sessions for each LU. The LUCOUNT parameter in AAUPRMLP provides a way to estimate the number of LUs which will be known to NetView; using this operand properly can help improve performance.

```
NLDM.LIST                                                     PAGE    1
                            RESOURCE NAME LIST
LIST TYPE: ACTIVE    SLU                               DOMAIN: CNM23
---------------------------------------------------------------------
 SEL#     NAME    STATUS    SEL#     NAME    STATUS    SEL#     NAME    STATUS
( 1)  AEYR0001  ACTIVE   (16)  K06NJ027  ACTIVE   (31)  K06NJ17F  ACTIVE
( 2)  IBM0IB2D  ACTIVE   (17)  K06NJ028  ACTIVE   (32)  K0686D    ACTIVE
( 3)  ISTPDCLU  ACTIVE   (18)  K06NJ038  ACTIVE   (33)  K0687A    ACTIVE
( 4)  K05NJ001  ACTIVE   (19)  K06NJ039  ACTIVE   (34)  K0687B    ACTIVE
( 5)  K05NJ002  ACTIVE   (20)  K06NJ050  ACTIVE   (35)  K0687C    ACTIVE
( 6)  K05NJ003  ACTIVE   (21)  K06NJ051  ACTIVE   (36)  K06876    ACTIVE
( 7)  K05NJ004  ACTIVE   (22)  K06NJ055  ACTIVE   (37)  K0688004  ACTIVE
( 8)  K06NJ003  ACTIVE   (23)  K06NJ056  ACTIVE   (38)  K0688011  ACTIVE
( 9)  K06NJ004  ACTIVE   (24)  K06NJ057  ACTIVE   (39)  K0688012  ACTIVE
(10)  K06NJ009  ACTIVE   (25)  K06NJ078  ACTIVE   (40)  K0688019  ACTIVE
(11)  K06NJ011  ACTIVE   (26)  K06NJ079  ACTIVE   (41)  K0688020  ACTIVE
(12)  K06NJ012  ACTIVE   (27)  K06NJ100  ACTIVE   (42)  K0688026  ACTIVE
(13)  K06NJ013  ACTIVE   (28)  K06NJ105  ACTIVE   (43)  K0688027  ACTIVE
(14)  K06NJ014  ACTIVE   (29)  K06NJ140  ACTIVE   (44)  K0688056  ACTIVE
(15)  K06NJ026  ACTIVE   (30)  K06NJ142  ACTIVE   (45)  K1207001  ACTIVE

ENTER TO VIEW MORE DATA OR TYPE FIND NAME TO LOCATE SPECIFIC NAME
ENTER SEL# (SESS LIST), SEL# RTS (RESP TIME SUM) OR SEL# RTT (RESP TIME TREND)
CMD==>
```

Figure 12.6 List of secondary logical units known to the session monitor.

The data for individual sessions can be accessed by the operator from three main LU lists:

- Active LU
- Primary LU (PLU)
- Secondary LU (SLU)

Figure 12.6 provides an example of a list of secondary LUs. Figure 12.7 lists the sessions for one of the LUs from the list.

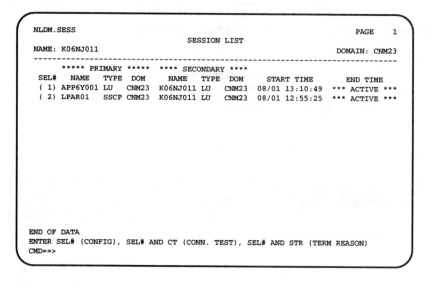

```
NLDM.SESS                                                        PAGE    1
                                SESSION LIST
NAME: K06NJ011                                              DOMAIN: CNM23
-----------------------------------------------------------------------------
        ***** PRIMARY *****   **** SECONDARY ****
  SEL#    NAME   TYPE  DOM      NAME    TYPE  DOM    START TIME     END TIME
 ( 1) APP6Y001 LU    CNM23  K06NJ011 LU    CNM23  08/01 13:10:49 *** ACTIVE ***
 ( 2) LPAR01   SSCP CNM23  K06NJ011 LU    CNM23  08/01 12:55:25 *** ACTIVE ***




END OF DATA
ENTER SEL# (CONFIG), SEL# AND CT (CONN. TEST), SEL# AND STR (TERM REASON)
CMD==>
```

Figure 12.7 List of sessions for a specific SNA logical unit.

Alternative Access

In addition to the primary and secondary LU lists, there are several other access paths to the SNA session data. These include:

- Physical unit (PU) name
- SSCP-DOMAIN names
- SNA virtual and explicit routes

Figure 12.8 presents an example of the list of PUs in the domain.

12.4 Session Awareness

The SAW data, as mentioned above, provides the basis for the session monitor collection activities. This information can be processed or excluded from the session monitor depending on the keep class definitions. In addition, with VTAM version 3.3 (or version 3.2 with the appropriate maintenance), the SAW data can be filtered in VTAM before being sent to NetView.

```
NLDM.LIST                                                      PAGE   1
                            RESOURCE NAME LIST
LIST TYPE: ACTIVE    PU                               DOMAIN: CNM23
-------------------------------------------------------------------------
  SEL#     NAME     STATUS    SEL#    NAME    STATUS    SEL#   NAME    STATUS
 ( 1)    NCP011    ACTIVE
 ( 2)    NCP015    ACTIVE
 ( 3)    N06NJ0    ACTIVE
 ( 4)    N06NJ1    ACTIVE
 ( 5)    N06880    ACTIVE
 ( 6)    N110300   ACTIVE
 ( 7)    N120700   ACTIVE
 ( 8)    N121600   ACTIVE
 ( 9)    SA06      ACTIVE
 (10)    N10AC0    ACTIVE
 (11)    N14AC0    ACTIVE




 END OF DATA - TYPE FIND NAME TO LOCATE SPECIFIC NAME
 ENTER SEL# OR COMMAND
 CMD==>
```

Figure 12.8 Access to session data by SNA physical unit name.

Content of SAW Data

A message is generated by VTAM and sent to the session monitor when a session is started or terminated. The SAW data includes the following session information:

- Type
- Partner names
- Activation status, including failure information
- State, such as active or recovery pending
- Configuration data

The session configuration data provides an important framework for organizing and analyzing the other data. Figure 12.9 presents an example of the type of session configuration data that is available.

12.5 Session Trace Data

The session monitor provides the ability to trace sessions either selectively or on a global basis. The data consists of the session activation parameters, Path Information Unit (PIU) data, and NCP data.

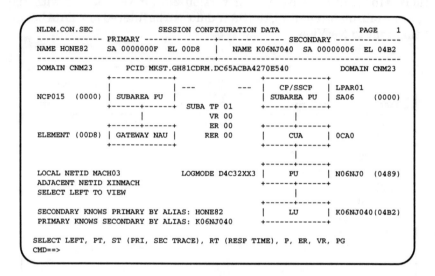

Figure 12.9 Configuration information for a specific session.

The NCP data applies to attached peripheral nodes, as well as data from the gateway NCP for cross-network sessions. Also, discarded PIUs are passed to the session monitor for trace processing. PIUs are discarded by VTAM when a protocol violation occurs or when they are not related to a specific session.

Enabling Global Trace

Global tracing must be enabled by the systems programmer before the data is available. There are three parameters related to the collection of this trace data, which take effect at session monitor initialization time:

- TRACESC - traffic for all SSCP sessions, including SSCP-to-SSCP, SSCP-to-PU, and SSCP-to-LU.
- TRACELU - all LU-to-LU sessions.
- TRACEGW - traffic through gateway NCPs for which NetView has received SAW data.

In most situations, global SSCP and LU tracing should be disabled due to the high consumption of processor resources involved. Tracing can then be activated selectively as required.

Tracing Sessions

The session monitor TRACE command is used to start and stop the collection of trace data. The MAXEND parameter in AAUPRMLP sets a limit on the maximum number of concurrent requests for trace data from the terminal operators.

After a trace has been started, the data can be viewed. The SNA Transmission Header (TH), Request Header (RH), and up to 11 bytes of data are collected for each PIU.

The tracing operation is performed based on where each LU is located. The data is displayed from a primary LU trace (PT) or secondary trace (ST).

```
NLDM.PIUT                    SESSION TRACE DATA                    PAGE    1
----------- PRIMARY --------------+---------- SECONDARY ---------------+- DOM -
NAME APP6Y001 SA 00000006 EL 0008 | NAME K06NJ040 SA 00000006 EL 04B2 | CNM23
----------------------------------+------------------------------------+-------
SEL#    TIME    SEQ# DIR    TYPE   ******** REQ/RESP HEADER ******** RULEN SENS N
( 1) 19:13:49 0056 S-P DATA       ....OC.ER............CD..........      3
( 2) 19:13:49 006A P-S DATA       ....OC.DR............CD..........   1333        T
( 3) 19:13:49 006A S-P (+)RSP     ....OC.DR........................      0
( 4) 19:13:58 0057 S-P DATA       ....OC.ER............CD..........      7
( 5) 19:13:58 006B P-S DATA       ....OC.DR............CD..........    987        T
( 6) 19:13:58 006B S-P (+)RSP     ....OC.DR........................      0




END OF DATA
ENTER SEL# OR COMMAND
CMD==>
```

Figure 12.10 Session trace data for a specific logical unit.

Figure 12.10 shows the PIU data captured by NetView. Each entry can be selected, and the detail data examined.

12.6 Response Time Monitoring

The response time experienced by terminal operators has traditionally been one measure of the level of service provided to network users. There are two major methods for gathering this type of information:

- Software estimation - this technique involves intercepting PIUs at the host, and then forcing a definite response indicator in the message that is returned to the terminal device. The time taken for a response to return is then taken as an approximation of the original inbound transaction request.
- Hardware statistics - the control unit measures the actual response time from the time a message is sent to the host, until a response returns. A set of "buckets," or counters, are maintained which contain the number of transactions falling within the specific ranges for each terminal. This Response Time Monitor (RTM) feature is a standard feature on the recent control units (e.g., 3174).

The RTM feature can be controlled, and the data displayed, either from a locally attached terminal or from the host. From the mainframe, the CNM interface, through the SSCP-to-PU session, is used to exchange NMVT request units with the control unit. There are two SNA/MS major vectors involved; refer to the appendix for more information.

The session monitor detects when a session starts (through SAW data). An NMVT is sent to the control unit when a session starts in order to dynamically set the proper response time objectives.

Several parameters are defined in the AAUPRMLP file which affect response time data collection. These include:

- RTM - enables the collection of RTM data.
- KEEPRTM - determines the number of RTM collection periods that can be kept in virtual storage for each session.
- PERFMEM - a member in DSIPARM containing the actual performance class objectives.
- RTMDISP - determines whether an operator, when RTM collection is activated by the session monitor, is able to display each transaction response time at the local terminal.

With the required hardware in place and the RTM feature enabled, the response time objectives can then be defined for each type of session.

Setting Performance Objectives

As with the keep classes discussed earlier, RTM data is also collected based on class definitions. Each session is mapped into a particular class based on its characteristics.

The parameter PERFMEM identifies the DSIPARM member containing the performance definitions. MAPSESS creates the mapping configuration, and the PCLASS statement defines the individual class definitions. Figure 12.11 contains an example of the PCLASS parameter statement.

```
TSOLCL   PCLASS OBJPCT=80,OBJTIME=1,+
                BOUNDS=(.5,1,2,5),+
                RTDEF=KEYBD,+
                DSPLYLOC=YES
```

Figure 12.11 RTM performance objectives are defined in separate classes.

The keywords control the response time objectives (OBJTIME and OBJPCT), boundaries for the buckets (BOUNDS), how the end of a transaction is defined (KEYBD - keyboard unlock), and whether the terminal user can display his response time locally for the last transaction (DSPLYLOC).

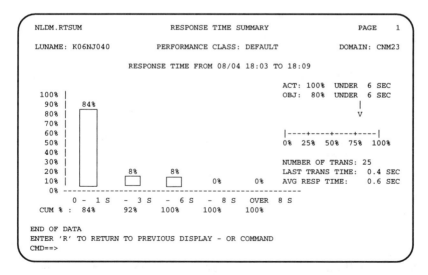

Figure 12.12 Response Time Monitor summary screen.

When RTM data has been collected for a session, the terminal operator can display the information with the session monitor. Figure 12.12 presents the RTM summary data for a 3270 terminal.

12.7 Virtual and Explicit Route Information

The performance of the SNA routing protocols can have an effect on overall session response time. The session monitor includes support for the virtual as well as explicit routes.

```
NLDM.VR                         VIRTUAL ROUTE STATUS                    PAGE    1
------------------------------------------------------------------------------
DOMAIN: CNM23                      NETID: MACH03                    DOMAIN: CNM23

      ORIGIN            WINDOW SIZE: MIN   3  CUR   9  MAX   9      DESTINATION
+----------------+                                             +----------------+
|                |         SEQ NUMBER: SENT   RECEIVED          |                |
| NAME: SA06     |         SAMPLE 1:   007B    007C             | NAME: NCP011   |
|                |         SAMPLE 2:   007C    007D             |                |
| SA:   00000006 | VR IS NOT BLOCKED                           | SA:   0000000B |
|                | |>>>--->----->----->---->----->----->--->>>| |                |
| PU TYPE: 5     |                                             | PU TYPE: 4     |
|                |            VR 00    TP 02                    |                |
|                |                                             | INBND PIU POOL |
|                | |<<<---<----<-----<----<-----<-----<---<<<| | CURRENT:    1  |
|                |         SEQ NUMBER: RECEIVED   SENT          | LIMIT:     25  |
|                |         SAMPLE 1:     00CE    00CE           |                |
| STATUS: 0000   |         SAMPLE 2:     00CF    00CF           | STATUS: 0000   |
|                | VR IS NOT BLOCKED                           |                |
|                |                                             |                |
+----------------+   WINDOW SIZE: MIN   3  CUR   9  MAX   9  +----------------+
SAMPLE 1 REQUESTED AT 14:06:38 ON 08/24 - SAMPLE 2 REQUESTED   7 SEC LATER
ENTER A (ANALYZE VIRTUAL ROUTE CONDITION)
CMD==>
```

Figure 12.13 An example of virtual route performance analysis.

Figure 12.13 contains an example of a VR selected for analysis from a list available to the terminal operator. The VR pacing window size information, PIU sequence numbers, and NCP-specific information, along with other data, is included.

The configuration of the physically mapped explicit route can also be displayed from the ER list data. Further analysis of the transmission groups is also possible from this panel.

12.8 Additional Functionality

There are other features available with the session monitor, and considerations for their implementation and use. The important areas for additional customization are presented below.

External Logging

The external log task, discussed in Chapter 8, can be used to record the information generated by the session monitor. This data then becomes available for performance and availability analysis, and can be passed into products such as the Service Level Reporter (SLR). The generation of this data is not affected by the keep class filtering statements.

A parameter statement in AAUPRMLP controls what data is sent to the external log for recording:

LOG=YES,SESSTAT=YES

The LOG parameter enables recording (YES), and will create the RTM, configuration, and session start/end data (for sessions with RTM records). SESSTAT is optional, and when used provides the session statistics (accounting and availability) as well as improved session start/end data.

Sense Code Filtering

Sense codes are SNA architected codes which exactly communicate error information. The session monitor has access to this sense code data, which can be used to filter the PIUs in which it occurs.

The job in CNMSAMP named CNMSJM10 can be run to analyze the session monitor database. The output provides a list of the sense codes contained, and the number recorded for each. This information helps to determine which sense codes to exclude.

To filter a sense code from recording, update the module DSICTMOD shipped in the samples library member CNMS0055. The first word is the number of sense code entries in the table. The individual entries follow, up to a maximum of 25. Finally the module must be reassembled, and the NetView program restarted.

13

Status Monitor

The status monitor component is a descendent of the earlier VTAM Node Control Application (VNCA). It collects and organizes status information regarding the SNA nodes within a VTAM domain. This allows the terminal operator to have a single view of the status of the network resources.

13.1 Features and Implementation

The status monitor provides several functions to the NetView user. Its operational characteristics and features fall into different categories. The status monitor allows you to:

- Browse the network log.
- Group network nodes according to a hierarchical arrangement, which mirrors the definitions established by VTAM.
- Collect and record status information for the resources based on definitions and a preprocessor.
- Recognize different states for each of the nodes being monitored.
- Use color, as well as other screen control techniques, when displaying the information.
- Control resources through VTAM commands and defined CLISTs.
- Automatically restart certain types of minor nodes.
- Gather information for the Graphic Monitor Facility (GMF).

The systems programmer has a number of options available when implementing the status monitor. Many of the functions provided operate with supplied default values, which can be changed based on the needs of an installation.

Parameter	Description
A (ALERT)	This statement is used to define the message characteristics (e.g., color) for the four classes.
C (CLIST)	The names of up to 16 CLISTs can be declared for display on the status monitor detail panel.
F (FILTER)	Messages processed by NetView can be assigned to one of the four classes for customized display.
O MONIT	This parameter enables the status monitor process of reactivating certain inactive nodes.
O SECSTAT	With this statement in use, the status monitor does not receive direct status updates from VTAM.
SENDMSG	For users of VTAM version 3.3 and above, using this option provides additional status information.
T (TIMER)	Used to establish the timed execution of inquiries to VTAM, which generate status update messages for NetView.

Figure 13.1 Parameters used to control the status monitor definition.

Configuration and Implementation

There are two subtasks that implement the status monitor component:

- CNM01VMT - VTAM status function, providing the monitoring capability
- CNM01BRW - log browse task

The last three characters of each name are fixed as 'VMT' and 'BRW', respectively. The first part of the names, shown in this case as 'CNM01', is the NetView domain ID. Both are optional tasks defined in the DSIDMN file with the TASK statement.

The subtask CNM01VMT reads an initialization member in DSIPARM, usually named DSICNM. Figure 13.1 contains a list of the parameter statements in the file which are used to establish the basic operational aspects of the component.

Another task to be performed when implementing the status monitor is to construct a view of which resources are to be monitored. This procedure involves using the STATOPT keyword parameter within the text of the VTAM definitions in the VTAMLST dataset. A special preprocessor must be run to create a definition deck which is then read at STATMON initialization.

Support for GMF

The data collected by the status monitor is passed over to the graphics task, CNMTAMEL. This task can then forward the updates, depending on its own GMF view definitions, down to the workstation.

In a multiple domain situation, a distributed host will not send the updates to the workstation directly. Rather, CNMTAMEL forwards the information to the central status focal point host through the LUC facilities.

This status forwarding process is controlled with the GRAPHOPT parameter which, like STATOPT, is recognized by the preprocessor. Refer to Chapter 19 for a description of GMF, and to Chapter 17 for an explanation of status forwarding.

13.2 Browsing the Network Log

The network log provides a record of the data generated and processed by NetView. Therefore, the ability to browse the log can be critical to the operation of NetView and the network in general.

As mentioned above, the log browse function is packaged with the status monitor. Both subtasks, VMT and BRW, must be active before a terminal operator can use the BROWSE command to access the log.

There are several operands that can be used when specifying which VSAM file to read; the active, inactive, primary, or secondary file can be named. Figure 13.2 presents a view of the active log file as seen from an operator's terminal. In this case, the command BR NETLOGA is used to access the active log. Chapter 8 also provides information on the network log.

```
STATMON.BROWSE       ACTS  NETWORK LOG FOR 08/02/93 (93214) COLS 017 094  13:00
HOST: HOST02           *1*   *2*   *3*   *4*  SEARCH MAX:          SCROLL: CSR
---2----+----3----+----4----+----5----+----6----+----7----+----8----+----9----
   CNM23     12:59:04    $HASP628 LINE1     SNA ACTIVE
   CNM23     12:59:04    $HASP628 LINE2     SNA ACTIVE
   CNM23     12:59:04    $HASP628 LINE3     SNA ACTIVE   (USMHSE2C)
   CNM23     12:59:04    $HASP628 LINE4     SNA ACTIVE   (MVSPS1)
   CNM23     12:59:11 3 DSI064A OPENACB FAILED, ACBOFLG = X'02', ACBERROR = X'58',
   CNM23   % 12:59:11    CNM039I AN IMPORTANT MESSAGE HAS BEEN LOGGED - PLEASE BROW
   CNM23     12:59:16    $HASP250 RSCS4218 IS PURGED
   CNM23     12:59:38    CCX001 TRANFER COMPLETED
   CNM23     12:59:38    IEC070I CATALOG.UCAT.MAIN
   CNM23     12:59:38    K2VSAMIO01  REQUEST=PUT  , RETURN CODE=08, FDBK=1C
   CNM23     12:59:38    DBF0023I INTEGRATION STARTING WITH RECORD =    21
   CNM23     12:59:38    DBF0161I COMPARE OF KEYS ENCOUNTERS ERROR
   CNM23     12:59:40    DBF0210E TERMINATION IN PROGRESS
   CNM23     12:59:40    CCX002 REQUEST RECEIVED FROM USER = OPER2
   CNM23     12:59:41    PDX0020 DEBUG MODE ENTERED
   CNM23     12:59:41    IEC070I CATALOG.UCAT.MAIN
   CNM23     12:59:41    K2VSAMIO01  REQUEST=PUT  , RETURN CODE=08, FDBK=1C
   CNM23     13:00:11 3 DSI064A OPENACB FAILED, ACBOFLG = X'02', ACBERROR = X'58',

CMD==>
1=HLP 2=END 3=RET 4=TOP 5=BOT 6=ROL 7=BCK 8=FWD 9=RPF 10=LFT 11=RGT 12=ALL
```

Figure 13.2 Sample output from the network log viewed from an operator terminal.

Each message contains the time it was generated, as well as the originating domain ID. The numbers running across the top of the screen provide a way to scroll ahead through the log and quickly locate the next message that has been assigned to one of the four message classes.

Several enhancements to the log browse facility have been included with version 2.3. These include more complete access and display capabilities, such as improved scrolling and FIND, as well as access by date/time. Also, the new global exit DSIEX18 can be utilized during log processing. The samples library includes the BLOG REXX-based system, which forms a panel-driven procedure for more precisely selecting the subset of records from the log for display.

13.3 Arrangement of Network Nodes

The status monitor tracks and displays resource information according to major and minor nodes. This arrangement is based on the structure of the actual SNA products.

Hierarchical Nature of SNA

The traditional SNA architecture is hierarchical in nature, with command and control concentrated at the central SSCP. The corresponding hardware and software products have therefore been created to emulate this same type of framework.

In an SNA network, VTAM implements the control point capability on the host. Each host maintains control over a single SNA domain through the SSCP-to-PU and SSCP-to-LU sessions.

The VTAM resource definitions which describe the network are arranged first into major nodes. Each of the major nodes definitions is contained within a member in the VTAMLST dataset. Within the major nodes are one or more minor nodes. The type of minor nodes used will depend on the major node type. Examples of major nodes include an NCP, local 3270 control unit, and host-based application program.

Each of the nodes defined in a specific resource definition path has a relation to the other nodes. One node can be said to be higher in the hierarchical structure, while another is lower. For example, consider the following structure:

- VTAM domain
- SNA 3174 control unit
- One or more attached terminal LUs

At the top of the path is the domain, followed by a lower major node definition for the 3174. The control unit can have several terminals defined, each at the lowest part of the hierarchy.

13.4 Definition of Resources

The resources to be tracked must be identified to the status monitor. This is done by first updating members in the VTAMLST dataset, and then running a preprocessor job supplied with NetView. The DSINDEF file created from the process is then read by the status monitor during initialization.

In order to control data collection and processing, the STATOPT keyword parameter is used. In a multiple domain environment, additional customization can be performed. In this case, the status monitor plays an important role in supporting GMF by gathering and then forwarding status information to a central site. The status monitor components in the distributed systems use the GRAPHOPT statement to control what information is to be forwarded. For an explanation of this parameter, as well as the concept of status forwarding, refer to Chapters 17 and 19.

STATOPT Statement

The STATOPT parameter controls the resources processed by the status monitor. It begins with an asterisk (i.e., '*') in column one, and therefore appears as a comment card to VTAM.

This statement is used in two manners by the systems programmer to include resources for the status monitor:

- Define optional descriptive names for VTAM major and minor nodes.
- Define nodes that are not activated at VTAM initialization, but should still be monitored.

Figure 13.3 includes an example used to identify an application for monitoring.

The STATOPT keyword must begin in column 16, and in this case declares a name for the application. Other parameters which are not shown, but can be used, are included in Figure 13.4.

Preprocessor and the DSINDEF File

The STATMON preprocessor JCL is shipped in the member CNMSJ007 of the samples library. The program draws on several sources of input in order to create the DSINDEF file:

- JCL parameter input
- Configuration member ATCCONxx
- Startup member ATCSTRxx
- Major nodes not activated at VTAM initialization, which should be tracked by the status monitor in CNMCONxx
- Actual major node members

Each line of the output DSINDEF member in the DSIPARM dataset contains one CNMDPREC control block. The fields are precisely defined by NetView, and determine how the status monitor is to process the information it receives.

```
CNM01    APPL  AUTH=(NVPACE,ACQ,PASS),PRTCT=CNM01,           X
               MODETAB=AMODETAB,DLOGMOD=DSIL6MOD,            X
               APPC=YES,PARSESS=YES,                         X
               DMINWNL=4,DMINWNR=4,DSESLIM=8,                X
               AUTOSES=2
   *           STATOPT='NETVIEW PROD'
```

Figure 13.3 Parameter used to define resources to the status monitor.

In defining the status monitor configuration, the systems programmer should carefully coordinate these activities with the GMF definitions.

13.5 Interfaces for Status Update

After the basic component features have been enabled and the network resources customized, the status monitor is prepared to track the defined network resources. The technique used to obtain the required information has evolved from the original interpretation of text messages received from VTAM to the more direct status updates available with NetView version 2.

STATOPT Operand	Description
NOMONIT	Provides the ability to exclude applicable nodes from automatic reactivation by STATMON.
NOACTY	Excludes the node from activity recording.
OMIT	Removes the node and all dependents from the view of the network provided by STATMON.

Figure 13.4 Additional keyword operands that can be used with STATOPT.

Original Message Access

The status monitor must be notified of the status of network nodes that are being monitored. For example, a line or terminal can go from active to inactive.

The technique used has traditionally been one where messages are accepted from VTAM across the program operator interface. Once received, the text is then parsed and examined. If a node in the message is recognized, its status is updated in the Resource Definition Activity Table (RDAT) data area, which is accompanied by a change to the operator's screen.

```
STATMON.DSS                    DOMAIN STATUS SUMMARY                      17:07
HOST: HOST01          *1*     *2*     *3*     *4*
                     ACTIVE  PENDING  INACT   MONIT   NEVACT   OTHER
.....3  NCP/CA/LAN/PK .....1  ......  ......  ......  .....2   ......
...28   LINES         .....5  ......  ......  ......  ...23    ......
...31   PUS/CLUSTERS  .....5  ......  ......  ......  ...26    ......
...61   LUS/TERMS     ...32   .....3  ....18  ......  .....8   ......
.....1  SWITCHED MAJ  ......  ......  ......  ......  .....1   ......
.....6  SWITCHED PUS  ......  ......  ......  ......  .....6   ......
...24   SWITCHED LUS  ......  ......  ......  ......  ...24    ......
.....2  LOCAL MAJ NDS .....1  ......  ......  ......  .....1   ......
.....1  PUS           .....1  ......  ......  ......  ......   ......
...14   LUS/TERMS     .....2  .....1  ......  ......  ...11    ......
.....4  APPL MAJ NDS  .....3  ......  .....1  ......  ......   ......
...66   APPLICATIONS  .....7  ......  ......  ......  ...58    .....1
.....2  CDRM MAJ NDS  .....1  ......  ......  ......  .....1   ......
.....4  CDRMS         ......  .....3  ......  ......  .....1   ......
.....2  CDRSC MAJ NDS ......  ......  .....1  ......  .....1   ......
...22   CDRSCS        ......  .....1  ......  ......  ...21    ......
------  ------------- ------  ------  ------  ------  ------   ------
..271   TOTAL NODES   ...58   .....8  ...20   ......  ...184   .....1

CMD==>
1=HELP  2=END  3=RETURN  4=BROWSE LOG  6=ROLL          9=REFRESH
```

Figure 13.5 The domain status summary screen.

The primary program operator (PPO) interface provides data which is available through the PPT in the form of unsolicited text messages. The status monitor also makes use of the secondary program operator (SPO) interface. In this case, solicited messages are returned in response to specific VTAM commands.

The 'T' statement in DSICNM, as mentioned in the figure above, allows the systems programmer to establish the execution of display commands on a regular basis. The solicited messages are accepted for processing by STATMON. There are two operands that can be used with the parameter, each causing a command to be issued every 'mm' minutes:

- APPLS - VTAM command 'D NET,APPLS'
- PENDING - VTAM command 'D NET,PENDING'

Of course, this entire technique of parsing and examining VTAM messages has several disadvantages. First, there can be significant overhead involved in translating the status information from text to internal control block format. Also, the timers used generate unneeded traffic and burden VTAM. Finally, the status information obtained from VTAM can change very rapidly, and might actually be inaccurate when finally presented to the terminal operator.

It would be more desirable to bypass this message parsing technique. Status information should be directly passed from VTAM to NetView.

VTAM-STATMON Interface

With NetView version 2.1, a more efficient method for communicating status information was introduced. Together with VTAM version 3.3 (on MVS), the VTAM-to-STATMON interface is now available. It should be used where ever possible in order to reduce overhead and improve the accuracy of the status information.

With this new interface, the PPO and solicited messages provided by VTAM are no longer needed. The updates to the STATMON control block structures are performed directly.

The load module ISTIECCE is shipped with the NetView product. As described in Chapter 6, it must be copied to the VTAMLIB dataset in the VTAM started procedure JCL. Therefore, although the module is a part of NetView, it is used by VTAM.

```
STATMON.DSD(DESC)              DOMAIN STATUS DETAIL (DESCRIPTION)      17:09
HOST: HOST01            *1*    *2*   *3*    *4*
                      ACTIVE  PENDING  INACT   MONIT   NEVACT   OTHER
?....66  APPLICATIONS ?.....7  ?...... ?...... ?...... ?....58  ?.....1
-----------------------------------------------------------------------------
? DISPLAY    |   NODE ID.  DESCRIPTION        NODE ID.  DESCRIPTION
? APPLS      |
? LINES      | ? AAUTCNMI  NLDMCNMI
? PUS/CLSTRS | ? DSIAMLUT  AMLUT TASK
? LUS/TERMS  | ? BNJHWMON  NPDA TASK
? CDRMS      | ? DSICRTR   CNM ROUTER
? CDRSCS     | ? DSIGDS    GDS TASK
  ? ACT      | ? DSIKREM   CSCF TASK
  ? EVERY    | ? DSIROVS   PUGW TASK
  ? INACT    |
? PENDING    |
? BFRUSE     |
? VARY INACT |
  ? I    ? F |
? VARY ACT   |
  ? ONLY  ? ALL |

CMD==>
1=HELP 2=END 3=RETURN 4=BROWSE LOG 6=ROLL          11=CLIST 12=MENU
```

Figure 13.6 A list of the active VTAM applications.

Any time the status of a network resource changes, the module is called by the VTAM code. The program uses MVS cross-memory (XMEM) techniques, and the VTAM Inline Exit Facility, to access the private area of the NetView application address space. In this way, the status monitor data areas can be updated immediately by VTAM.

```
NCCF                    N E T V I E W    CNM23 OPER1    08/25/93 17:19:51
* CNM23    D NET,ID=AAUTCNMI
  CNM23    IST097I DISPLAY ACCEPTED
' CNM23
IST075I  NAME = AAUTCNMI          , TYPE = APPL
IST486I  STATUS= ACTIV      , DESIRED STATE= ACTIV
IST977I  MDLTAB=***NA*** ASLTAB=***NA***
IST861I  MODETAB=***NA*** USSTAB=***NA*** LOGTAB=***NA***
IST934I  DLOGMOD=***NA***
IST597I  CAPABILITY-PLU ENABLED  ,SLU DISABLED ,SESSION LIMIT NONE
IST654I  I/O TRACE = OFF, BUFFER TRACE = OFF
IST271I  JOBNAME = CNM2PROC, STEPNAME = CNM2PROC
IST171I  ACTIVE SESSIONS = 0000000000, SESSION REQUESTS = 0000000000
IST314I  END
------------------------------------------------------------------------------




=X= ***
```

Figure 13.7 An example of a VTAM display command issued by the STATMON user.

There are a few restrictions to keep in mind when using this interface. First, the use of XMEM access requires that NetView run as a non-swappable address space. This had been previously recommended by IBM, but would be mandatory in this case. Also, only one NetView domain can make use of the interface on the same host. In the case where multiple domains are active under the same MVS operating system, the parameter:

O SECSTAT

should be included in DSICNM to disable the interface in all but one of the domains (i.e., primary domain). The SENDMSG parameter in DSICNM can also be used to request additional information for the primary domain which is using the interface.

13.6 Resource Display and Control

The terminal operator can type STATMON from the command line to access the status monitor. A summary of the resources in the VTAM domain is then displayed.

Status Summary

Figure 13.5 presents an example of the Display Status Summary panel. This screen provides a single view of the entire domain as monitored by the user. Each category of major nodes is shown. A color coding scheme is used to differentiate each of the states.

A specific class of resources can be selected by typing a character, such as 'S', in the column next to the resources listed. Or a subset, such as those in the active state, can be chosen.

Command Entry

After a resource category has been selected, a list of major nodes is displayed. From here, the resources can be operated upon through the use of either VTAM commands or NetView CLISTs.

Figure 13.6 includes an example of active VTAM applications being monitored; in this test environment only seven are shown on the screen.

```
STATMON.DSD(DESC)              DOMAIN STATUS DETAIL (DESCRIPTION)      17:10
HOST: HOST01          *1*    *2*   *3*   *4*
                      ACTIVE PENDING  INACT   MONIT   NEVACT   OTHER
?....66  APPLICATIONS ?.....7  ?......   ?......  ?......  ?....58  ?.....1
------------------------------------------------------------------------
? AUTOTR      |   NODE ID.  DESCRIPTION          NODE ID.  DESCRIPTION
? NODE        |
? EVENTS      | ? AAUTCNMI   NLDMCNMI
? INACTF      | ? DSIAMLUT   AMLUT TASK
? MONOFF      | ? BNJHWMON   NPDA TASK
? MONON       | ? DSICRTR    CNM ROUTER
? RECYCLE     | ? DSIGDS     GDS TASK
? REDIAL      | ? DSIKREM    CSCF TASK
? SESS        | ? DSIROVS    PUGW TASK
? STATIONS    |
? STATS       |
              |
              |
              |
              |
              |
              |
CMD==>
1=HELP 2=END 3=RETURN 4=BROWSE LOG 6=ROLL        10=VTAM        12=MENU
```

Figure 13.8 CLIST panel with same list of applications.

From here, a VTAM command can be issued through a simple point-and-shoot technique. Figure 13.7 shows the result of selecting a resource to perform a display command with. The command is constructed and executed by the command facility, which temporarily interrupts the STATMON user.

```
STATMON.DSD(DESC)            DOMAIN STATUS DETAIL (DESCRIPTION)      17:08
HOST: HOST01            *1*    *2*    *3*    *4*
                        ACTIVE PENDING  INACT   MONIT   NEVACT   OTHER
?....66  APPLICATIONS ?.....7  ?......  ?......  ?......  ?....58  ?.....1
-----------------------------------------------------------------------------
DISPLAY:        |  NODE ID.  DESCRIPTION        NODE ID.  DESCRIPTION
  HIGHER NODE   |
  ? SUMMARY     |  ? AAUTCNMI   NLDMCNMI
  ? DETAIL      |  ? DSIAMLUT   AMLUT TASK
 THIS NODE      |  ? BNJHWMON   NPDA TASK
  ? SUMMARY     |  ? DSICRTR    CNM ROUTER
  ? DETAIL      |  ? DSIGDS     GDS TASK
                |  ? DSIKREM    CSCF TASK
----------------|  ? DSIROVS    PUGW TASK
DETAIL FORMAT:  |
  ? DESCRIPT    |
  ? ANALYSIS    |
  ? ACTIVITY    |
                |
                |
CMD==>
1=HELP 2=END 3=RETURN 4=BROWSE LOG 6=ROLL          10=VTAM 11=CLIST
```

Figure 13.9 An example of the resource description panel.

Figure 13.8 includes the same list shown above, but now with the CLISTs that can be executed. This list of commands is defined in the DSICNM member with the 'C' statement.

Resource Analysis

Using the menu function key, a description panel with further options for analysis is displayed, as shown in Figure 13.9. There are actually a set of three associated screens used to provide analysis and activity information. Figure 13.10 includes a sample of the analysis information provided. These statistics are gathered by STATMON on a continuous basis; the buckets can be cleared by using the CLRSTATS command. Activity for the selected resources is displayed in Figure 13.11.

Automatic Restart

The user can configure the status monitor to automatically reactivate certain resources with the following DSICNM parameter:

O MONIT

The resources affected by this statement include:

■ Lines
■ Nonswitched PUs
■ BSC 3270 controllers
■ Channel-attached SNA control units
■ CDRM minor nodes
■ Channel-to-channel (CTC) connections

There are certain cases when STATMON will not reactivate a node, such as if it was deliberately inactivated with the VTAM vary command.

13.7 Evolution and Future Requirements

As the industry has evolved, NetView has been slowly enhanced to accommodate the requirements of its users. Over the past several years, the strategic importance and positioning of the status monitor has increased in some respects while decreased in others.

```
STATMON.DSD(ANALYSIS)           DOMAIN STATUS DETAIL (ANALYSIS)          17:13
HOST: HOST01            *1*    *2*    *3*   *4*              ELAPSED TIME   1:42
                       ACTIVE  PENDING    INACT    MONIT   NEVACT   OTHER
?....66  APPLICATIONS ?.....7  ?......   ?......  ?......  ?....58  ?.....1
-------------------------------------------------------------------------------
DISPLAY:              |            STATUS  |  ACTIVE   PENDING   INACTIVE    OTHER
HIGHER NODE           |  NODE ID.   SINCE  | COUNT  %  COUNT  %  COUNT  %  COUNT  %
  ? SUMMARY           | ? AAUTCNMI A 15:32 |   1 100    0  0     0   0      1   0
  ? DETAIL            | ? DSIAMLUT A 15:32 |   1 100    0  0     0   0      1   0
THIS NODE             | ? BNJHWMON A 15:32 |   1 100    0  0     0   0      1   0
  ? SUMMARY           | ? DSICRTR  A 15:32 |   1 100    0  0     0   0      1   0
  ? DETAIL            | ? DSIGDS   A 15:32 |   1 100    0  0     0   0      1   0
                      | ? DSIKREM  A 15:32 |   1 100    0  0     0   0      1   0
                      | ? DSIROVS  A 15:32 |   1 100    0  0     0   0      1   0
---------------       |
DETAIL FORMAT:        |
  ? DESCRIPT          |
  ? ANALYSIS          |
  ? ACTIVITY          |
                      |
                      |

CMD==>
1=HELP 2=END 3=RETURN 4=BROWSE LOG 6=ROLL          10=VTAM 11=CLIST
```

Figure 13.10 Analysis panel for selected resources.

As long as there are SNA networks, the collection of status information for the SNA resources will always be important. But the manner in which this data is currently stored and displayed by the status monitor will undoubtedly change due to the need for newer technologies in related areas.

```
STATMON.DSD(ACT)                    DOMAIN STATUS DETAIL (ACTIVITY)          17:17
HOST: HOST01              *1*   *2*   *3*   *4*
                         ACTIVE PENDING  INACT    MONIT   NEVACT   OTHER
?....66 APPLICATIONS ?.....7  ?......  ?......  ?......  ?....58  ?.....1
-------------------------------------------------------------------------------
DISPLAY:        |
  HIGHER NODE   |    NODE ID. DESCRIPTION        SENDS CHANGE |  RECVS CHANGE
    ? SUMMARY   |    ? AAUTCNMI NLDMCNMI             0     0   |    0      0
    ? DETAIL    |    ? DSIAMLUT AMLUT TASK           0     0   |  204      0
  THIS NODE     |    ? BNJHWMON NPDA TASK            0     0   |    0      0
    ? SUMMARY   |    ? DSICRTR  CNM ROUTER           0     0   |    0      0
    ? DETAIL    |    ? DSIGDS   GDS TASK             0     0   |    0      0
                |    ? DSIKREM  CSCF TASK            0     0   |    0      0
                |    ? DSIROVS  PUGW TASK            0     0   |    0      0
---------------|
DETAIL FORMAT: |
    ? DESCRIPT  |
    ? ANALYSIS  |
    ? ACTIVITY  |
                |
                |
CMD==>
1=HELP 2=END 3=RETURN 4=BROWSE LOG 6=ROLL             10=VTAM 11=CLIST
```

Figure 13.11   An example of the activity display for selected resources.

Current Deficiencies

The status monitor collects and displays information for the VTAM resources in a single domain. While it provides a valuable service in support of GMF, there are several deficiencies with its design when used alone (without GMF):

■ The use of 3270 technology, when current Graphical User Interface (GUI) display platforms are more useful.

■ Limited to the display of only one domain, which does not include the entire network.

■ The requirement for a manual definition process.

■ A growing redundancy of the data areas used to store the data, such as the VTAM Resource Definition Table (RDT) and the status monitor's Resource Definition Activity Table (RDAT). Not to mention possible future objects within RODM.

■ Lack of direct cooperation and communication with
NetView/6000 on the RS/6000 workstation.

It is clear that IBM is addressing these problems, however it seems
that the status monitor is being "overrun" by other technologies for
gathering and displaying status information.

The Resource Object Data Manager (RODM) provides an open,
object-oriented repository for network and system data. It is the natural
choice for all types of operational information, including SNA data. The
use of RODM also provides a consistency which would allow for easier
access from other platforms, such as NetView/6000.

Enterprise Network Management

14

Automation Facilities

Automation can be defined as the ability to reduce the amount of human involvement during the operation and control of a specific process. It has become an important part of data center operations over the past several years. Applying automation technology can have several benefits, including:

- Consistent and definable response to normal and abnormal events.
- Improved efficiency and reaction time.
- Reduced frequency of unplanned outages, and therefore better system availability.
- Reduction in the amount of information displayed and therefore a more usable operator interface.
- A larger number of devices and applications that can be managed by one domain, thus allowing for orderly network growth.

With version 1.2 of NetView, IBM began to implement the basic capabilities that would establish the product as a premier automation platform. Since then, each new release has included enhancements which further define the features needed to support both systems and network automation.

This chapter presents the basic automation facilities which are available with NetView. These features provide a platform on which the functional systems can be built in order to carry out automation.

14.1 Introduction

The first major characteristic of automation on the MVS host involves having access to data from several different sources. Through analysis of this information, in at least a very basic manner, a response can be issued. This paradigm is referred to as event-driven, or message-driven, automation.

NetView is the designated IBM product for providing automation within the SystemView framework. It is still in a phase of active development, with the recent enhancements pointing to a definite vision for NetView and its role as an automation platform.

Growth of an Industry

Much has been written about the importance of data center automation. Phrases such as "lights out operation" were adopted by automation advocates for what might be possible as the products began to enter the mainstream several years ago.

To some extent, the promise of the technology had been oversold. That is, automation does not completely eliminate the need for a well-trained operations staff. Users normally find that human intervention and supervision is still necessary. Also, the implementation of a product typically involves a major expense, therefore offsetting cost reductions in other areas.

However, automation is still a very important aspect of computer operations which can provide significant benefits. In fact, automation of some type is usually a necessity at larger sites.

There are several independent software vendors that offer automation solutions for the mainframe environment. These products, such as OPS/MVS (Legent) and AF/Operator (Candle), preceded NetView in some cases and helped to forge the market.

NetView's Position

NetView was originally designed to provide, through the consolidation of previously separate products, a system for SNA network management. Gradually, automation capabilities were added and then enhanced. At the same time, the number and types of interfaces available to access information about the status of network and systems resources grew.

Because of NetView's central position, it is ideally suited for supporting both network and systems automation. The product serves as a basis, or platform, for responding to a wide variety of conditions in the network. Any system constructed on top of NetView is composed of CLISTs, commands, and exits, as well as features particular to automation such as the message automation table.

Although it has taken some time for IBM to become established, a wide array of features and supporting products are now provided. And the new Resource Object Data Manager (RODM) technology, which diverges from the event-driven model, has raised the standards in this competitive market.

Transition to RODM

RODM is included with NetView version 2.3, and provides an all-purpose repository for operational data; refer to Chapter 18 for a more complete explanation. The information stored in the new MVS address space is arranged in an object-oriented manner, with documented APIs available for data access and update.

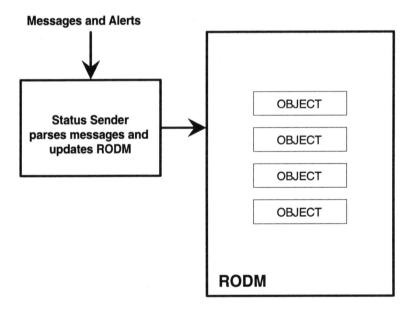

Figure 14.1 Illustration of a status sender application.

The NetView application, with its automation table, provides a solid basis for responding to messages and other events in the network. To the extent that RODM is utilized, there is a shift away from the event-driven to an object-status paradigm as provided with RODM.

Figure 14.1 provides an illustration of the primary migration technique that will be used between event-driven and object-status models. A status sender, usually resident within the NetView application, accepts messages and alerts. They are then converted into the appropriate RODM API calls to update the corresponding objects.

Source	Description
Operating System Interfaces	This includes the basic command and console message facilities, as well as SVC 76 (LOGREC).
VTAM POI	Both the primary and secondary operator interfaces can be used.
CNM Interface	The CNMI provides a way to accept and processing data from the devices and service points in the network.
NetView PPI	The PPI is used to send data, including alerts, into NetView; it is also used by the NetView database bridge.
Traditional Cross-Domain	Earlier communication techniques, such as TAF, NNT, and LUC sessions are still an important part of operations.
APPC Transports	With version 2.2, the two transports were added, both of which use LU type 6.2 to provide data to NetView applications.
TSCF	The Target System Control Facility (TSCF) intercepts console traffic, and provides remote control capability.

Figure 14.2 Major sources of data external to the application address space.

Automation Plan

Most large IBM shops already have NetView installed in order to perform SNA network management. It therefore makes sense to consider the product for use as an automation platform as well. Most of the time, NetView is suitable for at least network automation because of its close proximity to the network data. The product can be utilized for systems automation as well.

After determining the goals and assessing available resources, the manager or project leader can then begin to make decisions about the framework. This includes, for example, to what extent NetView will be used for automation. Will RODM be used ? What about the supporting products, such as AOC/MVS ? And for some larger users, two copies of NetView are actually activated, thereby allowing a separation of the problem determination from the automation functions. With the large decisions out of the way, a realistic project plan can then be drafted.

14.2 External Message Flow

The flow of messages into, and out of, the NetView application address space drive the traditional automation facilities. Figure 14.2 includes a list of the major sources of data which are accepted and processed.

These sources provide NetView components, and the NetView-based applications, with an awareness of activity on the system and in the network. A few of the connections provide the ability to forward information from one domain to another. In order to improve efficiency and reduce traffic, automation is usually carried out on the local host first.

14.3 Internal Message Routing

Both solicited and unsolicited messages are accepted by NetView for automation processing. The systems programmer can customize the product in order to control routing and processing of each buffer.

The path that a message takes depends on several factors, including its type and point of entry into the address space. There are three major techniques that can be used in controlling internal message flow:

- ASSIGN command
- Explicit MSGROUTE directive from a CLIST
- Automation table

The routing of messages through NetView can be fairly complicated. However, it is possible to make a generalization in order to allow for a basic understanding. Below is a description of each of the major processing steps that a typical unsolicited message goes through.

Global Exit DSIEX17

This exit point is invoked for all incoming MVS messages and Delete Operator Messages (DOMs), both solicited and unsolicited. The exit can update, replace, or delete the message before it proceeds any further.

ASSIGN Processing

There are several functions that can be performed with the ASSIGN command. These mirror the parameter operands, and include:

- GROUP - assigns one or more operators to a group known by a single name.
- MSG - identifies a set of messages that are to be directed to an operator or group of operators. The primary (PRI) and secondary (SEC) operands are used together for unsolicited messages, while the COPY parameter routes copies of solicited messages.
- DROP - deletes previously created group and routing assignments.

As far as the topic at hand is concerned, the PRI/SEC ASSIGN processing can be used to redirect an unsolicited message before it is processed by the automation table.

```
ASSIGN MSG=NVT*,PRI=(AUTO1,AUTO2),SEC=(MOPER1,OPER8)
```

Figure 14.3 An example of the ASSIGN command.

Figure 14.3 contains an example of an ASSIGN command using the PRI and SEC operands. The message is directed to the first active task in the group; it is not sent to multiple primary receivers. If a primary receiver is located, then all of the secondary subtasks also receive the same message. As seen in the figure, a wildcard technique is available such that all messages beginning with 'NVT' are routed.

Automation takes place on the primary subtask, as long as the receiver named is not SYSOP or LOG. Automation will never be performed on the secondary receiver, unless the message is sent to another NetView domain.

The ASSIGN mechanism is useful in several instances, including:

- Dividing messages among several subtasks for automation table processing.
- Quickly sending a message to the system operator.

For simple message routing, however, it is more desirable to route a message for display and processing using the automation table. The automation table provides more flexibility when examining a message; not only the message, but a wide range of other characteristics can be examined. The table is searched sequentially, therefore providing more control. The ASSIGN statements are not processed in the order that they were entered, but rather from the specific to the general case. Finally, the automation table provides a central location for the definitions which can easily be displayed and controlled.

Authorized Receiver

An operator task can be identified as an authorized receiver according to its profile definition. Namely, the parameter

AUTH MSGRECVR=YES

establishes the subtask as an authorized receiver. In most cases, an unsolicited message, with no specific destination provided by ASSIGN or automation table processing, is routed to the active authorized receiver. Multiple receivers can be defined, but only one is allowed to be active at a time for the purpose of routing.

Automation Table Routing

What is referred to as the automation table here actually involves several different processes, all of which are related. Each message will flow through the following steps:

- DSIEX02A global exit
- WAIT or TRAP processing, to determine if the message meets the criteria specified by the waiting task
- Automation table

- DSIEX16 global exit
- ASSIGN COPY processing, to send copies of the message
- Final logging and display

The automation table accepts a wide range of messages, both solicited and unsolicited. However, each message is only passed through the table once; secondary or copies of a message buffer are not automated (unless they are sent to another NetView domain).

14.4 Automation Subtasks

The automation subtask, or autotask, is basically an operator subtask (OST) without the dedicated terminal. It is started and runs in the background to perform some specific task, usually related to automation. The tasks can generally execute the same types of CLISTs, commands, and exits as operators, and are only limited by the fact that there is no direct display capability.

Resource Isolation

One of the major benefits that comes with using an autotask is resource isolation. That is, a large system can be divided into several smaller parts. For example, each component resource or process can be owned and controlled by a single autotask. Processing, in the form of message buffers, are then diverted to the autotasks as required by the design.

```
AUTOTASK OPID=AUTO24,CONSOLE=03
```

Figure 14.4 An example of the command used to start an autotask.

One example of this is MVS console support. An autotask can be associated with a specific console so that commands entered at the console are directed to the autotask for execution. Also, messages accepted by the autotask are redisplayed at the console.

Message Processing

There are several methods for processing messages, some of which were first mentioned above. These include, for example, WAIT/TRAP commands from a CLIST or HLL program. Also, the automation table is of course utilized for original copies of a message.

Command	Description
AT	Indicates that a command should be scheduled at a specified date and time.
AFTER	A named command is to be scheduled after a specific amount of elapsed time.
EVERY	A command is to be executed on a regular, timed basis.
LIST TIMER	A specific timer, or all timers, can be displayed and examined.
PURGE TIMER	A specific timer, or all timers, can be removed from the system.

Figure 14.5 Commands used to control and display NetView timers.

Commands can be generated by the autotask, either directly from the message table or with the EXCMD facility. For example, the command

EXCMD AUTO1,COMM01

will schedule the command COMM01 on the autotask named AUTO1.

Activation and Deactivation

An automation subtask must first be defined as any other operator would be. It is then activated with the AUTOTASK command, as shown in Figure 14.4.

In this case, the subtask is started and the console with ID 03, as known to MVS, is assigned. The DROP operand can be used to remove the console association without changing the subtask status.

To terminate the task, a LOGOFF command must be directed to the autotask. This can be done from the MVS console, or within NetView using the EXCMD facility.

14.5 Timing Services

The timing services enable commands to be scheduled based on the current or elapsed time. It is really a remnant of the previous releases, where the regular timed inquires were necessary in order to extract data so as to keep the NetView tasks updated. While still important, there is a clear shift away from this type of processing, due to the inherent inefficiencies.

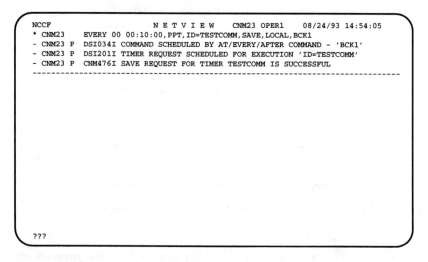

Figure 14.6 An example of the EVERY timer command.

Figure 14.5 contains a list of the commands which are used to control and display the timer settings.

Command Syntax

The format is similar for the AT, AFTER, and EVERY commands. It generally consists of supplying a command name and time value (according to either local or GMT time). In addition, the three commands also share the following operands:

- ID - allows a name to be assigned to the timer.
- PPT - the command can be scheduled on the PPT subtask, instead of the operator task where the timer command was issued.
- SAVE - determines if the timer should be stored on disk by the save/restore task, for later recovery using the RESTORE command.

Figure 14.6 presents an example of the EVERY command issued from an operator terminal. It is generally a good practice to establish the commands for execution on a stable subtask. This can either be the PPT, or a dedicated autotask.

14.6 Message Automation Table

The message table forms the basis for event-driven automation on the MVS host. Generally speaking, all messages arriving solicited and unsolicited are passed through the table for the original instance. The external sources were described above; in addition, NetView operator commands and messages are also used as input to the table.

Content and Processing

The table is composed of several different types of statements, as illustrated in Figure 14.7. The definitions are arranged so as to provide NetView with the logic necessary to determine how the selected messages should be processed

The most important of the definitions is the IF-THEN statement; Figure 14.8 provides an example. The general procedure used by NetView in processing a message is to compare the contents and/or characteristics of the buffer to each of the IF statements. The table processing proceeds sequentially, generally on the subtask where the message is received.

When a match occurs, the actions listed on the statement following the THEN operand are performed by NetView.

Message Comparison Options

As noted above, text messages arrive from several sources and are passed through the table. With version 2.2, the SNA Management Services Unit (MSU) can also be examined by the table. Three types of MSUs can be processed:

- NMVT
- MDS-MU
- CP-MSU

There are several different keyword operands that can be used on a single IF statement. Based on the comparisons used, an IF statement can be classified as applying to either a message or an MSU (or either).

Table Statement	Description
IF-THEN	Basic unit of the table, designed to trigger an action based on the contents and characteristics of each message.
BEGIN-END	Allows the table to be divided into sections, or subtables, thus improving overall performance.
ALWAYS	Where the IF-THEN statement is conditional, this parameter will always causes a specified action to take place.
%INCLUDE	Used elsewhere during NetView definition, this statement pulls in, or copies, other source members into the table.
SYN	The synonym definition provides a convenient method for defining values that will be used later in the table.

Figure 14.7 A list of the types of statements that can be used within the automation table.

Typical message comparisons involve the message ID, or actual message text. An MSU can be broken up, and the individual segments examined. The resource hierarchy for the MSU can also be extracted and compared to a specified name-type pair.

Automation Table Function

The Automation Table Function (ATF) was introduced with version 2.2, and provides a method for extending the comparison capabilities of the table. Instead of using one of the pre-defined keywords, a module can be invoked to examine the message buffer. Of course, the ATF has a greater flexibility, and can access data outside of the automation table processing and even outside of NetView (on the same host).

```
IF  MSGID='NVT2048I'  THEN
    EXEC(CMD('NVMSEND')
    ROUTE(ONE AUTO1));
```

Figure 14.8 An example of an automation table IF statement.

IBM provides ATFs which can be used to examine common and task global variables. Or, the user can design and code his or her own function. The contents of the parameter buffer can be updated by the routine, or a return code set that forces the IF statement to be "false" (i.e., no match).

Actions

When an IF statement match occurs, there are several types of actions that can be performed. They fall into three major categories, including:

- Message display and logging
- Command execution
- Message and command routing

The display characteristics of a message can be altered for quick identification by the operator. Because messages and MSUs are processed differently, there is a separate set of display options for each.

A match can also generate the execution of one or more command procedures. The command can be scheduled on a specific task, or allowed to execute where the match occurred (by default). Also, the message itself can be routed to another subtask, usually for display. When a message is redirected, it is not passed through the automation table a second time.

Operation and Use

Figure 14.9 contains an example of how the AUTOTBL (originally AUTOMSG) command can be used to display the status of the table, and then activate a new one.

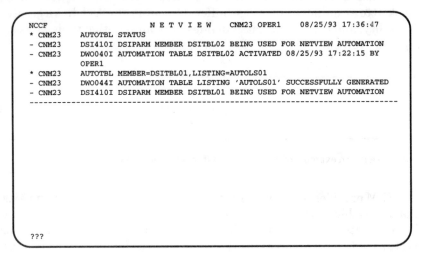

```
NCCF                      N E T V I E W    CNM23 OPER1     08/25/93 17:36:47
* CNM23    AUTOTBL STATUS
- CNM23    DSI410I DSIPARM MEMBER DSITBL02 BEING USED FOR NETVIEW AUTOMATION
- CNM23    DWO040I AUTOMATION TABLE DSITBL02 ACTIVATED 08/25/93 17:22:15 BY
           OPER1
* CNM23    AUTOTBL MEMBER=DSITBL01,LISTING=AUTOLS01
- CNM23    DWO044I AUTOMATION TABLE LISTING 'AUTOLS01' SUCCESSFULLY GENERATED
- CNM23    DSI410I DSIPARM MEMBER DSITBL01 BEING USED FOR NETVIEW AUTOMATION
--------------------------------------------------------------------------------



???
```

Figure 14.9 The AUTOTBL command is used to control table operation.

While several tables can be defined in the DSIPARM dataset, only one is active at a time within NetView. Also, when a single table contains statements for both messages and MSUs, NetView "compiles" and stores the statements separately. When the automation table processing is performed, one table or the other is examined based on whether it is a message or MSU.

Design and Performance Considerations

Each message that is passed through the table proceeds sequentially until a match occurs. This can create a performance problem with a large table, especially when messages flow through the table with no match.

NetView version 2.2 introduced significant performance improvements in automation table processing. Namely, the BEGIN-END statements can be used in order to create sections, or subtables. In this case, the IF statement at the beginning of the subtable is used to examine the message. If a match occurs, processing continues within that section until the corresponding END. With no match, the entire subtable is bypassed.

In general, there are four areas to focus on when tuning the table operation. These include:

- Restrict the flow of messages into the table, therefore eliminating unneeded searches. Many sites can have a large number of messages flowing through the table with no match at all.
- Remove IF-THEN statements that receive no matches. This will reduce the size of the table.
- Reorganize the table, placing IF statements with frequent matches near the top.
- Utilize the BEGIN-END subtable structure with version 2.2 and above.

One technique that can be used in order to track the hits in the table is to examine the network log. For each match, NetView generates the message CNM493I which indicates where the match occurred in the table. The text contains a sequence number which is taken from the line (columns 73 through 80) containing the IF statement.

14.7 NetView Bridge

The NetView Bridge was introduced with version 2.1, and provides the ability for NetView-based applications to connect to an external database in the MVS environment. It is a collection of subtasks, commands, and APIs which together implement a transaction-oriented access to the external database. The Bridge is an important part of the overall strategy for providing a complete automation solution.

The user can develop a system to utilize the Bridge. IBM also supplies support to connect to its Information/Management product.

PPI Connection

Figure 14.10 provides an illustration of the overall architecture of the NetView Bridge. The Bridge structure can be broken into six elements:

- External database.
- Database server in a separate MVS address space.

- Program-to-Program Interface (PPI), which is supported by the NetView SSI address space.
- Bridge Dispatcher, which coordinates transaction activity and communications within NetView.
- Remote Dispatcher, which accepts requests from remote domains over the High Performance (HP) transport.
- User-written commands, designed to send transaction requests and data to the external database.

As seen in the figure, the PPI forms an important part of the NetView Bridge operation. It facilitates communication between the NetView application and the external database address spaces.

Database Server

The Database Server runs in a separate address space, and supports access to the external database. The user-written applications within NetView make requests that are funneled over the PPI to the server.

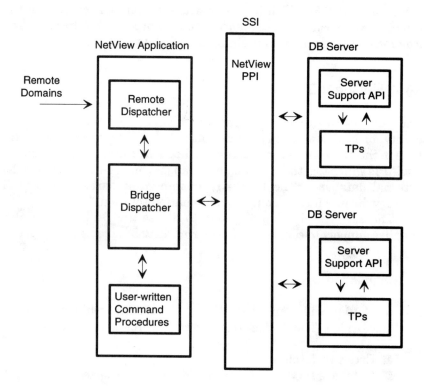

Figure 14.10 The NetView Bridge architecture within a single domain.

There are two main components to the database server:

- Server support API is used to communicate with the Bridge Dispatcher and manage the local environment.
- Transaction programs (TPs) are invoked by the server in order to directly interact with the database.

Multiple servers can be active on the same MVS host, each providing a connection to a different database.

Bridge Dispatcher

There are actually two types of dispatchers active within the NetView application address space:

- Bridge Dispatcher
- Remote Dispatcher

The Bridge Dispatcher is implemented as an automation subtask (i.e., autotask), and accepts requests from the local programs. These transactions are sent over the PPI to the target server. Responses then flow back to the dispatcher, and to the originating application.

The Remote Dispatcher enables requests to flow from remote platforms over the HP transport to the MVS host which contains the database. An autotask must be defined in each host. The Remote Dispatcher then communicates directly with the Bridge Dispatcher.

The user-written applications, whether on a local or remote system, must utilize the Bridge Requester API to send and receive transaction requests and data.

AutoBridge/MVS

IBM has steadily enhanced its connections to, and uses of, the NetView Bridge. An example of this is the AutoBridge/MVS product, which was announced in October, 1992.

AutoBridge/MVS accepts and transforms the alert, message, and application data available within NetView. This information is then used to create problem records in the Information/Management database using the NetView Bridge Adapter.

The product therefore allows for automatic generation of problem records. This can have several advantages, including less manual labor, as well as more accurate and timely updates.

14.8 IBM Automation Products

The rich set of tools and facilities provided by NetView must be fully utilized in order to construct a complete automation capability. This involves designing and implementing an application system which consists of automation subtasks, CLISTs, command processors, and exits on top of the NetView base.

For many large installations, an entire group of people might be dedicated to automation. This usually involves system development, as well as installation and configuration of additional software.

IBM provides several products which run inside of NetView, exploiting the basic automation features. They all have several common characteristics, and their implementation reduces the work that would otherwise be needed to take full advantage of NetView.

Automated Operations Console

The AOC/MVS product was announced in July, 1990 as an enhanced replacement for the earlier Automated Console Operations (ACO) SolutionPac. The product is designed primarily for system (i.e., console) automation, and complements the ANO/MVS product.

AOC/MVS uses passive and active monitoring to provide:

■ Subsystem management (e.g., JES)
■ Volume management
■ Target system management (i.e., central monitoring)
■ MVS dataset off loading
■ JES spool recovery
■ WTO buffer recovery

The product works with other systems, such as TSCF and RMF, to monitor and manage the system. A high-level policy is established by the user, so that automation objectives can be consistently executed.

Release 2 provided several enhancements, including an integration with several of the recent NetView features such as RODM and GMF.

Automated Network Operations

Like AOC/MVS, the ANO/MVS product formed the successor to the earlier ANO SolutionPac, and was announced in May, 1991. The product provides an automation capability for the management of network resources. In June of 1992, a version of the product was also announced to support the VM operating system (i.e., ANO/VM).

The product examines VTAM messages in order to automate the recovery of certain network resources. Using the LAN/AO option (described below), token ring statistics are also available. ANO/MVS also includes support for X.25 and Switched Network Backup (SNBU) automation.

Automated Operations Expert

The Automated Operations Expert (AOEXPERT/MVS) product is designed to augment NetView's operation by adding an expert systems capability.

Automation Option	Description
OPC	A two-way connection can be made between NetView and either of the Operations Planning and Control products (OPC/A and OPC/ESA).
CICS	CICS/AO provides a single point of control for the startup, shutdown, and recovery of CICS regions.
IMS	Both IMS and the IMS Extended Recovery Facility (IMS/XRF) are supported through links to NetView.
LAN	Supports the monitoring and recovery of IBM token ring networks from a centrally located NetView.

Figure 14.11 The automation options available from IBM.

The product has an interesting history. AOEXPERT/MVS was first announced in September, 1991, with a scheduled general availability of June, 1992. At the time it was to become available, IBM withdrew it, stating that it "is exploring ways to make this function available in the marketplace by working with Business Partners or through other means." Then, in December of 1992, the product was reannounced.

The goal of AOEXPERT/MVS is to reduce outages and improve overall system performance. It is designed to go beyond procedure-oriented automation by establishing business policies with respect to systems management. This technique allows more complex problems to be dealt with through the examination and analysis of information from several sources. The Integrate Reasoning Shell (TIERS) product from IBM is utilized with AOEXPERT.

Automation Options

The Automation Options (AOs) can be ordered and installed to extend NetView's reach into the network. The AOs establish connections to other mainframe products and systems, therefore supplementing NetView's data access and control capabilities.

Figure 14.11 contains a list of the current automation options. Most of these products operate in conjunction with AOC/MVS; LAN/AO works with ANO/MVS.

15

Central Resource Control

NetView has been positioned by IBM to provide a central point of command and control for the devices and alternative computing platforms within the network. Initially, this involved supporting SNA controllers and service point implementations. However, in recent years the product has been continually enhanced to provide better management for the large heterogeneous networks that many companies are building.

The links to the network devices have matured as well. Where the SSCP-to-PU session had been widely used, the newer Management Service transport, described in the following chapter, represents a superior technology for the future. Also, Chapter 17 discusses the implementation and operation of multiple NetView domains.

This chapter presents the major products which interface to NetView on the host to manage the enterprise-wide network resources. The first seven sections include the primary connection technologies, each with a generally acknowledged widespread usage and strategic importance. The final section contains a summary of the evolving second-tier interfaces that, while important, are perhaps less visible and widely used.

15.1 Network Asset Manager

Many of the IBM control units and other devices maintain a record of their local configuration; part of this data is entered by the user during normal configuration. This information is referred to as Vital Product Data (VPD).

As an example, the 3174 maintains VPD describing its local environment, including the attached 3270 terminal devices. This information can be dynamically transferred from the terminals to the control unit during the power on process.

There are two major categories of VPD: basic and extended. The basic information includes things like machine type and serial number. Extended VPD is available on the newer machines, and allows additional information to be retained, such as characteristics regarding the machine's location and users.

The VPD can be manually displayed by a local operator. With NetView release 3, IBM included the Network Access Manager (NAM) facility which allows this VPD to be collected, displayed, and recorded at a central location.

VPD Command	Description
VPDALL	Creates a collection of commands to gather data for the external log, with resources defined in VTAMLST.
VPDCMD	A command used to request VPD from a named PU for display at a terminal.
VPDLOG	A CLIST to request that the collected data be sent to the external log where it can be processed.
VPDDCE	This CLIST gathers data for DCEs connected to a named communications controller and writes it to the log.
VPDPU	This CLIST uses VPDCMD and VPDLOG to collect and record VPD from a specified PU.
VPDXDOM	A CLIST for use within the automation table which gathers VPD from a cross-domain resource.

Figure 15.1 A list of the Vital Product Data commands.

The NAM feature includes a single optional task, as well as several commands that must be defined to NetView. The commands, which can be issued by an operator or CLIST, generate requests for the information which flow over the SSCP-to-PU session. The NMVT request unit is used, and carries the Product Set ID (PSID) major vectors.

Accessing the VPD from a central NetView host, if implemented properly, can provide a convenient and reliable mechanism for tracking network resources.

NAM Definition

In defining the NAM facility, a subtask must be included in the DSIDMN file: VPDTASK. The initialization member named for the task contains the VPDINIT statement. The parameters used determine operational characteristics for the task, and limitations on processing requests from users.

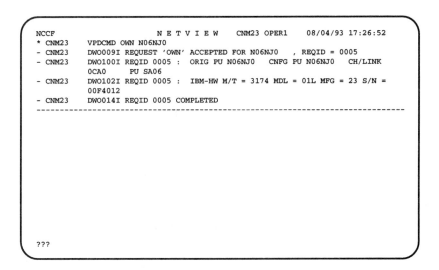

```
NCCF                    N E T V I E W    CNM23 OPER1    08/04/93 17:26:52
* CNM23     VPDCMD OWN N06NJO
- CNM23     DWO009I REQUEST 'OWN' ACCEPTED FOR N06NJO   , REQID = 0005
- CNM23     DWO100I REQID 0005 :  ORIG PU N06NJO   CNFG PU N06NJO   CH/LINK
            0CA0      PU SA06
- CNM23     DWO102I REQID 0005 :  IBM-HW M/T = 3174 MDL = 01L MFG = 23 S/N =
            00F4012
- CNM23     DWO014I REQID 0005 COMPLETED
--------------------------------------------------------------------------------



???
```

Figure 15.2 Example of a command used to extract VPD from a PU.

A VTAM APPLID must be defined for the task with CNM authority. This allows the requests and responses to be exchanged with the PUs in the network.

In addition to the NetView configuration, a configuration must also be performed at the control unit level as well.

VPD Commands

Figure 15.1 contains a list of the commands that can be used to request VPD from network devices. These commands operate together in order to solicit and record data.

Figure 15.2 provides an example of the VPDCMD command, which is used in this case to request data from a single PU.

15.2 Central Site Control Facility

The CSCF feature was introduced with NetView at the release 3 level. It provides a method for managing 3174 or 3172 control units from a NetView operator terminal. It is one of three facilities that can be used together in order to administer an SNA network:

- Central Site Customization Utility (CSCU) - this utility can be used to create customized control diskettes for the control units.
- Central Site Change Management (CSCM) - together with the NetView Distribution Manager, CSCM provides a method for distributing the customization data through the network over the SSCP-to-PU session.
- Central Site Control Facility (CSCF) - allows a NetView operator to gain access to a named control unit as if it were one of the locally attached terminals.

The CSCF feature, as with NAM, must be defined before it can be utilized. This includes adding a task (DSIKREM) to the DSIPARM dataset.

From an operator terminal, the following command can be issued to begin the CSCF session with a named control unit:

CSCF PU=P06CA0

This command results in the CSCF main menu being displayed, a copy of which is presented in Figure 15.3. As can be seen, there are several options available to the user. These include displaying information, running diagnostic tests, and resetting logs and counters.

For example, the VPD can be solicited and displayed, as shown in Figure 15.4. This panel includes a wide range of information, such as product characteristics and release levels, maintenance updates and RPQs, as well as user-defined location information.

15.3 NetView/PC

The NetView/PC product was first announced in June, 1987, and represented an extension to the scope of NetView's management capability. The product implements an SNA service point, which enables it to forward alerts, and to accept commands as part of the Service Point Command Service (SPCS) facility.

```
BKBCP200          _____ 3174 Test Menu (1TEST) _____        PU/P06CA0

     Test         Description                             (page 1 of 2)

       0          Terminal check
       1          Display event logs and response time log
       2          Display configuration panels
       3          3270 device status information
       4          Reset logs and cable errors
       5          Display vital data
       6          Display Control Areas
       7          Color convergence
       8          Extended functions and program symbols
       9          LAN tests
      10          Port wrap tests
      11,p        Trace control (p=password)
      12          Asynchronous emulation adapter tests
      A,n         Alert to Host ID n (n=1A-1H,2A-2D,3A-3D)
      D,n,m       Dump device on port n, HG m (n=0-31 m=26-27)


CMD===>
PF1= HELP              PF2= END            PF3= RETURN           PF6= ROLL
PF8= FORWARD                                                     PF12= RETRIEVE
```

Figure 15.3 Main menu for the Central Site Control Facility.

NetView/PC forms an important link between NetView and the non-SNA equipment. The product has been widely supported, especially by non-IBM hardware vendors seeking a tighter integration with the IBM mainframe.

The first version was DOS-based, and somewhat limited in its features and functionality. Release 2, announced in September of 1988, included several enhancements, such as support for OS/2, conversion of the user-written programs from macro assembler to the C language, the addition of a local display capability for the generic alerts, and enhanced communications and connectivity options.

Figure 15.5 provides an illustration of NetView/PC within the network. While the product provides an important bridge into the IBM world, it relies on the older SSCP-to-PU transport. The newer Management Services (MS) transport, based on LU type 6.2, provides a superset of the NetView/PC support; refer to Chapter 16 for a complete description.

Service Point Command Service

The SPCS facility allows commands, packaged in a precisely defined structure, to be sent to the workstation. From there, they are forwarded on to the specific device. These SPCS commands have been absorbed into the SNA/MS Common Operator Services (COS).

```
BKBCP206            _____ Controller Vital Data _____        PU/N06NJ0

JOHN JACOB 042892 3174 CONFIG SUPPORT C

Model Number:          01L                                   Active
Controller ID:         23F4012      Patches                  RPQs
Microcode Release:     C0100
Maintenance Release:   91206        93545
IML Drive/Type:        01/41        A47C5
                                    A47C6
DSL Information:                    A56C2
                                    A5981
3174 01.00 4040000000              A5991
AAAA 01.00 4040000000              A5992
                                    A5A51
                                    A5971


Location: _____

CMD===>
PF2= END                      PF3= RETURN              PF6= ROLL
PF11= Test Menu                                        PF12= RETRIEVE
```

Figure 15.4 A display of the control unit's vital data using CSCF.

The SPCS commands include:

- LINKDATA
- LINKPD
- LINKTEST
- RUNCMD

These are supported in the current version of the product.

15.4 LAN Network Manager

The LAN Network Manager suite of products are designed to replace the earlier LAN Manager offerings. They provide the capability to monitor and control the operation of multi-segment IBM token-ring and PC networks, as well as the 8209 LAN Bridge.

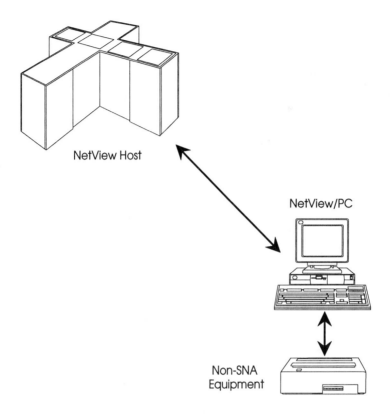

Figure 15.5 NetView/PC supports non-SNA equipment.

There are three related products operating with OS/2, including:

- LAN Network Manager, versions 1.0 and 1.1 - this is the comprehensive enterprise solution, capable of managing bridged segments either locally or from a central NetView host.
- LAN Network Manager Entry - more limited in features, this product can be used to manage a single remote LAN segment from NetView. It has no local user interface.
- LAN Station Manager - runs on an OS/2 or DOS workstation to provide configuration and environmental data to the LAN Network Manager V1.1 or LAN Network Manager Entry. Represents an implementation of the Heterogeneous LAN Management (HLM) standard which supports OSI standards.

Note that the LAN Network Manager was introduced with two releases. The first release provides an easy migration path from the LAN Manager version 2.0 product. It features the use of the Database Manager to store configuration information. The second release, version 1.1, provides a more comprehensive standalone offering where the LAN segments can be managed from a single workstation. The enhancements also include better host connections to NetView, ties to the LAN Station Manager, event filtering, and complete graphics capabilities.

LAN Manager CLIST	Description
ADAPTER	Used to control and display adapter connections.
BRIDGE	Accesses status and makes changes to the bridge configurations.
LAN	Generic interface which allows specific command to be named.
QNETWORK	Provides a way to query the network, including the LAN ring segments, buses, and bridges.
RESETLAN	Used to reset the LAN Network Manager at a named service point.
SEGMENT	Tests a specific segment to determine if it is capable of sending data.

Figure 15.6 Commands supported by the LAN Network Manager.

Figure 15.6 provides a list of the available LAN Network Manager CLISTs. There are several restrictions on their usage which should be observed. For example, some cannot be used with the Entry product, such as BRIDGE. Note that the connection to the NetView host can be established using either the Communications Manager or NetView/PC (as a service point).

15.5 TCP/IP Host Management

The implementation of applications using the TCP/IP communication protocol continues to grow. While many of the applications are found in the workstation and LAN area, the architecture is also widely implemented on the mainframe as well. This has created a challenge for the network manager, especially in the mixed SNA and TCP/IP environments found in many shops.

There are basically two methods to provide a monitoring and control capability from a central host. These include:

- Direct host management by bringing TCP/IP all the way up to the mainframe.
- Protocol conversion by a remote workstation, with the data forwarded in an SNA format.

Management and control by a workstation is performed by the NetView/6000 product, as described later in the chapter. This section briefly discusses TCP/IP management by NetView on MVS.

SNMP Support

While TCP/IP has been around for almost two decades, it wasn't until 1988 that the Simple Network Management Protocol (SNMP) was proposed. This standard is used to carry out the management of a TCP/IP network. It continues to mature - an extension named SNMP version 2 (SNMPv2) has already been proposed and is now in final review. Refer to Chapter 5 for more information on the SNMP and TCP/IP.

The operation and use of SNMP depends upon two major concepts:

- Network Manager Station (NMS). This is a display station which connects to the SNMP agents. It assembles a complete view of the network based on the information it receives, both solicited and unsolicited.

■ SNMP Agent. This entity is implemented on one or more platforms in order to manage the local environment. It accepts and responds to requests from the display stations.

The SNMP agent implements and maintains a Management Information Base (MIB). The actual resources are represented as objects in the MIB, which are operated upon using the SNMP protocols.

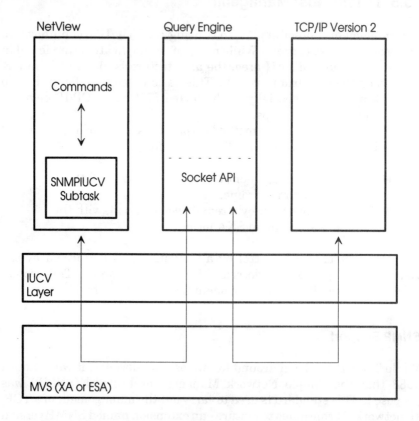

Figure 15.7 Structure used by NetView in managing TCP/IP devices.

NetView provides an interface into the TCP/IP network so that terminal operators can solicit and display data from the SNMP agents in the network. Also, NetView can receive unsolicited traps.

Host Components

The major elements include:

- NetView optional subtask and commands
- TCP/IP for MVS version 2
- Additional address space called the Query Engine

Figure 15.7 provides an overview of the TCP/IP management framework. The NetView code communicates with the Query Engine over the Inter-User Communication Vehicle (IUCV) protocol, which is native to the VM operating system. The TCP/IP for VM product, the first supplied by IBM, uses IUCV. For compatibility, it has been carried over to the MVS environment. The Query Engine then communicates with the TCP/IP address space using the supplied socket API.

Using this basic configuration, an application can be developed and implemented to manage TCP/IP from within NetView.

15.6 NetView/6000

The NetView/6000 product runs on an RS/6000 workstation, and provides the ability to monitor and manage the resources within a TCP/IP network. It can manage resources through the SNMP manager-agent model, where agents might be implemented in devices such as the IBM 6611 router.

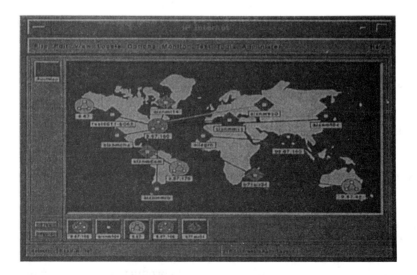

Figure 15.8 Version 2.1 of the NetView/6000 product.

The product was first announced in January, 1992, and is largely based on HP's OpenView. Version 2.1, announced in December, 1992, includes several enhancements and positions the product as more of an enterprise-wide solution. There is also an Entry version, designed to be used within smaller networks.

IBM continues to strengthen the NetView/6000 environment in an attempt to distinguish it from OpenView, and other similar network management systems. One example of this is the Systems Monitor/6000 product, which was announced in September of 1992. It is designed to complement NetView/6000 by monitoring the operation and performance of LAN nodes and segments. This offloads some of the work from the NetView/6000 workstation, especially the polling overhead associated with SNMP. System Monitor/6000 also provides a filtering and automation capability which can be customized by the user.

Basic Monitoring and Display Capabilities

The primary function of NetView/6000 is to monitor and display information about the devices in a TCP/IP network. It is able to support IP-addressable devices which contain an SNMP agent. Network resources can be dynamically discovered and recorded.

The product includes the necessary APIs and flexibility in its MIB implementation to absorb multi-protocol, multi-vendor devices. It provides the necessary tools for customization and enhancement.

The user interface is based on the Motif standard, as defined by the Open Software Foundation (OSF). Maps are utilized in order to display network topology - there is an internal topology manager which manages the workstation's view of the network. Individual resources are displayed as icons, which change color based on their status.

Figure 15.8 presents a screen image as seen from the product. In this case, a map is shown with the IP addressable devices.

The operator can use NetView/6000 to initiate specific tests from the workstation, and to manage the MIB information. Also, performance statistics are available for display.

Standalone or Host Integration

NetView/6000 can be positioned as the central point for network management and control within the network. Or, it can be coupled with NetView on the host in a mixed protocol environment.

When using NetView at the host, the AIX NetView Service Point must be installed at the workstation. This product enables communication with NetView through the service point interface. Version 2.1 of the product was recently announced in September of 1992, and includes several enhancements. Among them is the availability of an LU type 6.2 connection to the host.

Strategic Importance

Many sites are now actively pursuing a policy of moving applications off the mainframe and on to an array of more cost effective, distributed platforms. At the very least, the growth of mainframe development has slowed, with the new implementations being found on the LAN-based workstations.

One of the primary communication protocols used in this high growth area is TCP/IP. Because of this, SNMP-based management systems are becoming increasingly important.

NetView/6000 is poised for an expanding strategic role. IBM is building a complete environment around NetView/600, adding other products as required. For example, Trouble Ticket/6000 mirrors the Information/Management package at the host, and enables problem records and other data to be stored and accessed.

The decision of where to perform network management tasks depends on several factors. And in fact, the various functions can be separated and executed where appropriate.

The networking center has shifted somewhat from traditional SNA at the host to a mixture of TCP/IP, APPN, and OSI across the enterprise. As the workstation environment continues to mature and gain in strategic importance, some analysts are even predicting that NetView/6000 will eventually become the central focal point for network management, displacing NetView. Evidence of this trend can be seen in a recent IBM product, SNA/6000. It provides access to SNA data, and basic management capabilities from the RS/6000 workstation. Refer to Chapter 4 for additional information regarding the role of NetView/6000.

15.7 LAN NetView

The LAN NetView product family establishes a framework for the development of distributed systems management applications. Through these applications, the central management of both local and remote LAN-based PCs can be enhanced.

In October of 1992, the LANfocus Management/2 family was first announced. Soon after, in January of 1993, the name was changed to LAN NetView. This change more clearly aligned the new products with the global NetView focus, and to some extent simplified the product's packaging and distribution.

Standards Implementation

LAN NetView is based on several IBM and international standards, thus facilitating improved interoperability and customer acceptance. These standards include:

- Abstract Syntax Notation One (ASN.1)
- Basic Encoding Rules (BER)
- Common Management Information Services (CMIS)
- Common Management Information Protocol (CMIP)
- Guideline for the Definition of Managed Objects (GDMO), as well as other standards in the ISO 10165 series
- Simple Network Management Protocol (SNMP)
- X/Open Management Protocol (XMP)
- Systems Application Architecture (SAA)
- SystemView

While a new family of products, LAN NetView is designed to integrate with and be complementary to the current IBM offerings, such as the LAN Network Manager.

LAN NetView Family of Products

As mentioned above, LAN NetView is not a single product, but rather a family of products. Figure 15.9 includes a list of the core products, which establish a framework for the development of systems management applications.

The OSI paradigm of managing and managed systems is utilized. Consistent with this approach, LAN NetView Manager serves as the managing system in the OSI model. It includes several major services and components, such as an enhanced user interface, open APIs, resource discovery, topology mapping, and event management. The user interface is based on the Workplace Shell, and provides support for SystemView Integration level 2. In fact, a separate View component has been included which is shared by the LAN NetView applications.

LAN NetView Enabler provides services to the managed OS/2 systems. It includes a subset of the Manager features, such as a basic agent support for OS/2.

In addition, there are two other agent functions available. The Agents for DOS product supports both IBM and Microsoft DOS. Agents

Extended implements further support for the OS/2 platform, beyond what is supplied with the Manager and Enabler. Four OS/2 subsystems can be monitored and controlled, including:

■ OS/2 LAN Server V3.0
■ OS/2 Communications Manager/2 V1.0
■ OS/2 Extended Services Database Manager
■ IBM Database 2 for OS/2 (DB2/2)

The list of unique subsystems included with Agents Extended will probably grow as the OS/2 platform continues to mature.

LAN NetView Product	Description
Manager	Supports OSI concept of a managing system, providing central management from an OS/2 workstation using the Workplace Shell.
Enabler	Provides a subset of the Manager's features, such as a basic agent function, which enables the management of local or remote OS/2 machines.
Agents for DOS	Allows for the management of IBM and Microsoft DOS machines.
Agents Extended	An extension to the agent capability for OS/2 subsystems such as the OS/2 LAN Server product.

Figure 15.9 Members of the LAN NetView family of products.

Supporting Products

The LAN NetView provides a rich framework for application development. Several IBM products were created for this environment. In addition to the core products listed in Figure 15.9, IBM also supplies:

■ LAN NetView Start
■ LAN NetView Monitor

- LAN NetView Fix
- LAN NetView Tie

Start enables the administration of a collection of OS/2 platforms, with an emphasis on configuration, installation, and distribution. The Monitor, as its name implies, collects performance information. LAN NetView Fix serves as an event handler, and can be used to automate problem determination procedures.

Also, support for and integration with Novell's Netware is provided through the Netware Services Manager OS/2 application.

Finally, the LAN NetView Management Utilities for OS/2 product can be viewed as another application in the LAN NetView family. It provides a set of services designed to assist the LAN systems administrator, such as command execution and data transport.

Connection to NetView

LAN NetView can operate independently, without the need for any type of host-based software. However, many customers would like to consolidate their network and systems management activity with centralized access and control. In order to address this requirement, IBM provides the LAN NetView Tie product which connects the LAN NetView environment to NetView on the mainframe.

Using Tie, OSI alarms detected in the LAN environment can be converted to SNA alerts and forwarded to the host NetView. Certain event information can also be sent.

In addition, the NetView operator can issue commands through the Tie connection. For example, the user can create an event sieve through the REGISTER command, in effect controlling which LAN resources will be monitored.

The integration of LAN NetView with the host NetView is consistent with IBM's strategy to provide global, enterprise-wide systems management.

15.8 Target System Control Facility

The Target System Control Facility (TSCF) was announced in July, 1990, and enables a focal point NetView system on MVS to control one or more target systems. It provides a migration path from the earlier Inter-System Control Facility (ISCF).

The functions that can be performed with TSCF at the remote target system include:

- Power on and IPL
- Clock alteration, including setting and synchronization
- Configuration operations
- Problem detection and response
- System shutdown

The product runs within NetView at the host, and is designed to utilize its automation capabilities, such as the message table. Commands and display panels are provided for the terminal operator.

In April, 1993, IBM released an announcement that stressed the strategic role of TSCF within SystemView, and its closer integration with AOC/MVS in order to enable better support for automation.

Components

TSCF must first be installed at the focal point system running NetView. The OS/2 portion, called distributed feature code, is included on the tape and must be downloaded.

The target processors that can be managed by TSCF, running on the MVS, VM, VSE, and TPF operating systems, include:

- ES/9000 machine type 9021
- 3090
- 4381
- 308x

An LU type 6.2 communication link is established between the focal point system and the OS/2 platform supporting the target system. One or more target systems are directly attached to the PS/2 computer, and accept commands indirectly from the NetView operator.

15.9 Additional Product Support

The primary NetView interface products, for centralized control, are described in the above sections. In addition, there is a set of what might be called second-tier technologies used with NetView. While still important, these connections generally have less visibility and market penetration.

In addition to the topics presented below, support for the 3710 Network Controller is also provided by NetView.

Command	Description
CANCMD	Used to cancel most of the outstanding LPDA-2 DCE commands.
DISPCMD	Displays a list of the currently outstanding LPDA-2 DCE commands.
LPDA	Used to change or display the status of a line attached to a node.
MDMCNFG	Can be used to examine and update the modem configuration data.
MDMCNTL	Controls status of modem characteristics and operation, such as line speed.
THRESH	Used to control threshold values for stations that are downstream of a modem.

Figure 15.10   LPDA-2 DCE commands available with NetView.

Link-Level Management

The Link Problem Determination Aid (LPDA) architecture, as with other aspects of the IBM network management strategy, has steadily evolved. The current LPDA-2 framework provides the means for central management of Data Circuit-terminating Equipment (DCE), or IBM modems.

NetView includes a set of commands which are compatible with the LPDA-2 standard. Figure 15.10 includes a list of these operator commands.

X.25 Networks

The Consultative Committee on International Telegraph and Telephone (CCITT) is an international organization that works to develop and distribute network and network management standards. X.25 is one such architecture, which is designed to provide a consistent interface to packet switching networks. X.25 specifies the interface standard, while the packet division and routing within the network can be implemented in any number of ways.

IBM includes several products that support the X.25 architecture. The primary offering runs within the NCP communication controller, and is named NCP Packet Switch Interface (NPSI). NetView provides support for these types of connections, and can receive alerts and statistical information.

Open System Interconnection

The model for Open Systems Interconnection (OSI) provides an open framework for communications and network management; refer to Chapter 5 for more information.

OSI-compliant products have been slow to emerge, and even after their creation are slowly accepted for use. IBM developed the host-based OSI/CS (Communication Subsystem) product, which is rumored to have a low market penetration. However, OSI/CS does provide connectivity into OSI-based networks, with a basic support from NetView.

It seems unlikely at this point that OSI will, after years of sluggish implementation, rapidly grow to become the dominate networking architecture. However, it is clear that bits and pieces of the OSI model are being absorbed and utilized. For example, the SNMP (i.e., TCP/IP) standard has accepted aspects of OSI.

In the long term, certain OSI protocols, such as CMIP, will most probably become integrated with non-OSI architectures for transport. For example, CMIP over TCP/IP (CMOT) was at one time deemed the target long term architecture. Other possibilities include shipping CMIP over SNA with the newer APPN nodes.

16

APPC Transport Implementations

Until very recently, access to SNA network management data on the MVS host had been facilitated primarily through the SSCP-to-PU session, as detailed in the original CNM specifications. Although this structure has been absorbed and enriched within the SNA Management Services (SNA/MS) framework, it is still in many ways inflexible and inadequate for addressing the evolving network and system management requirements of today's enterprise networks.

With NetView version 2.2, IBM has introduced a more comprehensive implementation of the SNA/MS architecture on the MVS mainframe. This MS capability provides NetView-based applications with a wider access to network resources through LU type 6.2 connectivity. With an adherence to this single cross-platform standard, a tighter degree of integration becomes possible among the various systems management applications. As the gradual process of upgrading network devices and distributed platforms continues, it is clear that the NetView MS transport will form an important part in the future for communicating network and systems management information with a centrally located MVS host.

Along with the MS transport, NetView also includes a more general APPC implementation designed to facilitate the transmission of larger files and other data. This High Performance (HP) transport is an extension and modification of the basic communication and dispatching capabilities found with the MS transport.

16.1 Implementation Overview

The NetView Management Services implementation is based on a direct LU type 6.2 session connection between NetView and the other platforms and system resources in the network. Any device or application with at least a basic APPC capability is positioned to exchange systems and network management information with NetView. The data, once received at the host, can be processed by the full range of facilities available with NetView and its related applications. Through this open and integrated approach, the NetView Management Services implementation provides the basis for a set of complementary MS applications located both within NetView and the enterprise as a whole.

APPC Transaction Programs

The SNA logical unit type 6.2, as outlined in Chapter 1, is IBM's strategic protocol for program-to-program communication. In the APPC model, transaction programs (TPs) utilize a well-defined set of generic verbs in order to communicate with one another, thus shielding developers from the complexities of the underlying SNA protocols. Transaction programs can be supplied by IBM as service TPs, or can be written by the user.

The NetView SNA/MS implementation is an extension of this basic APPC model. Several TPs are included in the LU to carry out the MS functions as requested by either a local NetView-based application or one of its remote partners. The management data flows over the LU 6.2 sessions in the form of General Data Stream (GDS) variables. These very well-defined structures form a common language for the connected MS applications.

The MS architecture defines a VTAM logmode table entry for the sessions, and therefore the exact LU 6.2 parameters used when sending and receiving data. The session characteristics have been selected so as to guarantee a high level of error detection and notification.

Management Service Transport

As described in Chapter 2, the functional specifications of the SNA/MS architecture are arranged in discrete groups called function sets. A function set is a collection of services and features which performs a specific MS function for the node. The Multiple Domain Support (MDS) function set provides the transport mechanism enabling the flow of data between NetView and the various network resources. The MDS implementation within the NetView product used to support the transmission of structured MS data is referred to as the MS transport.

The MS transport features an open and consistent high-level API through which system management data can be accessed and collected from the network. This API removes the programmer from the complexities of the MDS APPC transaction programs, which are scheduled automatically as required, and even further from the low-level SNA protocols. Because of the API's relative simplicity, the development of MS applications within NetView has been greatly expedited.

IBM provides a group of applications which implement functions as specified by SNA/MS. Users can also develop their own systems within NetView using the MS transport, or applications which are based on these supplied applications.

Operations Management Applications

Another layer of functionality has been built on top of the MS transport which is designed to support remote operations. In this way, NetView serves as an operations management platform, and provides an implementation of the architected focal point for remote operations.

A program on a NetView subtask can register as an operations management (OM) application, which qualifies it for additional support and services, thus better facilitating the operation of the enterprise network. Such an application is considered to be OM-served.

The OM functions are maintained and administered by an MS transport application named OPS_MGMT, which serves as a second level router (i.e., above the MS transport). With the required routing information, multiple applications can access the same network devices.

High Performance Transport

The second type of APPC transport provided is the High Performance (HP) transport. This communication facility is an implementation of an optional subset within the MDS function set. Some of the operational characteristics have been modified to improve performance for larger files and bulk data.

While several session-related parameters for the HP transport are different, the API used in developing applications is very similar to that used with the MS transport. Data is sent and received in the same manner, with MDS-supplied transaction programs. In the process, some compromise of data integrity may become possible. The HP transport is therefore positioned to be used for large data transfers where performance is important and error detection is not as critical.

Application Structure

As pointed out above, there are two similar transport APIs available to the application developer. In addition, the OM facility can be utilized. The structure of an application in each case is fundamentally the same. It consists of a set of command processors which are scheduled to send and receive the network data.

The transport application must first register with NetView. At this time, several of its characteristics are recorded, including the application's name. After this, data can be sent and received as required.

```
NCCF                      N E T V I E W    CNM23 OPER1      08/03/93 14:02:08
* CNM23      REGISTER QUERY
' CNM23
DWO468I TYPE APPL        COMMAND  TASK     FPCAT      FOCALPT LOGMODE  NOTIFY
DWO469I MS   NVAUTO      DSINVGRP DSINVGR  --NONE--   NO      SNASVCMG NONE
DWO469I MS   LINKSERV    BNJNETOP BNJDSERV --NONE--   YES     SNASVCMG NONE
DWO469I MS   ALERT       BNJNETOP BNJDSERV --NONE--   YES     SNASVCMG NONE
DWO469I MS   OPS_MGMT    DSIOURCP DSI6DST  --NONE--   YES     SNASVCMG NONE
DWO469I MS   EP_OPS      DSIOURCP DSI6DST  OPS_MGMT   NO      SNASVCMG ALL
DWO469I MS   MS_CAPS     DSIFPRCV DSI6DST  --NONE--   NO      SNASVCMG ERROR
DWO469I MS   SPCS        DSIYPRTL DSIGDS   --NONE--   YES     SNASVCMG NONE
DWO469I OM   NVAUTO      DSINVGRP DSINVGR  --NONE--   N/A     SNASVCMG NONE
DWO469I HP   RMTCMD_S    DSIUDST  DSIUDST  N/A        N/A     PARALLEL NONE
DWO469I HP   RMTCMD_R    DSIUDST  DSIUDST  N/A        N/A     PARALLEL NONE
DSI633I REGISTER COMMAND SUCCESSFULLY COMPLETED
------------------------------------------------------------------------------




???
```

Figure 16.1 NetView command used to display registered transport applications.

Figure 16.1 provides an example of the NetView REGISTER command, used in this case to list all of the applications currently using the MS and HP transports.

Platform Implementations

An MS transport implementation, regardless of the platform, provides a higher level access to and simplification of the required APPC protocols. Such a transport, with its published API, facilitates the development of custom-built MS applications. Currently, there are three MS transport implementations provided by IBM:

■ NetView version 2.2 and above

■ OS/2: either EE V1.2 or V1.3 with the Networking Services/2 product installed, or Extended Services (ES) V1.0 and above; or the new Communications Manager/2 (including OS/2 V2)
■ OS/400 version 2.2 and above

While an MS transport API implementation can make application development easier, it is not required by a platform when communicating with NetView. In order to exchange MS data with NetView, a node or device need only have an APPC capability which has been expanded and tailored to include at least a minimum of the basic SNA/MS functionality.

16.2 MS Transport Applications

The MS transport API is utilized by several IBM-supplied applications to implement the various Management Services functions; Figure 16.2 provides a list of these applications.

Many of the MS transport applications run under the DSI6DST task, which is required in order to activate the transport capability.

Focal Point Administration

The focal-to-entry point relationships are tracked by an MS application named MS_CAPS, short for "Management Services capabilities." For example, when an MS application registers as a focal point for some aspect of the SNA/MS functionality, the MS_CAPS records this and notifies any entry points of the new focal point. This feature becomes important for recovery, or when a focal point changes.

The three focal point categories supported by NetView include:

■ Alerts
■ Operations management
■ Common Operations Services (COS)

The applications implementing this support are described below.

Hardware Monitor Alert Receiver

The ALERT_NETOP application serves as an architected focal point which implements one of the problem management subsets dealing with alert data. It receives alerts and passes them to the hardware monitor.

MS Application	Description
MS_CAPS	Management Services capabilities maintains the focal point / entry point relations among applications.
ALERT	Application registered as an architected focal point to receive MSUs for the hardware monitor.
LINKSERV	Defined by the SNA/MS architecture and positioned to assist in managing the various link connections.
OPS_MGMT	Focal point for operations management; providing services and support to connected applications.
EP_OPS	Defined entry point for operations management; associated with the application OPS_MGMT.
SPCS	Focal point providing support for Common Operations Services (COS); extension of basic SPCS feature.

Figure 16.2 Management Services transport applications supplied with NetView.

The alert data, and other major vectors, are enveloped within a CP-MSU and are processed by the hardware monitor as if they had been received from any of the other data sources, such as the CNM interface or PPI.

The LINKSERV application, also detailed by the SNA/MS architecture, is poised to assist the hardware monitor in gathering link-related error information.

Operations Management

The OPS_MGMT application formally implements an additional layer on top of the MS transport. It has been included to support NetView applications that require a higher degree of operations management capability.

There are several advantages to using the MS transport as the basis for an operations management platform. Figure 16.3 provides a list of the major services provided.

OM Services	Description
Architected Commands	A set of commonly used commands are defined and available for the operations management applications.
Extended Definition and Registration	Primary and backup focal points can be defined in DSIPARM and then recorded by the save/restore facility.
Enhanced Routing	The routing and targeting major vector is used within the CP-MSU sent to remote applications.

Figure 16.3 List of the major services provided by NetView-based operations management.

The EP_OPS application is registered as an entry point providing operations management support.

Common Operations Services

As mentioned in Chapter 15, the Service Point Command Service (SPCS) facility allows command and other control information to be sent to a service point through the SSCP. This allows an application on the host to maintain control over the service points in its domain. Most typically, a service point is implemented by the NetView/PC product.

This functionality has been extended with multiple domain support, and absorbed under a consistent COS umbrella. The operator access commands can now be transferred to other NetView domains where they are routed to the proper service point.

Generic Automation Receiver

The generic automation receiver is an MS application registered with the name NVAUTO. It provides no architected focal points services. Rather, the application can receive an MSU and simply pass it through the NetView message automation table.

This application has dual citizenship, being registered as both a vanilla MS application and an OM-served application. This enables it to be utilized by a wider range of network applications and devices.

16.3 HP Transport Applications

The high performance transport provides a generic LU type 6.2 connectivity for the NetView-based applications. The transport capability is implemented by the subtask DSIHPDST, which is also used by several of the actual IBM-supplied applications.

Comparison to the MS Transport

When creating a system which will use one of the two APPC transports, it is important for the designer to first define the characteristics of the application. For example, what platforms will be used? What type of data will be exchanged? Are any of the well-defined SNA/MS disciplines required? How important are the operational characteristics of the underlying SNA sessions? How important is performance? From questions such as these, the proper connectivity option(s) can be selected.

The high performance transport is different from the MS transport in several areas. It is more of a general-purpose APPC transport facility which does not require any of the specifically architected SNA/MS functions. For example, no support is provided for the focal point categories (e.g., problem management). At the same time, it enables more flexibility than the MS transport, and has the following characteristics:

- Confirmation is not required for each message sent over the SNA session.

- Persistent (i.e., active) conversations over dedicated sessions can be used.
- The name of a logon mode table entry can be specified for the session.
- Higher transmission rates are possible.

NetView supplied applications which use the HP transport fall into two major areas, as described below.

Remote Command Execution

The NNT, as discussed in Chapter 17, is the older method to communicate text messages between NetView domains. For example, the ROUTE command can be used to send a command to a remote domain. Each OST-to-NNT connection uses a separate session.

IBM has used the HP transport as a basis for remote command execution. The NetView command RMTCMD can be issued to forward commands and receive replies.

There are three applications which work together in providing the remote command support: RMTCMD_O, RMTCMD_R, and RMTCMD_S. These applications assist the OST in registration, message routing, and end of task processing (i.e., connection termination).

Remote Bridge to Database

The Information/Management database has long been the IBM repository for configuration, change, and problem data on the MVS host. There are other databases which also play an important role in the operation of a large enterprise. Access to and control of this centrally stored information from both local and remote platforms has become increasingly important.

The HP transport has been customized in order to allow remote access to the NetView bridge. The reach of the many alternative platforms has therefore been extended.

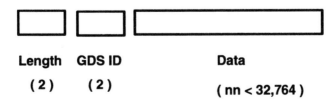

Length	GDS ID	Data
(2)	(2)	(nn < 32,764)

Figure 16.4 Structure of a single GDS variable.

The HP transport application R_BRIDGE provides the connection to the databases, particularly Information Management, based on the requests that it receives. The command REMOTEBR is used by both the requesting task and the server task to control access to the bridge.

16.4 GDS Variable Usage

All data flowing between the MS transport applications consists of GDS variables which are defined by the SNA/MS architecture. Figure 16.4 provides an illustration of the basic GDS structure used to carry data, which can include more imbedded GDS variables.

The Multiple Domain Support Management Unit (MDS-MU) is the main GDS variable used to package the information flowing among the MS transport applications. The MDS-MU contains other variables, such as the Control Point Management Services Unit (CP-MSU).

GDS Variable	Description
MDS-MU	The MDS-MU variable is used as an envelope to carry the other data structures, and begins the header.
MDS Routing Information	Always the first variable, it helps define the entire flow including the origin and destination.
AUOW	The Agent Unit of Work Correlator is used for the solicited requests when matching replies.
CP-MSU	Carries a few main GDS variables (e.g., R&TI and SNACR) as well as various major vectors.
SNACR	The SNA Condition Report is used to report abnormal conditions or errors to the MS applications.

Figure 16.5 Most commonly used GDS variables within the MDS-MU.

This section presents the GDS variables that are commonly utilized over the MS transport LU type 6.2 sessions.

MDS Message Unit

Figure 16.5 provides a list of the GDS variables that are usually carried within the MDS-MU.

The MDS header consists of the MDS-MU, immediately followed by the Routing Information and then Agent Unit of Work Correlator (AUOW) GDS variables. The AUOW provides a method for correlating several outstanding requests and replies.

After the header, there is usually either a CP-MSU or an SNA Condition Report (SNACR).

The CP-MSU is an envelope for major vectors. One of the important vectors used by the MS transport applications is the Routing and Targeting Information (R&TI), which is followed by user data. The R&TI provides an addressing mechanism for the multiple applications usually found in the operations management (OM) environment.

16.5 Application Development

A transport application is comprised of one or more command processors, each of which is scheduled to perform a specific function. The routines can be written in assembler or a HLL (e.g., PL/I or C), although certain features can be accessed from the CLIST language as well. There is also a limited operator interface, namely the REGISTER command, which was presented in the first section.

This section presents some of the more important aspects of developing a transport application. There are slight differences between the MS, HP, and OM interfaces. However, each operates in basically the same manner.

MS Router within MDS Function Set

A set of command processors are assembled to construct an APPC transport application. Each application is a logical element within NetView. That is, there is not necessarily a one-to-one correspondence between an MS application and a specific NetView subtask; multiple applications can be registered and active on a single subtask.

During the registration process, which must be performed first, an application identifies itself by a unique name to the transport. Among other things, the type of transport to be used is also specified.

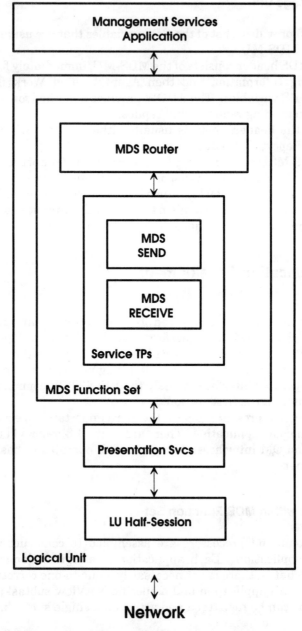

Figure 16.6 Structure and implementation of the MDS function set within an LU.

Once active, an application can issue the API requests. These requests, which are then funneled through the MDS router, result in one or more of the service TPs being scheduled. The router manages the execution and operation of APPC service TPs. There are several TPs defined by the MDS function set:

- MDS_RECEIVE
- MDS_SEND
- MDS_SON
- MDS_HANDLER
- MDS_HP_RECEIVE
- MDS_HP_SEND

The two sets of send/receive programs are used for the MS and HP transports, respectively. Session Outage Notification (SON) is used to handle session outages. The MDS_HANDLER program accepts messages from back-level nodes (i.e., those not supporting the latest level of the SNA specifications) and passes them to the MDS router for processing.

Figure 16.6 provides an illustration of the MDS function set implementation within NetView, showing the position of the MDS router. The two major TPs that are used most often, and establish the basic function of the node, are shown in the figure: MDS_RECEIVE and MDS_SEND.

Transaction Processing Considerations

There are two major levels where transaction processing takes place: the NetView application and the APPC TPs. At the transport application level (within NetView), several different types of transactions are possible. These include:

- Request expecting reply
- Request not expecting reply
- Reply not last (more data to follow)
- Reply last
- MDS error message

Another aspect of application processing is the nature of the API request being made: synchronous or asynchronous. When using a HLL, it is possible to issue a synchronous request. That is, the application is effectively suspended until the request has been completed. At this time, the next instruction after the API request is then processed. Asynchronous requests are made without suspending the sender. The work will complete some time later.

Application Registration

In addition to selecting the appropriate transport and provides a unique application name, other information must be provided. This includes the name of command processor to be asynchronously scheduled for unsolicited MS data, whether the MS application provides a focal point service, whether to receive information from a focal point (listener), and whether to receive outage notifications for the underlying SNA sessions. During HP transport registration, a command processor is provided for receiving replies for solicited requests.

17

Multiple Domain Access

The use of NetView's functions and features can be enhanced within a multiple domain environment. This situation usually consists of configuring the product on several different hosts, although more than one domain can be active on a single MVS system as well.

With multiple domains, there are several different vehicles used in order to exchange the various categories of network management data. They roughly fall into one of two major models:

- Component-to-component couplings - messages and commands are exchanged in both directions between similar, paired NetView elements.
- Focal point architecture concept - where data is generally forwarded in a one-way direction from a distributed to a central location.

The communication technology provided with NetView for interdomain exchanges has continually been expanded and enhanced by IBM. The LUC facility is still widely used, however LU type 6.2 provides a strong basis for the future.

17.1 NetView-to-NetView Messages

The NetView-to-NetView (NNT) communication uses a simple LU type
0 session to exchange text messages between domains. The command:

    START DOMAIN=xxxxx

creates the session, where 'xxxxx' is the name of the remote NetView
domain. An NNT subtask is started in the target system, which directly
communicates with the local operator task. Commands can then be
routed to the remote domain, with replies returned to the terminal
operator.

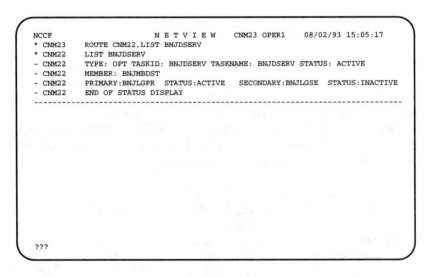

```
NCCF                    N E T V I E W    CNM23 OPER1    08/02/93 15:05:17
* CNM23    ROUTE CNM22,LIST BNJDSERV
* CNM22    LIST BNJDSERV
- CNM22    TYPE: OPT TASKID: BNJDSERV TASKNAME: BNJDSERV STATUS: ACTIVE
- CNM22    MEMBER: BNJMBDST
- CNM22    PRIMARY:BNJLGPR  STATUS:ACTIVE    SECONDARY:BNJLGSE  STATUS:INACTIVE
- CNM22    END OF STATUS DISPLAY
         ---------------------------------------------------------------------




???
```

Figure 17.1 Command output returned from a remote NNT subtask.

Figure 17.1 contains an example of a LIST command sent to domain
CNM22 with the reply returned to the operator in domain CNM23. As
seen in the sample, the ROUTE command includes the remote domain
and the command name. The DSIPSS macro can also be used, with the
type XSEND operand, to forward commands from an assembler language program.

In addition to the command-response model, the NNT task can also
be used to forward messages to the OST domain for automation. That is,
any messages queued to the NNT are automatically sent back to the OST
where they are passed through the automation table.

Message Forwarding

The NetView samples library includes the definitions required to setup the framework for forwarding messages from one domain to another. The user can implement the definitions, and customize them as required.

Several different subtasks are used, both autotasks and NNTs. The OST-to-NNT session serves as a basis for forwarding the messages. Once available at the central host, the data can then be automated and recorded as needed.

17.2 RMTCMD and ENDTASK Commands

As discussed in Chapter 16, the APPC transports were added to NetView with version 2.2. One of the two available options, the High Performance (HP) transport, serves as the basis for allowing operators to exchange commands and messages with remote NetView domains in a manner similar to NNTs.

The command RMTCMD establishes a connection over the HP transport. A distributed autotask in the remote domain is created, and permanently associated with the local operator. The connection, including the distributed autotask, can be terminated using the ENDTASK or LOGOFF command.

Figure 17.2 presents the parameters available with the RMTCMD operator command. The operands LU, NETID, and OPERID determine where the command is sent. If OPERID is omitted, an autotask with the same name as the sending task is started (if not already active).

After a command has been sent, the reply and any other messages queued to the distributed autotask are returned to the operator. In this way, the RMTCMD connection facility can be used for both command execution and message automation.

Improvement over the NNT

If all of the domains in the network that are exchanging commands and messages are at the version 2.2 level or higher, it is recommended that RMTCMD be used instead of the NNT for several reasons:

- Improved performance - the pair of LU type 6.2 sessions between domains is an improvement over the individual sessions used with the NNTs.
- Larger message sizes - the HP transport allows a maximum of 32K bytes instead of the 256 limit with the NNTs.

■ More complete data - when using the extended MCS console facility, data can be lost if the NNT connection is used.

Overall, the RMTCMD feature provides a significant improvement in terms of flexibility and usability over the older NNT session.

Configuration and Security

In order to use RMTCMD, the HP transport task (DSIHPDST) must first be active. In addition, DSIUDST, which is dedicated to the support of remote command execution, must also be defined and activated.

RMTCMD Operand	Description
LU	Name of remote NetView domain (also VTAM APPLID).
NETID	Network ID for the target system.
OPERID	Name of autotask in target domain to receive and process command.
EXP	Determines automation processing at an intermediate node (if any).
Command Text	The actual command to be processed by distributed autotask.

Figure 17.2 Operands on the RMTCMD operator command.

The TASK statement for DSIUDST usually names the member DSIUINIT, which contains the parameter RMTSECUR. This statement defines the security, if any, to be used for RMTCMD and ENDTASK processing. The possible options include:

- SAF - the security access facility is to be used, such as RACF.
- TABLE - the DSISECUR table, which is stored in the DSIPARM dataset.
- NONE - no restrictions on which operators can create or terminate sessions.

The security table (TABLE option) consists of RMTSEC statements which are read and "compiled", much like the automation table. Each line is designed to allow or block operators from using the RMTCMD or ENDTASK commands.

Command Chaining

Command chaining can be used to improve the access to messages and automation capabilities across multiple connected NetView domains. In this case, the command sent to the remote domain is RMTCMD, which in turn generates another send operation to a third domain. The EXP parameter, described in the figure mentioned above, can be used to control the extent of automation processing as the messages pass through the intermediate systems.

17.3 LUC Session Support

The LUC communication vehicle actually uses an LU type 0 session. However, a conversational model has been implemented on top of the basic session which provides a more formalized access to the connection from the multiple subtasks in the NetView address space.

The internal NetView macro DSILCREQ is designed to allocate and deallocate the sessions, as well as send and receive the data as required. This communication vehicle is used throughout NetView for several purposes, including cross-domain access to the hardware and session monitor data by an operator, as well as status and alert forwarding.

To enable LUC sessions, the user must first define and activate the LUC support subtask.

Subtask Definitions

The CNM01LUC task, where CNM01 is the local domain id, manages the LUC communication facility. The initialization member, usually named DSILUCTD, can contain two parameter statements. These statements define the LUC connections with the other domains, and include:

- CNMAUTH
- CNMTARG

CNMAUTH establishes a limit on the number of LUC sessions possible. Also, it can be configured to allow connections to be made with any domain (GLOBAL), or only with those defined in the subsequent CNMTARG statements (SPECIFIC).

The individual domains can be specified with CNMTARG, including whether the sessions are persistent. If not persistent, each session will be terminated after an interval as defined in the NetView constants module.

```
 NCCF                        N E T V I E W    CNM23 OPER1      08/16/93 14:43:46
 C CNM23    DISPLAY NET,ID=CNM23LUC,SCOPE=ALL
   CNM23    IST097I DISPLAY  ACCEPTED
 ' CNM23
 IST075I  NAME = CNM23LUC          , TYPE = APPL
 IST486I  STATUS= ACTIV       , DESIRED STATE= ACTIV
 IST977I  MDLTAB=***NA*** ASLTAB=***NA***
 IST861I  MODETAB=AMODETAB USSTAB=***NA*** LOGTAB=***NA***
 IST934I  DLOGMOD=DSINLDML
 IST597I  CAPABILITY-PLU ENABLED  ,SLU ENABLED  ,SESSION LIMIT NONE
 IST654I  I/O TRACE = OFF, BUFFER TRACE = OFF
 IST271I  JOBNAME = CNM2PROC, STEPNAME = CNM2PROC
 IST171I  ACTIVE SESSIONS = 0000000002, SESSION REQUESTS = 0000000000
 IST206I  SESSIONS:
 IST634I  NAME       STATUS        SID          SEND RECV VR TP NETID
 IST635I  CNM22LUC ACTIV-S   F51C7B1452E64C14 0002 0000  0  0 MACH03
 IST635I  CNM22LUC ACTIV-P   F51C7B1452E64C15 0000 0002  0  0 MACH03
 IST314I  END
 ------------------------------------------------------------------------------

 ???
```

Figure 17.3 VTAM display command showing LUC sessions.

Figure 17.3 shows the active LUC sessions with a VTAM display command.

17.4 Accessing Component Data

The terminal operator can access data for the session and hardware monitor components from remote domains. In both cases, the user must first roll into the desired component display for the local domain, and then issue the command:

SDOMAIN xxxxx

where 'xxxxx' is the target domain ID. The LUC session communication is used in both cases.

Session Monitor Configuration

Before viewing session monitor data in another domain, the systems programmer must first perform customization for both the session monitor task (AAUTSKLP) and the access method LU task (DSIAMLUT).

INITMOD Operand	Description
AUTHDOM	Establishes cross-domain authorization for which domains can access data in this (local) domain.
AUTHORIZ	Limit access to configuration and trace data in this (local) domain for cross-network operators.
NETID	Specifies the SNA network ID for this network when cross-network communication is possible.
AMLUTDLY	Determines the number of seconds NetView waits before trying to access the DSIAMLUT table again.

Figure 17.4 Session monitor parameters in AAUPRMLP related to cross-domain access.

Figure 17.4 contains a list of the parameter statements included with the member AAUPRMLP.

The subtask DSIAMLUT maintains a table which is defined by statements in the initialization member, usually named DSIAMLTD. For each remote NetView to be accessed, the parameter CDRMDEF maps the domain ID to the corresponding VTAM CDRM name.

17.5 Forwarding Status and Alert Data

The NetView product is constructed in such a manner that a central focal point host can collect information from the distributed systems in the network. There are different types of focal points. Usually they are all located on the same host, but this is not necessary.

```
DEFFOCPT PRIMARY=CNM13LUC,TYPE=ALERT,BACKUP=CNM21LUC
DEFFOCPT PRIMARY=CNM21LUC,TYPE=STATUS
```

Figure 17.5 An example of the parameters used for alert and status forwarding.

The CNM router subtask (DSICRTR) maintains the focal point definitions for alert and status forwarding, as used by the hardware and status monitors respectively. The TASK statement usually names the member DSICRTTD, which contains the necessary definitions. Figure 17.5 displays the statements used to establish the status and alert relations. A backup host for alert forwarding is optional, but is not supported with status forwarding.

Status Focal Point

Status forwarding was introduced with NetView version 2 in order to support the new GMF feature. While the DSICRTR definitions establish the focal point connection, NetView must also be made aware of what data to forward. This is done with the GRAPHOPT statement, which will be discussed in Chapter 19.

Figure 17.6 contains an example of GRAPHOPT parameters, showing that the forwarding of status information can be either enabled or blocked by resource name or type.

These definitions are placed in the VTAMLST ATCCONxx member, and can be used at the distributed as well as focal point hosts. After preparing the parameters, the STATMON pre-processor job must be run and the STATMON (and GMF) subtasks recycled. Note that status must be collected first by the status monitor. For example, the STATOPT statement with the OMIT option overrides a forwarding specification.

Alert Focal Point

Originally, alerts were forwarded from one domain to another by first converting them into a text message format and then using the OST-to-NNT connection. With version 1.3, alerts could be forwarded directly to a focal point over the LUC sessions.

```
*                GRAPHOPT FORWARD NAME L1*
*                GRAPHOPT BLOCK   NAME L1CA*
*                GRAPHOPT BLOCK   TYPE APPLS
```

Figure 17.6 An example of the different types of GRAPHOPT statements.

Most of the alerts are accepted by the CNM routing task (DSICRTR) in the domain where they originate, which are then passed over to the hardware monitor task, BNJDSERV. As described in Chapter 11, each alert is subjected to filtering. The OPER filter determines if a text message for the alert is generated (i.e., BNJ146I), which can then be forwarded if desired. The ROUTE filter is used to select which alerts will be sent to a focal point host over the LUC connection.

If an alert passes the ROUTE filter, it is sent back to DSICRTR and then on to the LUC subtask for transmission over the SNA session.

At the focal point host, the alert is filtered again and can be recorded or discarded. It cannot, however, be forwarded again using the LUC facility.

Intermediate Focal Point Support

As mentioned immediately above, the alert forwarding framework does not recognize nested focal points. However, it is possible to design a network with intermediate hosts which appear as nested focal points.

In this case, the distributed hosts forward LUC alerts to what appear to them as the main focal point. In really, this is an intermediate focal point host. The filtering can be configured to convert the alerts into text messages, which can then be forwarded to another, central mainframe.

17.6 Operations Management

The MS transport provides, among other things, the basis for communicating operations management data. The subtask DSI6DST normally uses the initialization member DSI6INIT to hold the configuration parameters.

Focal Definition

The DSI6INIT member can contain the following statements, both of which pertain to operations management:

- DEFENTPT
- DEFFOCPT

The entry point parameter is unique to the MS transport subtask, and allows the user to designate a particular host as being an entry point only.

FOCALPT Operand	Description
ACQUIRE	Allows the entry point to obtain a primary and/or backup focal point.
CHANGE	Used to change the architected focal point for MS transport users.
DROP	Provides a method for disconnecting a primary and backup focal point.
QUERY	Used to display focal point for alerts, operations management, status, or user-defined categories of data.

Figure 17.7 A list of the major functions provided by the FOCALPT command.

The focal point statement is the same one used for the DSICRTR subtask, and includes a TYPE operator, as well as PRIMARY and BACKUP hosts designations for the operations management data.

17.7 Focal Point Commands

After a configuration has been defined and activated, the terminal operator will usually need to be able to display and control the various focal point relationships. There are two commands available to perform these operations. This includes changing the focal point associations while NetView is still active.

CHANGEFP

This CLIST was introduced with version 1.2, and while still useful, is limited in its capabilities. It can be used to change the primary focal point for alert, message, and status information.

```
NCCF                    N E T V I E W    CNM23 OPER1    08/01/93 17:13:31
* CNM23     FOCALPT QUERY FPCAT=OPS_MGMT
' CNM23
DWO170I DISPLAY OF CURRENT FOCAL POINT INFORMATION

CATEGORY (EBCDIC): OPS_MGMT         CATEGORY (ARCH): X'23F0F1F7'
LOCAL  FOCAL POINT:
     APPL NAME: --NONE--            ACTIVE: N/A
REMOTE FOCAL POINT:
  PRIMARY NAME: MACH03.CNM22        ACTIVE: Y      PENDING: N
  BACKUP  NAME: --NONE--            ACTIVE: N/A    PENDING: N/A
RETRY TIMER SET: N

END OF CURRENT FOCAL POINT INFORMATION
--------------------------------------------------------------------------------




???
```

Figure 17.8 An example of a query for a particular focal point category.

FOCALPT

The FOCALPT command was added with version 2.2, and provides a more complete, strategic interface to be used when controlling the focal point operations. Figure 17.7 provides a list of the operations available.

Figure 17.8 displays an example with the query option, showing the focal point information for the operations management category.

18

Resource Object Data Manager

The Resource Object Data Manager (RODM) was introduced with NetView version 2.3. It implements a real-time repository for operational and control information, where the status of each system or network resource is defined and maintained. The data values can be updated and accessed by host applications through an open and supported set of APIs. This new technology enables a common representation of resources which is available to multiple users.

RODM represents a turning point for NetView, both in terms of its new capabilities and strategic importance. Ironically, this comes at a time when the mainframe seems to be under attack from all sides, and most IBM customers are at least considering less expensive alternatives.

However, RODM does provide a solid technical base for users who believe in the advantages of central control from a reliable mainframe. The technology helps to facilitate the management of the complex connectivity relationships and operational situations found in today's increasingly multi-vendor, multi-protocol networks.

Although initially geared towards supporting the management of non-SNA network resources through the GMF Host Subsystem data model, RODM also provides an expandable platform for the development of automation applications. Perhaps its most important characteristic is that it provides a shift from the traditional event-driven (e.g., messages, alerts) to an object-status model.

18.1 New Foundation for Automation

RODM represents a shift in the nature of automation technology on the MVS host. The message automation table, as discussed in Chapter 14, will still remain important for some time to come. In fact, it will be instrumental in helping to support RODM by converting the incoming messages to RODM updates.

However, the table is ideally suited to handling isolated events that usually require a simple response. RODM, on the other hand, is a more sophisticated tool for applying automation logic to more complex network and system problems.

CIB Implementation

The RODM feature enables the implementation of the SystemView Control Information Base (CIB) structure on the mainframe. It is therefore a strategic element within IBM's systems management framework.

Based on the CIB definitions, RODM provides a model for the resource activity across the enterprise. Each entity, such as a workstation or link, is represented as a data object within RODM.

Each of these objects can be thought of as a type of sophisticated control block. An object can maintain links to other objects, and is managed by one or more method programs that are loaded into the RODM address space. Therefore, the data and code within RODM are associated with each other, and logically stored together.

Using this technique, a more advanced approach to programming becomes possible. For example, logical relationships, as well as the simple physical characteristics, of the enterprise can be represented and managed.

Additional Address Space

RODM is implemented as a new address space running on either the MVS/XA or MVS/ESA operating system. The two different versions function in basically the same manner in each environment. All of the object and control data is maintained in virtual storage. However, the ESA derivative is designed to utilize dataspaces to hold most of the actual object data.

User applications on the same MVS host can access and manipulate the information managed by RODM through an external user API.

Multiple applications can connect to a single RODM region at the same time. Also, there can be more than one RODM address space active per MVS image.

Implementation and Use Scenarios

RODM provides two major functions that have been merged using the object-oriented programming model. These include:

- Data repository - as mentioned above, RODM maintains information in virtual storage, and can be thought of as a type of real-time database.
- Automation technology - changes to the status of data objects can trigger their associated method programs, thus providing a way to automate events in the network.

Together, this combination creates a new paradigm for monitoring and managing the enterprise resources.

While RODM has a few similarities to traditional database managers, it also differs in several important respects. For example, the information within RODM is held in virtual storage during normal operation, and not written to disk (there is, however, a checkpoint facility which is discussed later in the chapter). This provides for faster access, but could also limit the database size in extreme situations. Also, because programs are coupled to the objects, the data in effect becomes "active."

In speculating where RODM might be best applied, it must be noted first that the address space has been tightly coupled to the NetView application address space. There are a series of automation services, including a task within NetView, which support the link. This can make it more attractive to develop NetView-based applications. And in fact, the first major RODM application supplied by IBM, the GMF Host Subsystem (GMFHS), is designed to manage non-SNA network resources through these connections with NetView.

However, the RODM technology can be used for a variety of purposes. Anywhere that a benefit can be had by storing and updating operational data in a real-time mode represents a potential application. IBM has already announced that several of its products, such as AOC/MVS, will support RODM. In the future, other products, both from IBM and the independent vendors, could be updated to use RODM.

18.2 An Object Orientation

The concept of object-oriented programming (OOP) has recently gained widespread interest and support. There are several different characteristics associated with this technology. The RODM design contains a few of the more prominent features, such as:

- Class structure
- Objects
- Inheritance
- Data abstraction
- Encapsulation

The RODM data is arranged in a structured fashion, based on the classes and objects, and uses the principle of inheritance for the data and associated method programs. A high-speed data cache implementation is used to manage the information model.

Class Hierarchy Structure

Figure 18.1 provides an illustration of a typical class and object structure, designed as a hierarchy. The dark rectangles represent classes, while the smaller squares are the objects. The UniversalClass at the top is reserved by the system, and forms the root for the entire RODM data model.

Together, the classes form a template, and are analogous to a database definition. They represent a blueprint structure for how the information stored in RODM is arranged and accessed.

A class can be defined to have one or more children in the tree structure. Each child for a specific class must be of the same type, either another class or an object, but not both.

The objects are the actual instances of data within a specific class, and do not have children. Where the classes might be viewed as branches of a single tree, the objects are the leaves.

Classes and objects are composed of fields, containing the actual data. The classes, objects, and fields all have names by which they can be addressed.

Object Instances

Each class can have one or more objects. They represent specific instances of the type of resource defined by the class. Moving down the class structure, fields are passed on to each of the children, which are said to inherit the structure defined above. Public fields can be inherited, while the private class fields cannot.

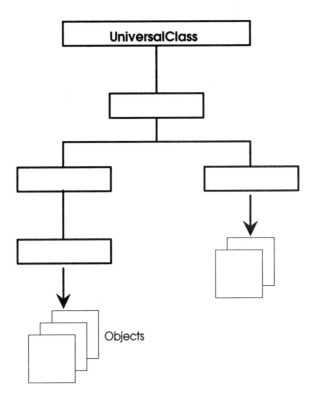

Figure 18.1 An illustration of the RODM class and object structure.

For example, consider a class which defines display devices. This could have a child class, inheriting its fields and defining more of its own, which describes 3270 display devices. A final class in this path might represent the 3179 terminal. The children of the class are objects, representing specific 3179 terminals. As can be seen in this simple illustration, as the navigation proceeds down the hierarchy the classes move from general to more specific; finally the objects describe actual instances of the terminal class type. Objects are created by naming the class to which they belong, as well as the object itself.

Fields and Sub-fields

Each field contains up to six subfields. The VALUE subfield is mandatory, while the other five are optional. Figure 18.2 contains a list of the subfields that are supported.

Subfield	Description
VALUE	The actual value for the field.
QUERY	Method, and parameter list, which is invoked when field is queried.
CHANGE	Method, and parameter list, which is invoked when field is changed.
NOTIFY	A method which is triggered when the field is changed to notify one or more users.
TIMESTAMP	The time value when the field was last changed.
PREV_VALUE	The previous value of the field; the VALUE subfield holds the current value.

Figure 18.2 A list of the subfields that can be defined for each field.

There are several system-defined fields that are pre-defined by RODM, and included within every class and object. These fields include:

- MyPrimaryParentID
- MyPrimaryParentName
- MyID
- MyName
- WhatIAm

In addition, every class also contains the MyClassChildren and MyObjectChildren fields, which identify the characteristics of its children.

Data Abstraction

In general, abstraction involves the creation of new and more complex entities from the available basic building blocks. This can have several benefits, including the ability to more closely represent the complexities of the real world systems.

There are several types of abstraction utilized by RODM, including class abstraction and data abstraction. Data abstraction is the process of creating more complex data areas, what are called structures in the C language, from the pre-defined data types (e.g., integer). Also, compound objects can be formed by linking multiple objects together; this is also a form of data abstraction.

18.3 Application Development

RODM is a transaction processing platform which is suitable for several different types of systems. These applications can be provided by a vendor such as IBM, or developed by the user.

Programming Options

There are two categories of programs that can be developed and scheduled to interact with RODM. These have been mentioned above, and include:

- Methods - within the RODM address space
- User applications - in a separate address space, external to RODM

Methods are associated with the fields in a class or object, and therefore provide encapsulation of data and logic. There are object-independent methods as well. The method routines are usually small programs which are used to manipulate the RODM data, but do not change the data model itself. They provide a way to interrelate the objects within RODM. For example, a method could be assigned to a particular field so as to gain control when the field is updated. The routine can then examine and/or update other related objects.

Control Block	Description
Access	Identifies the external user to RODM; needed by methods.
Transaction Information	Specifies details about the transaction, including transaction ID and return codes.
Function	Further defines the transaction by identifying the function and parameters.
Response	Required when data is returned to the caller by the called function.
Entity Access Information	Provides information regarding the specific class or object target.
Field Access Information	Further defines the target in terms of the exact field to be used.

Figure 18.3 Control blocks used during API requests for RODM services.

User applications are designed to execute outside of the RODM address space, and allow applications of all types to access the repository. They have more control over the contents of the data, as well as the structure of the data model itself.

Both types of programs have been designed to take advantage of the PL/I and C language; methods must be written in one of these two.

RODM Functions

When a call to RODM is made using one of the two APIs, a function module is identified. There are several different types of functions, each of which provides a particular service to the caller. Restrictions exist for which functions can be used based on the characteristics of the application (i.e., method or user) and security.

Transaction Processing

Methods and user applications interact with RODM using the two APIs, one for methods and the other for user applications. A single entity within RODM, such as a class, object, or field, can become the target of each operation.

For a specific request, information is provided by the caller in the form of control blocks. These control blocks are described briefly in Figure 18.3. The technique used to invoke each of the APIs is fundamentally the same, however there are slight differences in the data areas used and their contents.

Upon return, RODM passes back, among other things, a return code and a reason code. This single request-response action is considered to be a transaction. IBM states that RODM has been designed to support a high rate of transactions.

Navigation Through the Cache

As mentioned above, each class, object, and field has a name assigned to it. The developer accessing these items can use the fully qualified name. For example, in the case of a class, the name must be unique and can be up to 64 bytes long.

RODM also assigns an abbreviated identification (ID) to each item. This ID can be used instead of the name when referencing the data. For example, objects can be located in any of the following manners, proceeding from most to least efficient:

- ObjectID
- ClassID and ObjectName
- ClassName and ObjectName

There are routines available for translating between the two types of names. Using the IDs where possible can help to improve overall performance.

Serialization with the Lock Mechanism

A concern with any multiple usage platform, such as RODM, is serialization. It becomes particularly important that a technique be implemented for serializing the RODM data resources, such as objects and classes. This enables the integrity of the data to be maintained.

RODM provides a locking mechanism that operates in basically two manners for methods and user applications:

- Implicit locking
- Explicit locking

Each API request that accesses a class or object must first lock the entity before updating it. RODM provides this locking service automatically, or implicitly on the API requests. Also, a developer may explicit request that one or more objects be locked.

After the successful lock of a class or object, the program has exclusive access to the entity. There are several customization parameters that affect locking, as described below.

18.4 Implementation Details

As mentioned above, a new address space (i.e., started task) was introduced to support RODM. The system is a complex transaction processing platform, which has several major internal components. In order for the systems programmer or developer to properly utilize the functions provided by RODM, at least a basic understanding of the composition and operation of the entire system is necessary.

Major Component Functions

After being activated, the RODM address space performs several major functions to support its users. These components provide management of the following major resource areas:

- Storage
- API requests
- Object and methods, including locking
- Subtasks
- Event notification
- RODM log

Of the functions listed, storage management is perhaps the most complex and far-reaching. This is because of the potentially large amounts of virtual storage that can be used by RODM.

Storage Management

RODM can be considered to be manager of a large and complicated data cache that is maintained in high speed storage. The virtual storage map is broken up into several windows; Figure 18.4 describes the different window types.

Window Type	Description
MASTER	This control area contains the EKGMWCB, and records all cell pool allocations used by RODM.
TRANSLATION	Another control area, this window provides a mapping of the data in the RODM data cache.
DATA	Multiple data windows are allocated, and contain the actual data elements (e.g., objects).

Figure 18.4 Types of windows used by RODM in managing storage.

The master and translation windows reside in the virtual storage area of the RODM address space. The data cache, as defined by NetView, is composed of multiple data windows. These windows are allocated in virtual storage (MVS/XA) or data spaces (MVS/ESA). The data cache can expand as required; there can be up to 253 data spaces allocated by RODM under ESA.

A cell pool allocation mechanism is used by RODM; each of the data windows is divided into a group of one or more cells. Each cell contains a fixed number of bytes. The systems programmer can define the storage characteristics of RODM, including the windows and cell pools.

Customization

The RODM samples library contains an example of the RODM started task. After installing the product and setting up the JCL, the systems programmer must then customize its operational characteristics. The major areas for configuration include:

- Storage characteristics, including windows
- Class management
- Tasks and users activity
- Checkpoint and log I/O activity
- Security
- Shutdown characteristics

Refer to the appendix for a list of the definition parameters used by RODM.

18.5 Data Model Design

In the process of developing an RODM-based application, the designer must create a data model if one is not already provided. The model allows for a consistent structure in the definition and access of information.

The construction of a data model is in some ways similar to a database definition, where a hierarchical structure is logically layered out for optimal efficiency.

The general procedure involves analyzing the entire collection of data items to be included in the model. They are then arranged into groups, moving from general to specific. Finally, the object instances are allocated for the final (i.e., most specific) classes in the tree.

Below are some additional aspects of RODM processing that should be considered when building a data model.

System Classes

RODM pre-defines several classes that are constructed during a cold start of the address space. These classes are designed to contain information which supports the general operation of RODM and its connected users.

System Class	Description
UniversalClass	The root of the entire data model.
EKG_SystemDataParent	Child of UniveralClass and parent of all other system-defined classes.
EKG_System	Contains data which describes the RODM system environment.
EKG_User	Defines the user applications that are connected to RODM.
EKG_NotificationQueue	Contains the lists required to facilitate the notification process.
EKG_Method	Provides the structure for maintaining the RODM methods.

Figure 18.5 System-defined classes reserved by RODM.

One of the system-defined classes, UniversalClass, was mentioned above. Figure 18.5 contains a complete list of the classes reserved by RODM for system use.

Object Linking

Many times, the resources of a network are interrelated. To mirror this situation, RODM allows its data objects to be linked together. This is accomplished by using multi-valued fields.

A multi-valued field, as its name implies, can have more than one value. This allows several object-to-object relationships to be established, including:

- One-to-one
- One-to-many
- Many-to-many

Only a few of the RODM data types can contain multiple values. These include ObjectIDList and ObjectLinkList.

Loading the RODM Data Cache

The data model is defined by an analyst as a collection of parameters in a sequential dataset. Once prepared, this file can then be read by the load utility in order to create or modify the data model within the RODM cache. In addition to the basic structure, the initial field values can also be set.

There are two types of statements used to define the data model:

- High-level load function statements
- Load function primitives

The high-level statements are converted into low-level primitives, which are then also interpreted in order to control the actual load operation. The high-level statements very closely follow the ASN.1 international data definition standard.

Figure 18.6 contains a list of the operations available with the RODM load function. The RODM address space must be active while using the first two.

The load function can be run as a batch job, RODM initialization method, or called from another program on the same host. Therefore, the data cache can be updated at RODM startup, or modified later.

18.6 RODM Methods

The method programs execute within the RODM address space, and perform operations on the object data in response to events and explicit requests. They can be dynamically installed, refreshed, or deleted. NetView supplies several methods which can be used as necessary, or the developer can write the method programs.

Load Operation	Description
LOAD	The RODM data cache is updated based on the contents of the named input file.
VERIFY	This operation functions like LOAD, except that the cache is not actually updated; used for comparison only.
PARSE	This provides a technique for testing the syntax of the RODM statements.

Figure 18.6 Operations provided by the RODM load function.

The methods are more limited than the user applications in the sense that the data model itself is generally not modified. Methods provide the ability to create a complex information model by linking the data which is scattered across multiple objects.

Types of Methods

Methods can be designed to operate with a specific object, or they can be object-independent. There are six types of methods, as shown in Figure 18.7, which are classified based on how they are invoked. The first four are object-specific in that they are associated with a particular object field, while the last two are object-independent.

The change and notification methods are similar, but there can be multiple notification methods defined. In fact, the notification process is an important aspect of RODM's processing which is serviced by a formally defined component and system class.

Method Type	Description
Query	Triggered in response to an API query request for a field.
Change	Triggered in response to an API change request for a field.
Notification	Triggered in response to an API change for a field; there can be mulitple listeners defined.
Named	A named method is scheduled when requested by another method or an external user application.
Object Independent	An object-independent method is not associated with a particular object.
Initialization	These methods can be included to perform initialization at RODM startup.

Figure 18.7 Different types of methods scheduled within RODM.

Object-independent methods allow more flexibility; for example, they can be used to create or delete objects. The initialization methods have slightly more control, and can create classes in the data model.

Method API

The Method API (MAPI) allows methods to access RODM data. It is more limited than the user API, but is sufficiently robust in order to fulfill its role in supporting the data model. There are several different types of services available to examine and update the RODM data.

These API calls are generally performed synchronously, however there is a function that can be called to dispatch an asynchronous unit of work within the address space. Also, the Access Block is not required, since the program executes within the RODM address space.

18.7 User Applications

User applications can access RODM from other address spaces on the same host using the User API (UAPI). An important aspect of RODM's operation is the notify process, which allows these external user applications to "listen" for specific network events propagated by RODM.

User API

The User API provides services to the application programs, which can be divided into the following major groups:

- Connect to and disconnect from RODM.
- Create and delete classes and objects.
- Query the contents of fields and subfields.
- Change field and subfield contents.
- Trigger a named method to carry out an action.
- Establish a notify routine.
- Link and unlink objects.

The services available to a particular user depend on its authorization, which is usually administered by the system security program (e.g., RACF).

18.8 NetView Automation Services

RODM is designed to have a close association with the NetView product, therefore providing a special synergy for automation. A set of services are available which help support this connection. Figure 18.8 contains a list of the automation services provided.

Service	Description
DSIQTSK Subtask	This optional subtask forms the basis for the RODM-to-NetView link.
ORCONV Command	A command invoked within NetView to send updates to and trigger methods in RODM.
EKGSPPI Method	IBM-supplied method which can send commands into NetView.
CNMQAPI Routine	Provides the user API services to NetView-based application with less programming work.
DSINOR Macro	An assembler language macro which provides the same services as the CNMQAPI routine.
ORCNTL Application	NetView-based application that manages the DSIQTSK links which are established to RODM.

Figure 18.8 Automation services which closely link RODM to NetView.

Defining DSIQTSK

The optional subtask DSIQTSK must be defined in the DSIDMN member with the TASK statement. The initialization file, usually named DSIQTSKI, contains three types of parameter statements:

- CMDRCVR
- REP
- TASK

The task communicates with RODM through the NetView PPI; CMDRCVR defines the PPI (command) receiver name used by DSIQTSK. This statement can appear more than once, but only the first name is used.

There can be up to 64 RODM address spaces defined to the task. Each REP statement configures the connection to one RODM region. Among other things, an application name is declared by which RODM will address the NetView-based application.

Each command sent over to NetView must be scheduled on a particular subtask. The sender within RODM has flexibility in determining where the command executes. For example, the name of a task can be provided, or ANY task could be allowed to process the command. Where a task is not specifically named, DSIQTSK must select the subtask to run the command.

Each of the TASK statements in the initialization member identifies a task available for command execution. DSIQTSK distributes the commands across the defined tasks in order to balance the overall NetView workload.

18.9 Support for GMF Host Subsystem

The GMF Host Subsystem feature is a part of the NetView system, and the first RODM application provided by IBM. A data model is shipped by IBM in order to facilitate the management of non-SNA network resources.

GMFHS Data Model

Objects supplied by GMFHS, and used in the RODM data model, fall into one of three major categories:

- Management
- Managed
- View

Management objects represent devices or platforms in the enterprise that provide some type of management and control functionality. Examples include NetView/PC and the LAN Network Manager. Also, an SNA domain, represented by a single NetView domain, qualifies as a management object. Shadow resource objects can be defined in RODM to represent the SNA resources, however their actual status is not maintained by RODM.

These management objects work together in order to manage the actual network resources, which are modeled by RODM using the managed objects. Connectivity relationships among the management and managed objects can be established as well.

The view object can be created to supplement the dynamic construction of views already supported by RODM. There are two types of views that can be defined:

- Network view
- Peer view

As described above, the views are also RODM objects.

Network Configuration Application

In defining the network configuration, the analyst must provide the sequential file, with the appropriately formatted statements, to the RODM load function. There are a few different ways that this file can be constructed. The recommended approach is to utilize the new Network Configuration Application/MVS product.

NCA/MVS became available in March of 1992. It extends the Information/Management product, version 4.2.2 or later, by allowing the non-SNA resources and their connectivity relationships to be stored into the database. A utility can then be run which extracts the information and translates it, therefore producing a flat file suitable for the RODM loader.

Application Support and Processing

The GMF Host Subsystem operates as a separate address space and utilizes the user API. It accepts alerts and other data from the NetView application over the PPI.

The RODM data model is examined to determine what, if any, action should be taken based on the data for the non-SNA device. One or more objects can then be updated, which in turn generates a status message to the GMF display workstation.

18.10 Performance and Support

As a major host subsystem, there are several concerns that customers will have as they implement RODM. This section describes the major facilities available from IBM to help support the operation and use of the RODM product.

Checkpoint Facility

As pointed out earlier, RODM differs from traditional database systems in several respects. For example, the data is kept in virtual storage and not normally written to disk. This can cause a problem when an unexpected outage occurs, because all of the data can be lost.

To help deal with such a situation, RODM includes a checkpoint facility. The checkpointing feature allows a snapshot of the various storage windows to be written to the pre-defined VSAM disk files. During this time, normal operations are temporarily suspended; requests sent from NetView using the ORCONV command are queued. The checkpoint process can be initiated through an MVS operator command (including from NetView), or with an RODM API call.

Log and Dump Utility

Both the log and dump utility are important tools provided with RODM to assist in problem resolution.

There are 11 types of records that can be written to the log. The systems programmer can customize RODM in order to determine what data should be captured and written. A log-level mechanism is defined which is based on the transaction return codes. When a transaction completes with a return code over a specified value, the messages are logged. Also, a method function exists which can be used to explicitly write a record to the log. The user applications, however, cannot directly record data, but must reply on their connections to the methods.

The ESA data spaces can be dumped using an MVS console command. In addition, RODM provides a utility which can be used to format and dump selected areas of its data cache, based on input parameters supplied by the user. The types of reports available include:

- Class listing
- Class index
- Object listing
- Object index
- Statistical report

Most of the reports are self-evident. The statistical report includes user API activity during the execution of the dump utility.

RODM Tool Support / MVS

The RODM Tools Support/MVS tool kit is supported by IBM as an RPQ. It includes two tools:

- RODMView
- GMFHS Definer (GMFHSDEF)

RODMView provides an on-line operator interface into an active RODM address space. A full-screen front end or command line capability is available.

The tool allows an active RODM address space to be more effectively managed by allowing the data to be displayed and changed without needing to reload RODM. It exploits the services provided by the API calls in order to provide a more usable alternative to developing RODM programs.

GMFHSDEF is a full-screen TSO application that is designed to assist the systems programmer in managing the network configuration established by the GMFHS data model. It writes the RODM load utility statements to a data set, which can then be edited, providing a convenient, time-saving tool.

19

Graphic Monitor Facility

The Graphic Monitor Facility (GMF) was first introduced with version 2 of NetView. It is IBM's declared strategic Graphic User Interface (GUI) solution for the NetView user, providing a means to display status and isolate failures throughout the enterprise network. GMF exploits the capabilities of the OS/2 presentation manager, and adheres to level 1 of the CUA 89 compliance within the SystemView framework.

IBM continues to evolve and enhance its product strategy with respect to the display and control of network and systems management information. Most notable is the creation of the Resource Object Data Manager (RODM), and the GMF Host Subsystem which is designed to utilize RODM in support of GMF on the workstation. Other areas of growth in the future include a more functional and mature link to NetView/6000 to provide access to the same type of host-based SNA information.

19.1 Implementation Options

For the network manager, one of the decisions that must be made when selecting and implementing network management technology is which GUI display tool to use. For the mainframe, the NetView product currently supports two options:

- GMF
- NETCENTER

NETCENTER was acquired by IBM from U.S. West and announced in November, 1989. Shortly after that, in September of 1990, IBM announced GMF as part of the NetView version 2 package. Both tools allow network status data to be displayed on a workstation when properly connected to its corresponding host component.

Using NETCENTER

The NETCENTER feature allowed IBM to quickly enter the market by providing its customers with a graphical solution. This move also enabled the company to stave off competition while working to develop and launch its own product.

The workstation component of NETCENTER runs under DOS, utilizing the GEM technology from Digital Research, Inc. to provide its windowing capability. The host portion, generally referred to as Graphic Network Monitor (GNM), includes a separate address space designed to collect and archive status information.

A subtask is used inside of NetView to accept data from the standard exits and forward it over an LU type 0 session to the GNM address space. The Service Point Interface (SPI) component of GNM is available to monitor and manage non-SNA network resources.

While NETCENTER was the first of the two products released by IBM, and does have certain advantages (e.g., better integration of SNA and non-SNA data display), it is still viewed as a tactical, shorter term solution. It is not closely aligned with IBM plans or its current technology, such as RODM and OS/2. In spite of this, NETCENTER is a solid offering that will continue to enjoy support from IBM.

GMF Network Overview

GMF is positioned as the strategic GUI technology supporting NetView. While initially only supporting SNA resources, GMF has been enhanced with version 2.3 to include the capability to manage non-SNA devices as well. GMF should gradually take over the display role from NETCENTER, with IBM assisting its customers in the migration. In fact, with version 2.3 a subset of the NETCENTER Batch Network Definition File has been converted for use by GMF (actually for use by the underlying GraphicsView/2 product).

One of the most important aspects of GMF is how the status data is gathered, and then sent to the workstation. The NetView status monitor component is used to gather the status information in each of the participating domains. The concept of a status focal point is used, so that the data is maintained at a central location. In a multiple domain network, updates are forwarded from one or more distributed hosts to a central focal point host. Figure 19.1 provides a simple example of the flow of status data.

Host Subsystem and Non-SNA Resources

One of the major deficiencies of the GMF feature in versions 2.1 and 2.2 is that only SNA resources are supported. With the introduction of RODM in version 2.3, GMF is now positioned to provide support for non-SNA devices as well.

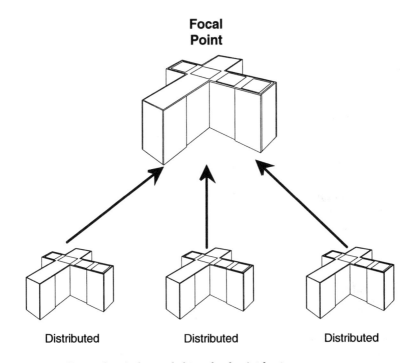

Figure 19.1   Status data is forwarded to a focal point host.

The GMF Host Subsystem (GMFHS) is the first major RODM application supplied by IBM. It functionally replaces and enhances the NETCENTER GNM host component, with the status and other supporting data and code stored within the RODM address space.

Alert data is accepted by the NetView application and then passed over to GMFHS through the PPI connection. At this point, the data is examined, with perhaps several API calls made to RODM. RODM object changes in turn can generate updates to the GMF display.

19.2 Resource Status Collection and Display

As mentioned above, the status data is gathered by the STATMON component in each NetView domain. This data is then forwarded to a central status focal point host.

Preparing the Status Monitor

The are several NetView subtasks involved in supporting status collection in a multiple domain network. These tasks, with 'xxxxx' representing the NetView domain ID, include:

- xxxxxVMT - Status monitor
- CNMTAMEL - Graphics (GMF)
- DSICRTR - CNM router
- xxxxxLUC - LUC support

All of these subtasks work together in order to capture and forward status information to the focal point host.

As described in Chapter 13, the status monitor is configured in each domain using the preprocessor. The STATOPT statement identifies which resources are to be monitored. In addition, a second parameter can be included with the STATMON preprocessor to determine what status information is forwarded to the focal point.

The GRAPHOPT statement should be included as a comment statement in the ATCCONyy member of VTAMLST. It is used with the preprocessor to forward status data for selected nodes.

Status Collection and Management

Once STATMON and the other subtasks are setup, the graphics subtask (i.e., CNMTAMEL) must be configured. This GMF host subtask implements the management of SNA status data for GMF, and can operate in one of two manners:

- Status manager
- Status collector

The distributed hosts in the network are defined as status collectors, while the focal point host acts as the status manager. In each case, the CNMTAMEL subtask is utilized; its exact role depends on the initialization parameters used, as specified on the TASK statement.

The product is shipped with the CNMTAMEL task pointing to one of two initialization members in DSIPARM. When DUIISC is utilized, the domain is a status collector; the use of member DUIISFP establishes it as a status manager (i.e., focal point).

Status Manager Parameter	Description
MAXNETWORKS	The maximum networks expected to be managed; performance is degraded if limit is exceeded.
MAXRESOURCES	The estimated maximum number of resources to be managed within each network.
MAXSSCOUNT	The estimated maximum number of status collectors from all networks that will be forwarding data.
SC	An optional parameter that can be used to name each resource status collector sending updates.
STATUSTABLE	Determines the status reported to GMF workstation when arriving from multiple collectors.
CODEPAGE	Specifies host code page value, which determines format (i.e. language) of data sent to workstation.

Figure 19.2 Parameters used to define the resource status manager.

The AMELINIT statement in DUIISFP points to the actual parameters for the resource status manager; the member DUIFPMEM is usually used. Figure 19.2 contains a list of the statements that can be specified during initialization of the resource status manager host.

Workstation Server and Clients

The GMF workstation code runs under OS/2 version 1.3 and above. There are two major types of workstation configurations:

- Server
- Client

The server connects with the resource status manager at the host in order to accept status updates and other data. The clients, usually locally attached through a token ring connection, rely on the server in order to access data for display. The client workstations are also referred to as "monitors" because they provide the actual presentation capability.

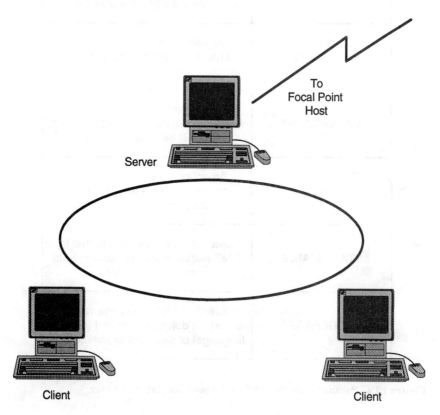

Figure 19.3 A server workstation can support multiple clients.

Figure 19.3 presents an example of a typical workstation configuration. Note that both server sessions, to the host and to its clients, use LU type 6.2. The server can access the host with an SDLC line or a token ring connection through a communication controller.

With versions 2.1 and 2.2, there can be server, client, and combination workstations. A combination is configured with both the server and client installed together on the same machine. With version 2.3, the standalone server no longer exists; in this case the "server" is actually a combination workstation, containing both server and client functions.

Status Updates and Pre-Defined Views

The information maintained by the resource status manager can be sent to the server workstations. The exact content and arrangement of the color displays at the clients is determined by user-defined views. These views are defined at the host, and created through a preprocessor. They are then downloaded to the server workstation where they can be further processed and customized. As information arrives at the resource status manager, it is sent down to the connected server workstations.

19.3 Creating Static Views

In order to customize the GMF workstation display, the user can create static views. These views contain pictorial representations of SNA network resources, and are based on the VTAM configuration data stored at the host.

Types of Views

Figure 19.4 contains a list of the major types of GMF views. The top three are most commonly associated with the use of GMF. From the cluster view, the user can proceed lower into the network hierarchy down to the peripheral level.

The retained view is created and saved at the workstation for later display when monitoring the active network; it is a customization of an already existing view. A snapshot view is simply a copy of a view, captured and saved on disk for later analysis.

In addition, the version 2.3 user can display dynamically built views. As its name implies, this type of view is not statically constructed at the host. Rather, it is dynamically built from currently available information. For example, version 2.3 supports the display of data for

SNA resources down to the LU level. These LU displays, except for those containing VTAM applications, are created dynamically. Another new view is the configuration parents view for SNA resources. This view presents the configuration of resources depending on the parents' relationships.

Preprocessor Job

The VIEW preprocessor is similar to the job run to customize the status monitor. Figure 19.5 contains a pictorial example of the procedure used in creating the GMF views.

View	Description
Cluster	Highest-level view that can be displayed, composed only of aggregate resources.
Backbone	Shows SNA backbone network, including subarea hosts, NCPs, transmission groups and links.
Peripheral	Contains real resources, such as PUs and VTAM applications.
Retained	A view that has been customized and saved at the workstation which can later be used for monitoring.
Snapshot	A copy of one of the views, usually containing problem data, which has been saved for analysis.

Figure 19.4 Major types of views used by GMF to display status information.

The first step is to construct the user profile definitions which direct the operation of the preprocessor. Next, the VTAM and NCP definitions can be updated in order to allow the preprocessor to create complete and integrated views of the entire backbone network. Figure 19.6 contains a list of these statements, which are added to the VTAMLST data set and appear as comments to VTAM.

The output from the preprocessor job consists of unformatted views, as well as other mapping information that is useful in tracking and administering the views. The unformatted views must then be downloaded to the server workstation where they can be further processed, as described in the next section.

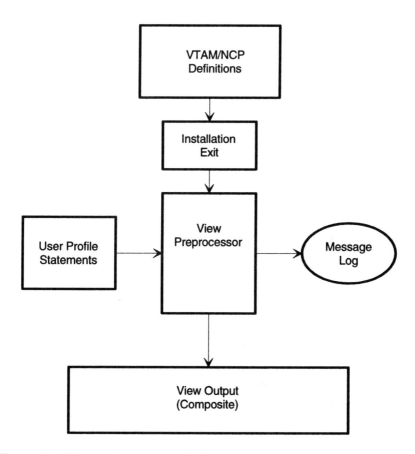

Figure 19.5 View creation process with the preprocessor.

Utilizing Aggregation

Aggregation is a technique for combining multiple resources together as one logical entity, represented as a single symbol. The advantage of this technique is that a much larger number of resources can be monitored with a single icon symbol. A real resource is an actual control unit or line. An aggregate resource, on the other hand, can depict multiple resources. The status shown for an aggregate resource depends on the state of the resources of which it is composed.

VTAM/NCP Parameter	Description
ADJLINK	Allows connectivity relationships between subarea nodes to be explicitly defined.
ADJNODE	Similar to ADJLINK, this parameter specifies the adjacent node name.
AGGPRI	Determines how a failure of a specific resource affects the parent resources.
NGFINC	Allows resources to be explicitly included or excluded from the view preprocessor.
NGFOPT	Controls the placement of resources into cluster views; also determines if a peripheral view is generated in certain cases.
NGFTXT	Can be used in order to add text information for each resource defined in a view.

Figure 19.6 Parameters used to establish and control view integration.

With versions 2.1 and 2.2, a weighting technique is used where an aggregate resource is affected by the real resources directly below it. Each real resource is assigned a weight value, which determines its influence during aggregation.

Version 2.3 has been enhanced to include an algorithm based on threshold values and aggregation priority values. Status mapping can also be used in order to affect the interpretation of status values. All three of these values can be set at the server workstation.

The thresholds are used to determine the subordinate resources that must enter an unsatisfactory state before the aggregate resource enters degraded, severely degraded, or unsatisfactory.

Workstation Component	Description
Graphic Data Server	Provides support in administering the views and workstation profiles; communicates with focal point host.
View Administrator	Task that controls downloading and conversion of views from the host.
Graphic Communication Server	An interface that manages the APPC sessions used by the workstation.
Graphic Monitor	Communicates with the graphic data server in order to accept configuration data and status updates.
GraphicsView/2 Version 1.1	An IBM product which is used as a base by GMF for displaying and manipulating the graphical data.
Command Exit Facility	Provides a technique for calling exits based on command invocation at the workstation, depending on profile.

Figure 19.7 Components of a GMF server workstation.

As part of GMF customization, described above, it is possible to effect aggregation with the AGGPRI parameter. This parameter was used in a slightly different manner with versions 2.1 and 2.2, but is still compatible with version 2.3.

The AGGPRI parameter value can range from 0 to 3, indicating the number of parent levels above the resource that are affected by a change to the resource. The IGNORE value allows the resource to be totally excluded from aggregation calculations. In addition, aggregation can be temporarily suspended and then reinstated at the workstation for each resource.

19.4 Workstation Configuration

The GMF workstation code is shipped and maintained using SMP/E at the host. During product installation, it must be downloaded to each of the workstations that will use the feature.

As discussed above, both a server and client workstation can be configured. With version 2.3, the server is actually a combination server-client, and connects to the GMF resource status manager. Figure 19.7 contains a list of the components found within a server workstation.

All of the components listed in the figure are also found in a client workstation, except the first two. The graphic data server and view administrator are only used in the server workstation.

GraphicsView/2 is included with GMF, and is actually a separate IBM product designed to support the display of data on an OS/2 workstation. It is used as the basis for data display with GMF.

Basic Installation Procedures

There is a step-by-step procedure outlined which must be used to properly install GMF on the workstation. The steps can be summarized as follows:

- Prepare OS/2 system.
- Download and customize the Installation Administrator files.
- Invoke and utilize the Installation Administrator, which handles the actual workstation installation.

The NetView Graphic Monitor Facility workstation code provided with NetView Version 2 Releases 1 and 2 is not upwardly compatible. NetView Version 2 Release 3 workstation code must be used in conjunction with the NetView Version 2 Release 3 host.

After the feature has been installed, the Communications Manager portion of OS/2 must be setup in order to provide the LU type 6.2 and 2 sessions required.

Editing and Customizing Views

The preprocessor creates the unformatted views, which must be downloaded to the server workstation after the GMF feature has been installed. This is done with the View Administrator, which uses a 3270 file transfer mechanism over the LU type 2 session. Then the unformatted views can be converted so as to be usable by the workstation.

After this, the views can be further customized. For example, resources can be copied/pasted between views, or deleted altogether. Views can be enhanced by adding text and background graphics. Also, status mappings for SNA resources can be adjusted.

And actually, there is a wide range of options for GMF customization at the workstation. The global characteristics of the display can be affected, such as colors, symbol sizes, font types and sizes, icons, status text, and help panels. This allows the systems programmer to implement GMF based on the needs of the installation.

19.5 Basic Operation and Use

As can be seen from the above discussion, there are several different sets of skills required to properly implement GMF. After the feature has been installed, and the views created, downloaded and customized, the operator can then activate GMF.

GMF Startup And Logon

With NetView and the prerequisite subtasks started, the GMF server is ready to use. First make sure that the workstation with OS/2 is active. Then establish an LU type 2 session with NetView, logging on as an operator. Select the Graphic Data Server icon to activate the server.

Next, the LU type 6.2 link between the resource status manager host and the server workstation is started with the following NetView command, where 'pcluname' is the name of the independent logical unit defined for the workstation:

NETCONV LU=pcluname ACTION=START

In this case, the connection is being started. The same command, with ACTION=STOP, is used to terminate the communication link.

A similar procedure can then be performed for any clients dependent on the server.

Object Colors and Characteristics

The monitor function allows the operator to open view windows for display. Each symbol shown within the views has a significance as conveyed by both in its shape and color. For example, a square represents a host.

In addition, the colors have significance. Their use depends to some extent on whether the resource is real or an aggregate. There are a total of eight colors defined, that range from green representing satisfactory, to red indicating severe problems.

View Navigation

The highest level view is the cluster view; an example is shown in Figure 19.8 with a background map of the United States.

From here, one can navigate using the mouse down through the SNA hierarchy to the backbone and then peripheral views. With version 2.3, more data is available, including:

- Peripheral LUs
- Host VTAM applications
- Cross-domain resources
- Cross-domain Resource Managers (CDRMs)
- Major nodes

In addition to accessing resource data in a hierarchical fashion, the user also has the option of quickly zooming to the desired resource. For example, a fastpath to the failing resource is available. Also, the operator can initiate a global find based on the resource name.

Command Entry

With version 2.3, commands can be entered directly from the resource views. There are three generic commands that can be issued for a resource:

- Activate

■ Inactivate
■ Recycle

In addition, the operator can select the NETWORK option in order to enter any line command which is sent up to NetView.

Before using this commands facility, a sign-on procedure must be initiated. This involves identifying the NetView operator subtask that will accept and process the commands.

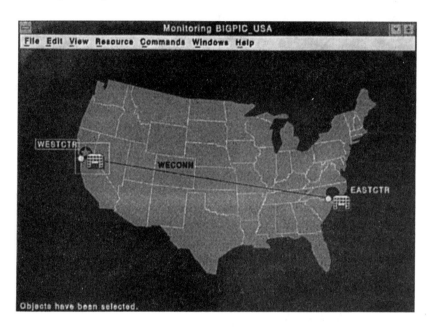

Figure 19.8 An example of a cluster view displayed by GMF.

The commands then flow from the monitor to the data server, where exits can be called to examine and affect the input. Also, a profile customization option is available in order to limit the operator commands issued.

The text then flows from the server up to the resource status manager host over the APPC session. The command is passed to the designated operator, with the response messages flowing back over the 3270 emulation session. Commands can be issued to other NetView domains using the RMTCMD facility, which requires NetView version 2.2 or above.

Another option is to implement the new Command Tree/2 product from IBM. This provides a more sophisticated technique for constructing and forwarding commands from the OS/2 workstation.

19.6 Support and Problem Diagnosis

The support of a typical GMF configuration can be slightly more challenging than many on-line, interactive systems. This is because of the many variables involved, including:

■ Multiple operating system platforms
■ Communication links
■ View creation and manipulation
■ Multiple domain status collection

There is a potentially large number of diagnostic procedures available. However, the majority focus on first verifying that the installation and implementation were done properly, and then on analyzing the available log and trace data.

Log and Trace Files

In the host environment, the system and NetView logs can contain information that is useful in debugging GMF problems. Also, the NetView internal trace might be needed in order to track information as it flows between the subtasks.

Because of the communication aspect involved, the standard VTAM traces are available for use, such as the buffer trace.

At the workstation, the file EXQERROR.LOG is used by GMF and its underlying GraphicsView/2 product to record error messages.

The Graphic Service Facility Support option allows events within the OS/2 environment, relating to the operation of GMF, to be traced. There are four variables that must be set in the CONFIG.SYS file which affect the operation of the feature:

■ EXQTRACEFILE - identifies the output file name.
■ EXQTRACEBUF - determines the size of the trace buffer.
■ EXQTRACEOPT - controls activation of trace, and processing options.
■ EXQTRACEDATA - identifies what data is to be captured.

This data is written to disk, and can later be formatted for use by IBM service personnel.

Evolution of NetView Features and Functions

This appendix provides a chronology of the major events in the evolution of the NetView product. Consistent with the focus of the book, MVS will be emphasized although many of the features apply to (affect) the other operational environments as well.

NetView Version 1 Release 1

Announced: May, 1986

The first release of NetView provided a repackaging of the various IBM network management offerings that were available at the time. Each of the products became a "component" running within the single NetView region. The major features included the command facility, hardware monitor, session monitor, status monitor, on-line help, helpdesk, and browse function.

In addition, the Terminal Access Facility (TAF) was included, along with support for certain IBM modems. A basic automation capability allowed for CLISTs to be scheduled based on message ID. Also, the network management architecture, consisting of an Open Network Management (ONM) framework and SNA/MS encodings, was implemented within the product.

By packaging these products together, IBM signaled the strategic importance of network management, and NetView. It also provided other benefits, such as easier installation and support, a consistency of use and operation, and a mutual benefit, as derived from leveraging similar and related functionality.

NetView Version 1 Release 2

Announced: June, 1987

Release 2 had several major enhancements, with the focus being improved automation capabilities. Also, a tiered control structure was established with the option to install a "distributed" version of the product that would report to a central site.

Support was provided for the MVS subsystem interface (SSI) through a new address space. This allowed MVS write-to-operator (WTO) messages to be accessed. In addition, a two-way console connection was established, where MVS commands could be entered from NetView, and NetView commands could be issued from an MVS console. The automation subtask (AUTOTASK) could now be implemented, thus allowing the internal workload to be further divided. Finally, the message automation table was introduced as a more sophisticated method for providing event-driven automation.

Access to network management information was also improved with the introduction of a new type of generic alert carried by the Network Management Vector Transport (NMVT) request unit. Connections to the SNA service point agents was expanded with the Service Point Command Service (SPCS) formats, allowing commands to be sent from the host out into the network.

Version 1.1 of the NetView/PC product also became available and worked with NetView release 2. NetView/PC acted as a service point by supporting non-SNA equipment. Events and other data could be translated into corresponding SNA messages, and sent to NetView through the access method on the host.

The CNM router function, implemented as a task, allowed for more control within NetView regarding the routing of unsolicited network management data. Alerts, once received, could be converted to messages and then forwarded for centralized automation and control.

NetView Version 1 Release 3

Announced: September, 1988

This release included a wide range of enhancements. Although several new features were added, release 3 focused on improvements to existing capabilities.

Support for the C and PL/I high-level programming languages were added, so that command processors and user exits could more easily be written and implemented. Also, the SAA procedural language REXX could now be utilized.

The Network Asset Manager (NAM) feature was added, as well as support for the LAN manager and new IBM modems. OSI-based network management was possible through a connection to the IBM OSI/ CS product.

Alerts could be forwarded to a central site from a distributed host without the need to first convert them to text messages. Also, improved internal message routing was introduced.

Finally, usability issues were addressed by improving the technique for creating, maintaining, and displaying 3270 panels (i.e., VIEW). Also, for the first time, performance was recognized as an issue, as IBM included a few basic commands designed to help analyzed the performance of the NetView address space.

NetView Version 1 Release 3 for MVS/ESA

Announced: October, 1989

Up until this point, the MVS/ESA operating system had not been explicitly supported. That is, previous releases could run under ESA, but would not take advantage of its capabilities. This new release included the features in the previously announced release 3. In addition, the functions of ESA were exploited. Also, several new features were added.

First, the major components such as the hardware monitor and session monitor were enhanced. This focused on performance and usability. For example, the path for SAW and trace data was changed to bypass VTAM by using the ESA dataspaces. The session monitor KEEPSESS parameter, as well as pattern matching for the hardware monitor also improved operation and performance.

The Program-to-Program Interface (PPI) was implemented as a method for better integrating host applications. Messages passed through the NetView SSI address space. Other features included Switched Network Backup (SNBU) support and the Central Site Control Facility (CSCF).

Finally, the new features could also be added to the release 3 for MVS/XA through a Small Programming Enhancement (SPE) maintenance package.

NetView Version 2 Release 1 and Release 2

Announced: September, 1990

Both releases 1 and 2 of the version 2 product were announced in the same letter, more clearly establishing NetView as an important part of the overall SystemView strategy.

Release 1 included the introduction of the Graphic Monitor Facility (GMF), as well as an option to acquire the DOS-based NETCENTER solution. It has been clearly articulated that GMF is IBM's strategic, long-term product for the monitoring and control of the resources through NetView using graphical technology. Also included with release 1 is the VTAM-STATMON interface, where status updates are made directly to the NetView address space using MVS cross-memory techniques. The Bridge allows access to the Information/Management database from NetView applications, and the NetView Installation Facility (NIF) provides (in theory, at least) a smoother product installation.

Release 2 provided a wider, and more consistent, access to SNA and non-SNA resources through the implementation of two APPC-based transports: Management Services (MS) and High Performance (HP). The automation table was also upgraded to allow not only text messages, but architected MS data to be processed.

NetView Version 2 Release 2 Enhancements

Announced: September, 1991

Prior to the actual availability of release 2, IBM provided more information on that level of the product. This included a re-emphasis of the APPC transport technology and automation table enhancements, with further details on how it supports the IBM strategy for systems management. A few additional features were also outlined, such as support for compiled REXX code.

NetView Version 2 Planned Enhancements

Announced: September, 1991

This was a pre-announcement of version 2 release 3. In the letter, IBM indicated that its next NetView release will focus on graphics and automation. In particular, the Resource Object Data Manager (RODM) will be shipped as a new, separate MVS (XA and ESA) address space. RODM will be designed to manage information describing the system and network resources in a heterogeneous network. The data will be structured in an object-oriented fashion, with a set of open APIs for vendor and user application development. This will enable a shift from event-driven to object-oriented automation.

RODM will form the basis for collecting and managing non-SNA resource information for display and control from the GMF workstation. In this way, NetView will gradually absorb techniques and technology that was previously available with NETCENTER.

Additional enhancements will also be included, such as closer links to the Information/Management database.

Planned APPN Enhancements

Announced: March, 1992

At this time, IBM announced its intent to provide comprehensive support for its future Advanced Peer-to-Peer Networking (APPN) technology through the use of NetView-based applications. No availability dates were provided, although the new features will, as usual, be thoroughly field tested. It is anticipated that the APPN enhancements will be provided with version 2 release 4.

The functionality provided will enable direct management and control of APPN network resources through a dynamic user interface, remote operations and automation, and collection of relevant accounting information.

NetView Version 2 Release 3

Announced: May, 1992

A major turning point for the NetView product came with the announcement of version 2, release 3. While several enhancements were included, the major focus of this release was the addition of the Resource Object Data Manager (RODM).

RODM on the MVS host is an implementation of the SystemView Control Information Base (CIB) structure. Running in its own address space, RODM is an on-line, real-time database for configuration and operational information. The data is stored in the form of objects, and can include not only data but defined methods (i.e., subroutines). This new paradigm allows a shift to be made from event-driven to object-oriented automation.

RODM forms an open repository for all types of information on the host. Initially, it is used to contain data representing non-SNA network resources. The GMF Host Subsystem (GMFHS) is the first RODM application, maintaining the non-SNA information for display on the GMF workstation. This feature was not available immediately, but instead provided through maintenance.

Other enhancements were made in the area of 3270 display capabilities, access to more detailed message data, and improvements in remote operation and automation.

NetView Version 2 Release 3 Additional Enhancements

Announced: May, 1993

Additional enhancements to version 2, release 3, to be available concurrent with the shipment of the GMFHS feature, were announced. These included improvements to assist the automation developer (i.e., "pipeline automation"), improved visibility to LU session data from the graphical display, and enhancements to remote operation through the inclusion of a Common Operation Service (COS) gateway.

B

SNA Management Services Major Vectors

This appendix provides a listing of the important major vector data structures that are used in order to communicate SNA Management Services (SNA/MS) data. The name of each vector is provided, along with its hexadecimal identifier. These vectors are carried in the Network Management Vector Transport and/or the Control Point Management Services Unit (CP-MSU).

There is a pattern where most of the major vectors are grouped together to form a request/reply protocol. Also, in a few cases there is a request, request acceptance, and then reply.

Alert (x'0000') - Provides an unsolicited notification of a problem, including detailed information regarding its cause and possible resolution.

Resolution (x'0002') - For a specific alert, this vector supplies an unsolicited notification of the problem's resolution.

Request Change Control (x'8050') - Requests that a specific change control function be executed.

Change Control (x'0050') - Returns the result from a previously received Request Change Control vector, or makes a request in an unsolicited manner to the focal point.

Execute Command ('x8061') - Sends a message to be interpreted and processed.

Reply to Execute Command (x'0061') - Used to return reply, including sense code if required, for a previously received Execute Command vector.

Analyze Status (x'8062') - A sophistication technique for requesting status data, with analysis performed by the receiving partner.

Reply to Analyze Status (x'0062') - Returns reply for a previously received Analyze Status request.

Query Resource Data (x'8063') - Used to collect information regarding one or more named resources.

Reply to Query Resource Data (x'0063') - Carries the reply for a previously issued Query Resource Data request.

Test Resource (x'8064') - Enables a remote test of one or more resources to be performed.

Reply to Test Resource (x'0064') - Transports the reply for previous Test Resource vector.

Request Activation (x'8066') - Used to initiate a specific activation procedure at the remote node.

Activation Acceptance (x'0066') - Indicates the (initial) acceptance of a Request Activation request, with final result still pending.

Activation (x'0067') - Carries notification of the Request Activation vector, with an indication of the resource state.

Request Initiation (x'8068') - Names a command procedure to be initiated (executed).

Initiation (x'0068') - Returns results of the previous Request Initiation request.

Send Message to Operator (x'006F') - Carries an unsolicited request to a named operator.

Operate (x'8070') - Sends an implementation-specific command from one control point to another for execution.

Operate Report (x'0070') - Carries outcome of previous Operate, including acceptance and successful execution.

Request Deactivation (x'8071') - Receiver is to schedule a named deactivation procedure.

Deactivation Acceptance (x'0071') - Conveys initial acceptance or rejection of a deactivation request.

Deactivation (x'0072') - Final outcome of deactivation request is passed to original issuer.

Set Clock (x'8075') - Used to change value of clock at remote node.

Set Clock Report (x'0075') - Carries results of previous Set Clock request.

Request Cancellation (x'8076') - Previously issued and outstanding requests can be canceled.

Cancellation (x'0076') - Returns results of the previous cancellation request.

Routing/Parsing Report (x'0077') - Carries error information describing a problem either routing or parsing a previously received MDS-MU.

Request RTM (x'8080') - Used to control the operation of the Response Time Monitor (RTM) feature of participating control units (i.e., PU type 2).

RTM (x'0080') - Data is returned to SSCP from control unit, either unsolicited or in response to a previous request.

Request Product Set ID (x'8090') - Carries request for information about the nature and configuration of a specific node.

Reply Product Set ID (x'0090') - Carries results of query request; can also be forwarded in an unsolicited fashion in certain cases.

MS Capabilities (x'80F0') - Exchanged between control points in order to established focal to entry point relationships.

C

Internal Trace Events

The NetView trace can be used to capture information regarding its internal operation, which is useful when solving product or application problems and errors. The collected data can be recorded in a wrap-around table in virtual storage (INT mode), or queued and written to a disk dataset (EXT mode).

This appendix presents the major events that can be collected for analysis using the NetView trace. In addition to the records shown, the Lost Trace record might also be encountered by the systems programmer analyzing the trace. This record is created in place of a record received for processing (i.e., writing to disk) after a pre-defined queue limit has been reached. Using lost trace records helps to limit the trace's use of virtual storage.

Each of the records is between 32 and 96 bytes long. In order to conserve space, the entries typically contain pointers instead of the actual data. For example, the address of a buffer or Task Vector Block (TVB) are found in many records.

LUC Communications

LUC communication links are utilized between NetView domains in order to carry several types of information, including alerts, status updates, and cross-domain access requests. A basic conversation model is implemented where access to a session link can be acquired and then released as needed by the internal applications.

There are four types of LUC operations, each of which is described in its own trace record: allocate, send data, receive data, and deallocate. The actual record for each has a slightly different format, providing a description of relevant fields such as the address of a sending buffer and Request Parameter List (RPL) return code.

Message Queuing Service

The Message Queuing Service (MQS) enables message buffers to be queued between NetView subtasks for processing. For example, these buffers can include text messages received for automation, or internal commands. In fact, the passing of internal messages between tasks is the foundation of NetView processing.

The trace provides an entry for each message queued. The fields include information identifying the sender and receiver, as well as the actual buffer.

SNAP Trace

The Vital Product Data (VPD) commands include an option to allow retrieved data to be passed to the internal trace for recording. This data is captured as a direct user request, and formatted as a SNAP trace record.

User Exit Processing

As discussed earlier in the book, there are a large number of exits that can be written in order to customize the NetView product. The trace can be used to create an entry each time one of the exits is scheduled for processing. Both the global and DST exits can be traced.

The type of information recorded includes the type of exit, input buffer being presented, and the task where the routine will run.

Module Entry and Exit

Many times it can be difficult to follow the exact internal processing path followed by NetView. In order to help isolate the sequence of events, the entry to and exit from a subset of the NetView product modules can be recorded.

Storage Management

Storage management problems, such as "creeping storage," can frequently be a problem, either with applications or NetView itself. During the course of normal processing, storage can be dynamically obtained and then released using the DSIGET and DSIFRE macro instructions. A record of each of these invocations can be made, and includes the buffer address and length.

Wait and Post Dispatching

For most MVS-based systems, applications are designed to use a wait and post model of processing. In fact, there are two MVS macro (i.e., WAIT and POST) which use a common data structure called an Event Control Block (ECB) in order to coordinate activity. A subtask can be suspended until another process wakes it up with a post operation.

Within NetView, each subtask can have several dispatching queues. A task can use DSIWAT to wait for incoming work requests, while another task issues DSIPOS to activate it after passing a work element. These two macros, along with DSIPATCH (i.e., dispatch), can be captured and recorded by the trace.

Presentation Services

Input from and output to a terminal screen is controlled with the macro DSIPSS. There are several different operations available with this macro, depending on the component or application being used.

Each call to NetView presentation services (i.e., DSIPSS) can be recorded. The data describes the exact operation, including the type of action and the buffer being used.

Status Monitor Processing

The status monitor continues to evolve, most recently in support of the Graphic Monitor Facility (GMF). It is used to collect and forward status updates in a distributed environment to a central host. From there, the GMF task can send the data to the GMF server workstation.

In order to support this complex arrangement, NetView can record several types of entries relating to the operation of the status monitor.

Assembler Data Areas

The NetView product, as with all other MVS-based systems, relies on a collection of control blocks to maintain and describe the processing structure. These data areas support its processing and operation. Many times, the assembler language programmer must have an awareness of at least some of these NetView control blocks in order to properly design and develop an application. And even if development is not done in assembler, an appreciation of the nature of these control blocks can increase the understanding of NetView's internal operation.

BUFHDR   The buffer header, as its name implies, is located at the beginning of every NetView message and command buffer. It describes the contents of the data, with fields such as the buffer's size, type, and origin. BUFHDR is a separate MVS DSECT packaged with DSITIB.

DSIAIFRO   Extensions can be appended to the automation IFR (see DSIIFR) arranged in vectorized object format. For example, details regarding the message being processed and its source can be included.

DSIART   The authorization and routing table contains entries which map a specific resource to the span network table, as defined by DSISNT. This enables the implementation of a framework for internal security.

DSICBH   The control block header is used at the beginning of all NetView control blocks (except where BUFHDR is used). It contains information describing the data area, such as its type and length.

DSICWB   The command work block provides an anchor for the specific instance of a command. It contains command parameters, workareas, as well as pointers to other work-related control blocks.

DSIDSB   A data services block is used with the disk services macro (DSIDKS), and describes the state of the I/O connection, including each individual request.

DSIDSRB   Each Data Services Command Processor (DSCP) utilizes this request block to anchor its execution. The number of these control blocks allocated for a specific subtask can be controlled by the user.

DSIDTR   The NetView Program-to-Program Interface (PPI) is accessed through a series of API calls using the data transport request data, mapped in this control block.

DSIELB   The external logging block data area is contained in each buffer passed to the external log for processing.

DSIIFR   The Internal Function Request (IFR) contains information describing the nature of a specific NetView function or process. There are four types of IFRs: automation, command, full-screen panel command, and user-defined. An IFR must be formatted before the buffer can be passed from one subtask to another using the Message Queuing Service (MQS).

DSILOGDS   This control block maps a record which is sent to the network log.

DSIMVT   The Main Vector Table (MVT) is the single main control block which anchors all of the other data areas in the NetView address space. Along with values affecting NetView's operation, it also contains points to other control structures. For example, the TVB queue (see DSITVB) is anchored from the MVT.

DSIOIT   The operator ID table is used to hold operator identifications that have been defined to NetView.

DSIPDB   NetView includes a service which is available to parse commands into tokens before presentation to user routines and other processes. This common function, implemented as a part of NetView, facilitates quicker, more consistent development. The parse descriptor block data area contains the description of a message in parsed format.

DSISCE   The system command entry carries information related to the content and nature of a command. Fields used include command name and corresponding module address.

DSISCT   The system command table holds multiple DSISCE entries, one for each of the commands defined at NetView startup.

DSISNT   Information supporting the operation of the SPAN security feature is contained in the span name table.

DSISVL   Each NetView service routine (except presentation services) is anchored from the service routine vector list.

DSISWB   A service work block is part of the structure
                  passed to most work requests. It contains a
                  parameter list area, as well as savearea and a
                  workarea. Pointers to other structures (e.g.,
                  DSTIB) are also included.

DSITECBR   This data area holds a list of processing mod-
                  ules for wait-post processing via the MVS Event
                  Control Block (ECB).

DSITIB   In addition to a TVB (see DSITVB), each active
                  subtask has one Task Information Block (TIB).
                  The TIB contains information similar to the
                  TVB, but is only present for active tasks.

DSITVB   Each NetView subtask is anchored and de-
                  scribed by a single Task Vector Block (TVB).
                  The TVB contains information describing the
                  task, as well as pointers to other control blocks,
                  such as the public work queues. A queue of
                  TVBs for all defined subtasks is allocated and
                  anchored from the MVT.

DSIUSE   The installation exit parameter list contains
                  information which is particular to the user exit
                  processing. Several pointers are used which
                  identify other NetView data structures, such as
                  the DSITVB and DSIPDB.

DUITRXCM   This data area passes resource status informa-
                  tion to the XITCM exit.

DUITSTAT   This data area passes resource status informa-
                  tion to the XITST exit.

Internal Message Types

As described earlier, each command and message buffer begins with the Buffer Header (BUFHDR) control block. BUFHDR describes the contents of each buffer, including its type. Listed below are the various types of internal buffers that are processed within the NetView address space. For each type, the equate symbol from the IBM assembler macro is provided, along with a brief description.

HDRTYPAC   Message that has been automated to drive command procedure.

HDRTYPDT   Internal non-message data type.

HDRTYPEB   Command or Command List (CLIST) that has been suppressed from display and logging. The suppression character defined in the DSIDMN member can be used, before the command, for this reason.

HDRTYPEC   Command or message generated from a CLIST.

HDRTYPED   Message from an immediate command processor.

HDRTYPEE   Message from the operating system interface (i.e., Subsystem Interface (SSI)).

HDRTYPEF   VSAM record; used by the Data Services Task (DST).

HDRTYPEG   Record received from the Communication Network Management (CNM) interface; used by the DST.

HDRTYPEI   An Internal Function Request (IFR), used to transfer buffers between subtasks. There are four different types of IFRs.

HDRTYPEJ   Multiple line Write-to-Operator (WTO), in title-line mode.

HDRTYPEK   Same as HDRTYPEJ, except for IBM non-NetView products.

HDRTYPEL   Same as HDRTYPEJ, except for non-IBM products.

HDRTYPEM   Message from the NetView message command processor.

HDRTYPEN   Normal single-buffer message from the NetView product.

HDRTYPEP   Message from command procedure running under the PPT subtask.

HDRTYPEQ   Single-buffer message received from the VTAM primary program interface in an unsolicited fashion.

HDRTYPER   Operator reply entered in response to the NetView message DSI802A.

HDRTYPES   Buffer that has been exchanged, or swapped.

HDRTYPET   Command entered to the NetView product from an operator terminal.

HDRTYPEU   Used by non-IBM programs for multiple-line and action WTO messages (WTO with reply required).

HDRTYPEV	Single-buffer message received from the VTAM program interface in a solicited fashion.
HDRTYPEW	Single-line message from an IBM product.
HDRTYPEX	Command received from another NetView domain over the NNT-to-OST interface.
HDRTYPEY	Single-line action WTO message, requiring a reply.
HDRTYPEZ	Normal single-buffer message from the NetView product, specifically from a DST subtask.
HDRTYPE$	Non-displayable message used to transfer information between command procedures written in a high-level language.
HDRTYPE1	Echo of a console command from primary operator log.
HDRTYPE2	Echo of a console message from primary operator log.
HDRTYPLS	Contains command that has been substituted.
HDRTYPLT	Internal trace record.
HDRTYPOR	Buffer used for pipeline automation.
HDRTYPQC	Command with all synchronously generated messages suppressed from display (also called a "quiet" message).
HDRTYPWT	Message that, when processed against outstanding &WAIT requests, generated a match.
HDRTYP10	Buffer containing a Management Services Unit (MSU).

Tutorial on the VIEW Command

The VIEW command processor provides a powerful tool that can be used in the development of NetView-based applications. It allows the user interface for a 3270 terminal operator to be created and displayed through the use of pre-defined screen images. The dynamic content of these panels, held in NetView variables, is updated and accessed by the controlling application.

The VIEW facility is invoked from a command procedure, including a CLIST or command processor written in the C or PL/I language. This appendix provides a brief overview of this NetView feature. The interested reader should refer to the bibliography for the relevant NetView product manuals - namely, the NetView Customization Guide (SC31-6132).

Elements and Operational Overview

There are three major elements of the overall VIEW architecture. This distinct separation of function has allowed the tool to be widely utilized within NetView by the various components. The architectural elements include:

- Panel templates, defining the input and output fields, as well as the screen attributes such as text color and highlighting.
- Techniques for defining and refreshing global and local variables that are named in the panel definitions.

■ Actual VIEW command processor, scheduled to
   display the output screen images, and pass user input
   and commands back to the calling program.

Figure F.1 provides a basic illustration of the process, where a user
command procedure updates the variable values and then schedules the
VIEW command to handle the actual terminal I/O based on the named
panel.

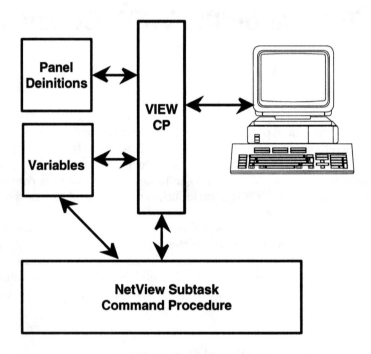

Figure F.1   Basic structure of the VIEW processing model.

Panel Contents and Creation

Each panel image is stored in a dataset member, and contains data that
is interpreted to represent the final screen format. The definitions
contained in these text members consist of VIEW directives, attribute
symbols, NetView variables, and text strings. The VIEW command
scans each line in order to create the final 3270 data stream sent to the
terminal.

Attribute Symbols

An attribute symbol is a special character, recognized by VIEW, that is used to designate a 3270 field attribute (e.g., highlight). These symbols are explicit declarations placed in the panel definition which do not change dynamically.

To allow for flexibility, there are two sets of attribute symbols. The group used for a particular panel depends on the "text indicator line" used near the top of the panel text. This line separates the actual displayed panel text from the preceding prologue, help, and general panel definitions.

Symbol	Field Type	Intensity	Description
%	Text	High	White
}	Text	High	White (reverse video)
!	Text	High	White (underscore)
~	Input	High	White
$	Text	Normal	Turquoise
\	Text	High	Turquoise (underscore)

Figure F.2 First set of attribute symbols, as controlled by the text indicator line (Part 1 of 2).

When "***" is declared, attribute set one is used; the text indicator line "*** AT2" causes symbol set two to be used. Figures F.2 and F.3 contain a list of the first set of attribute symbols that are recognized by the VIEW processor.

Symbol	Field Type	Intensity	Description
+	Text	Normal	Blue
{	Text	High	Blue (reverse video)
@	Text	Normal	Green
¬	Text	Normal	Yellow
|	Text	Normal	Pink
¢	Text	High	Red

Figure F.3 Remaining attribute symbols in first set, as controlled by the text indicator line (Part 2 of 2).

NetView Variables

Variables are used by NetView and its applications to hold information, usually on a temporary basis, that can change dynamically. Task variables are established for each subtask, while common variables are addressable by the other NetView tasks as well. Both task and common variables are considered to be "global" in the sense that they remain after the transaction which defined them terminates. In addition to global variables, local variables can be utilized by command procedures (written in C or PL/I) for the duration of the command.

These variables are defined and updated through documented API calls for code written in REXX, NetView CLIST, C, and PL/I. All use the same basic naming standard, except that NetView CLIST variables are preceded by the "&" character.

The application code can update the contents of these variables with text for subsequent display. The strings can include attribute symbols, which control the aspects of the display, such as color and highlighting.

Attribute Variables

The attribute symbols can be directly coded in the panel description. However, to allow the characteristics of a particular field to change dynamically, these symbols may be dynamically inserted into one or more of the NetView variables by the application before panel display. For example, when a field value exceeds a pre-defined limit it can change from normal to high intensity. While this approach provides the programmer with more control, NetView provides an even more convenient method for controlling the field attributes. The use of attribute variables allows the text data to be separated from attributes for a particular field.

An attribute variable can be defined for each corresponding NetView variable. The name used for the attribute variable is derived from the variable itself by adding a preceding "$" character. For example, the NetView variable VAR1 would have an attribute variable by the name of $VAR1. In the case of the NetView CLIST language, the pairing would be &VAR1 and &$VAR1.

The attribute variable consists of a string of 2-byte tokens, each separated by one or more blanks serving as delimiters. These tokens have pre-defined meanings, and collectively determine the field attributes.

The first byte of each token determines the major category, including:

- F - general field attribute, such as protected or unprotected.
- I - intensity, such as normal or high.
- C - color.
- H - highlighting, such as blinking or reverse video.
- U - cursor positioning.

The second byte of the token defines the actual value within the class. For example, "HB" falls under the highlighting category and signifies blinking. Similarly, "CT" designates the field as having the color turquoise.

The user does not need to place the attribute variables on the screen (i.e., in the panel definition). If one exists for the text variable, it is located and used. When an attribute variable has been defined, the text variable is not scanned for attribute symbols.

Variable Access and Operations

The variables named in each panel definition must first be updated before the panel can be properly displayed. This is accomplished differently for each variable type.

NetView Function	Variable Type	Language
&TGLOBAL	Global	NetView CLIST
&CGLOBAL	Global	NetView CLIST
GLOBALV	Global	NetView CLIST, REXX, PL/I, or C
CNMVARS	Global or Local	PL/I Language
Cnmvars	Global or Local	C Language

Figure F.4 Functions that can be used from the various languages to access variables.

Updating Variables

As mentioned above, there are several languages that can be used with the VIEW command. Figure F.4 contains a list of the functions used to update the different types of NetView variables.

Accepting Terminal Input

The VIEW command, described below, can be invoked to display a panel for output only; this might be used for HELP panels. Or, it can be used for input and output.

When input is expected, NetView utilizes a set of control variables to pass data to the application. These variables include:

- VIEWAID - the Attention Identifier (AID) field, which indicates which key (e.g., PF1) generated the interrupt.
- VIEWCURROW - row position of the cursor when the key was pressed.
- VIEWCURCOL - column position of the cursor when the key was pressed.

By examining these variables, as well as those defined specifically for the application, the command procedure can determine exactly what input was entered at the terminal.

VIEW Command Procedures

Once the panels have been defined and the variable names coordinated with the application for update, the final step is to schedule the VIEW command processor itself. From that point on, the terminal input and output passes through VIEW.

Figure F.5 provides an example of the VIEW command, showing each of the possible parameters. The " | " character indicates that one or the other of the listed options is selected, but not both.

```
VIEW   name1 name2 [INPUT | NOINPUT] [MSG | NOMSG]
```

Figure F.5 Example of the VIEW command showing the parameter options.

The first name identifies the application to NetView, and must be unique for each rollable application. The second parameter is the panel name to be used. INPUT allows user input to be accepted and passed to the command, while NOINPUT designates an output-only panel. The last parameter is supported for compatibility with previous releases, but has no meaning or effect on the command's operation.

As mentioned above, each line is scanned by VIEW to create the screen output. In order for an attribute to be assigned to a field, column one of the line must have an attribute symbol. This can be provided explicitly, or within a named variable.

Rollable Component

One of the advantages of using VIEW is that a rollable component can be created. Once established, such an application can be temporarily suspended while another component is activated. This is accomplished through the ROLL command.

The UNIQUE command can be used to help enforce the uniqueness of a VIEW application name. This is required for panels passing input to the application. UNIQUE can scan for an application name, and remove or promote it within the rollable (long-running command) stack.

G

RODM Customization Parameters

The Resource Object Data Manager (RODM) runs as a separate MVS started task. The systems programmer has several options available when defining and implementing this function. The major parameters, stored in the DSIPARM dataset member EKGCUST, are described below. Each parameter statement is briefly described, followed by an example.

ASYNC_TASKS - used to determine the number of concurrently active subtasks running asynchronously to service the RODM method API function requests.

ASYNC_TASKS nnnn

where 'nnnn' is the number of tasks, which can range from 1 to 2048.

CELL_POOLS - RODM implements its own storage management technique based on cell pool allocation, where large areas of storage are allocated and then sub-divided. This parameter can be included up to 200 times.

CELL_POOLS (cellsize:poolsize, ...)

where 'cellsize' is the cell size in bytes (8-512) and 'poolsize' is the number of 4K pages allocated for the pool.

CLASS_AGING_LIMIT - class IDs, once freed, can be reused by RODM after the specified amount of time has elapsed.

CLASS_AGING_LIMIT (nnnnnnn)

where 'nnnnnnn' is specified as the number of seconds to wait (decimal), with a maximum of 12 days (1036800).

CONCURRENT_USERS - specifies the maximum number of transactions that can be concurrently active within the RODM address space.

CONCURRENT_USERS (nnnn)

where 'nnnn' is the transaction limit, with a maximum value of 2048.

EXTEND_HEAP_SIZE - the size of the PL/I extended storage heaps can be defined.

EXTENDED_HEAP_SIZE (nnnK)

with 'nnn' being the number of 1024-byte increments, ranging from 4K to 256K.

IO_QUEUE_THRESHOLD - the number of log requests to queue before posting the log task.

IO_QUEUE_THRESHOLD (nnnnn)

where 'nnnnn' is the number of requests, from 0 to 32767.

LOCK_LISTRETRY - determines the number of retries that RODM will attempt in obtaining locks for a specified list of objects before failure.

LOCK_LISTRETRY (nnnn)

with 'nnnn' being the maximum retries, from 0 to 2000.

LOCK_LOOPLIMIT - there are several different levels of RODM locks. For each level (1, 2, and 3), this statement sets a limit for the number attempts that RODM will try to obtain the lock resulting from a direct LOCK API request. The lock level is determined by examining the Transaction Information Block (TIB).

LOCK_LOOPLIMIT (xx, yy, zz)

where 'xx' is the level 1 limit (0 to 128), 'yy' is the level 2 limit (0 to 4096), and 'zz' is the level 3 limit (0 to 32767).

LOCK_SLEEPTIME - after an unsuccessful attempt to obtain an object lock, RODM can be configured to wait a certain amount of time before trying again. A value, specified in 0.01 second increments, can be provided for each of the three lock levels (see LOCK_LOOPLIMIT and LOCK_SPINLIMIT).

LOCK_SLEEPTIME (xx, yy, zz)

where 'xx' is the level 1 wait time, 'yy' is the level 2 wait time, and 'zz' is the level 3 limit; the values for all three can range from 1 to 100.

LOCK_SPINLIMIT - used to define the number of lock attempts that are made for an object before entering a temporary wait state.

LOCK_SPINLIMIT (xx, yy, zz)

where 'xx' is the level 1 count (1 to 100), 'yy' is the level 2 count (1 to 500), and 'zz' is the level 3 count (1 to 1000).

LOG_LEVEL - this parameter determines which messages are written to the log by specifying a minimum severity level. Any API return code greater than or equal to the supplied value generates an RODM log message.

LOG_LEVEL (nnn)

where 'nnn' is the minimum value, which can range from 0 to 999.

MAX_CHUNK - in managing its internal storage, RODM will allow this many free "chunks" of storage to accumulate before collection.

MAX_CHUNK (nnnn)

where 'nnnn' can range from 16 to 4096.

MAX_SEGMENT_NUM - specifies the maximum number of storage segments available.

MAX_SEGMENT_NUM (nnn)

where 'nnn' is the number of segments, from 1 to 255.

MAX_WINDOW_NUM - specifies the maximum number of RODM windows available.

MAX_WINDOW_NUM (nnnnn)

where 'nnnnn' is the number of windows, from 1 to 32765.

MLOG_LEVEL - this parameter determines the level of messages sent to the RODM log for MAPI requests. Any method API return code greater than or equal to the supplied value generates an RODM log message.

MLOG_LEVEL (nn)

where 'nnn' is the minimum value, which can range from 0 to 99.

MTRACE_TYPE - through a bit map, specifies characteristics (enabling and disabling) of the method tracing.

MTRACE_TYPE (X'nnnnnnnn')

where 'nnnnnnnn' represents the seven major events in method processing that can be traced (e.g., entry, exit, and QUERY method processing).

PLI_ISA - determines the size of the internal storage area for PL/I processing.

PLI_ISA (nnnK)

with 'nnn' being the number of 1024-byte increments, ranging from 0K to 256K.

POST_RQST_BLK_NUM - used to define the maximum number of requests on the input request processing queue that will accumulate before an additional subtask is posted.

POST_RQST_BLK_NUM (nnnnn)

where 'nnnnn' is the request queue limit, with a range of 1 to 32767.

PRIMARY_HEAP_SIZE - the primary heap size for each RODM thread using PL/I.

PRIMARY_HEAP_SIZE (nnnK)

with 'nnn' being the number of 1024-byte increments, ranging from 0K to 256K.

QUIES_WAIT_TASK_TIME - the time allowed for an RODM transaction to gracefully terminate, before it is canceled.

QUIES_WAIT_TASK_TIME (nnnnn)

where 'nnnnn' is the wait value, specified in 0.01-second increments, with a range of 1 to 32767.

QUIES_WAIT_USER_TIME - the time allowed for a user to gracefully disconnect from RODM, before being forcibly disconnected.

QUIES_WAIT_USER_TIME (nnnnn)

where 'nnnnn' is the wait value, specified in 0.01-second increments, with a range of 1 to 32767.

SEC_CLASS - used to identify the class name used with the security facility (e.g., RACF).

SEC_CLASS (classname)

where 'classname' is a text string defining the applicable class, with a maximum length of 8 bytes.

SEC_RNAME - used to identify the resource name used with the security facility.

SEC_RNAME (resname)

where 'resname' is the resource name, with a maximum length of 43 bytes.

SEGMENT_POCKETS - the number of backup translation segments.

SEGMENT_POCKETS (nn)

where 'nn' represents the number of segments, from 1 to 16.

SSB_CHAIN - this statement defines the number of "same-name system" status blocks that can exist concurrently. A chain of SSBs is maintained in the Common Storage Area (CSA) of MVS which describes the previous activation requests; this chain can be deleted when the limit has been reached.

SSB_CHAIN (nnnnn)

where 'nnnnn' is the number of SSBs allowed for the RODM being defined.

TRANS_SEGMENT - the size of the translation segment can be defined in bytes.

TRANS_SEGMENT (nM)

where 'n' is the segment size in 1-megabyte increments; allowable values include 0.5M, 1M, and 2M.

WAIT_ALLOC_TIME - time that RODM will wait for allocation of window segments.

WAIT_ALLOC_TIME (nnn)

where 'nnn' is the wait value, specified in 0.01-second increments, with a range of 1 to 100.

WINDOW_CHKPT_TIME - defines the amount of time for taking a checkpoint of a specific RODM window.

WINDOW_CHKPT_TIME (nnnn)

where 'nnnn' is the wait value, specified in 0.01-second increments, with a range of 1 to 1500.

WINDOW_POCKETS - the number of backup windows.

WINDOW_POCKETS (nn)

where 'nnnnn' is defined within the range of 1 to 16.

WINDOW_SIZE - used to define the size of each data window in
bytes. RODM acquires storage for the object-oriented data
dynamically; this parameter in effect determines the expansion
size.

WINDOW_SIZE (nnM)

where 'nn' is the number of bytes, defined in 1-megabyte increments; allowable values are 2M, 4M, 8M, or 16M.

GMFHS Data Model and Usage

As explained in Chapter 18, the Resource Object Data Manager (RODM) is an object-oriented data cache shipped with NetView version 2.3. For each RODM application, a data model must be designed, created, and then loaded. The data model consists primarily of a hierarchical class structure, allowing the underlying data objects to be grouped and linked in an orderly fashion.

The first major RODM application provided by IBM is the Graphic Monitor Facility Host Subsystem (GMFHS). This application includes a data model and method routines which enable non-SNA network resources to be monitored and managed from NetView, through a participating GMF workstation.

The GMFHS data model, and its implementation, is a relatively large and complex subject area. The purpose of this appendix is to introduce the model, as well as to describe its general processing and identify additional areas for customization.

Management and Managed Objects

Consistent with the SystemView framework, RODM implements network management based on both management (i.e., manager) and managed (i.e., agent) objects. There are three types of management objects which assist NetView in controlling the network:

■ Network Management Gateways (NMGs)
■ SNA domains
■ Non-SNA domains

The NMGs act as agents of NetView, sending status information and executing commands.

The managed objects represent resources which, as their name implies, are managed by NetView and displayed by GMF. There are three major categories of managed objects:

- Non-SNA real resources
- SNA (shadow) resources
- Aggregate resource

The status for the SNA resources is not maintained by RODM. However, these objects are included to show, among other things, relationships with the real non-SNA resources.

Class Structure

Using an object-oriented approach, the RODM class structure is analogous to a database definition. The data objects are appended at the bottom of the class hierarchy. The highest classes, immediately below the RODM universal (root) class, are considered to be "parent" classes for the data model.

IBM supplies the GMFHS data model in source format; Figure H.1 presents the parent (highest) class definitions. Additional classes, which help to further refine the model, are defined under each of the parents. The object instances are anchored from the most specific (lowest) classes.

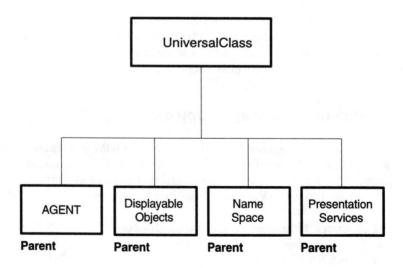

Figure H.1 Parent class structure for the GMFHS data model.

Agents

Figure H.2 illustrates the structure under the Agent parent class. As mentioned above, the NMGs are really agents of NetView, and represent one category of the GMFHS management objects.

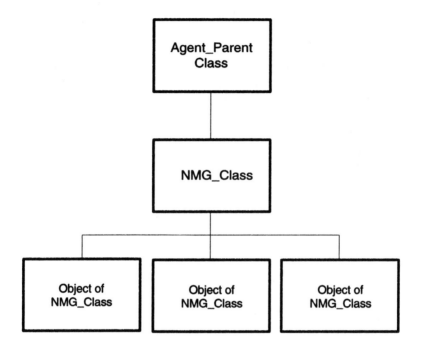

Figure H.2 Further definition of the data model under the Agent parent class.

There are several types of agents which manage a particular non-SNA resource under the control of NetView. Examples include:

■ NetView/PC
■ AIX Service Point
■ Host-based application using the Program-to-Program Interface to communicate with NetView
■ Operator Station Task (OST), or perhaps an autotask, running command procedures

Each of the agents is represented as an object within RODM.

Displayable-Objects

The GMFHS_Displayable_Objects parent class includes a diverse array of classes and objects, forming a complex branch of the data model structure. This data is maintained and available for display on the GMF workstation.

The two additional management objects, along with NMGs described above, fall under this parent class:

- SNA_Domain_Class - an SNA domain, as defined by a NetView domain based on the name in the DSIDMN member of the DSIPARM dataset.
- Non_SNA_Domain_Class - a "subnetwork" within the entire enterprise where a non-SNA protocol is used (e.g., DECNET); includes an NMG which provides the interface to NetView.

In addition, the three categories of managed objects are included:

- GMFHS_Shadow_Objects_Class - SNA resources included to illustrate connectivity relationships.
- GMFHS_Managed_Real_Objects_Class - non-SNA resources are represented with a one-to-one correspondence to each object.
- GMFHS_Aggregate_Objects_Class - one or more objects grouped together in order to provide a high-level status indicator (e.g., for a data center). The SNA shadow resources cannot be included because their status is not maintained by GMFHS.

Each object can contain several fields, including the resource name in each case.

Name-Spaces

The Name_Space parent class provides a technique for defining alternative names and types for the monitored resources.

Presentation-Services

Presentation of information at the GMF workstation is an important aspect of the GMFHS data model. The Presentation_Services parent class contains a wide range of classes and objects designed to enable the efficient display and interaction with a GMF workstation user.

One of the major features carried out by this part of the data model is the support of GMF views. There are several types of classes under the parent class which support the display of the RODM-based network data, including:

- NetView_View_Class
- Configuration_Parents_View_Class
- Configuration_Children_View_Class
- Configuration_Physical_Connectivity_View_Class
- Configuration_Logical_Connectivity_View_Class
- Configuration_Peer_View_Class
- Fast_Path_to_Failure_View_Class

This parent class enables other aspects of GMFHS presentation, including aggregation definition.

Object Definition and Processing

While the basic data model has been designed and included with NetView by IBM, each user installation is responsible for configuring the data cache. This involves defining the objects to RODM and their connectivity relationships. Also, views can be included.

Defining Network Resources

After understanding the data model and analyzing the target network, each user must define the object resources to RODM. This involves creating a text file consisting of statements for the RODM load function.

The RODM definitions in this file can be typed in by the user, or generated using an available utility. For example, if an installation's configuration data is stored in the IBM Information/Management database, the Network Configuration Application (NCA/MVS) product can be used to generate the file. If another configuration database product is used, then a routine must be written to extract the data and generate the load statements for RODM.

Figure H.3 contains an example of the statements contained in the RODM load file. In this case, a gateway in the NMG_Class by the name of "B3088P2" is defined.

Connectivity Relationships

The ability to establish connectivity relationships between objects can be an important aspect of the definition process. These links enable more realistic views to be displayed, and therefore provide a more comprehensive management capability.

```
CREATE INVOKER   ::= 0000004;
       OBJCLASS  ::= NMG_Class;
       OBJINST   ::= MyName = (CHARVAR) 'B3088P2';

       ATTRLIST
       Domain    ::= (OBJECTLINK)
       ('SNA_Domain_Class'.'B01NV'.'ContainsResource'),
       CommandRouteLUName ::= (CHARVAR) 'B01NV',
       NMGCharacteristics ::= (ANONYMOUSVAR) x'80',
       AgentStatusEffect          ::= (ANONYMOUSVAR) x'80',
       TransportProtocolName  ::= (CHARVAR) 'COS',
       WindowSize                 ::= (INTEGER) 8;
   END:
```

Figure H.3 Example of an object definition in the RODM load file.

There are several object fields that can be used to create the required connections. Examples of connectivity include physical, logical, and parent/child links.

Defining Views

As mentioned in Chapter 18, the two major types of views that can be created are network and peer. In each case, statements similar to those found in Figure H.3 are created to name the resources that are part of the view.

Processing

The GMFHS address space relies on both the RODM and NetView application address spaces to support the management of non-SNA network resources.

Unsolicited alerts are sent in to NetView for normal processing by the hardware monitor. During automation, a copy of each record is sent over to GMFHS.

The alert is then examined by GMFHS to determine, among other things, the name of the resource(s) involved. There is a correspondence between fields in each alert type, and the names of the objects in the data model. If an alert is received for a non-SNA resource being monitored, the object's status is updated in RODM. This can in turn generate other events based on the methods (e.g., change or notify) defined for the object, such as the revision of aggregation calculations or an update to the GMF display.

Automation Customization

The GMFHS data model can provide a basis for the automation of events in the network. It is included with NetView, and may be changed or upgraded if required. The user can take advantage of the RODM and GMFHS technology to implement additional automation functionality.

One of the major uses of the GMFHS data model with respect to automation is notification subscription for a particular object. After the proper initialization, a user application can then be notified when the status on a resource changes.

The GMFHS code receives unsolicited alerts, and then updates RODM objects as appropriate. Each update will generate asynchronous notifications to the user applications that are "listening."

The overall design of such an RODM application involves the following:

■ Setup
■ Wait
■ Notification
■ Shutdown

During the setup phase, an application connects to RODM, creates a notification subfield, and installs a method routine which will be driven when the object status changes. It must also prepare to receive updates from RODM by creating a notification queue. A notify request is initiated for each of the target objects. At this point, the user application can wait for incoming updates which are processed by GMFHS.

After one of the object status fields changes, the user's notification method is scheduled. The outcome is that a notification block describing the event is passed to the application; a previously defined Event Control Block (ECB) is posted. Based on the data, the application can take further action, such as inquiring about the status of other RODM objects.

Finally, the application must cleanup and withdraw from RODM during shutdown processing when its processing has been completed.

I

Abbreviations

ACB	Access Method Control Block
ACO	Automated Console Operations
AIX	Advanced Interactive Executive
ANO	Automated Network Operations
ANSI	American National Standards Institute
AOST	Automation Operator Station Task
API	Application Programming Interface
APPC	Advanced Program-to-Program Communication
APPLID	Application ID
APPN	Advanced Peer-to-Peer Networking
ARPA	Advanced Research Projects Agency
ASCII	American National Standard Code for Information Interchange
ASN.1	Abstract Syntax Notation One
BER	Basic Encoding Rules, or Box Error Record
BF	Boundary Function
CCITT	Consultative Committee on International Telegraphy and Telephone
CCS	Common Communications Support
CIB	Control Information Base
CDRM	Cross-Domain Resource Manager
CDRSC	Cross-Domain Resource
CLIST	Command List
CMIP	Common Management Information Protocol
CMIS	Common Management Information Services
CNM	Communication Network Management

CNMI	CNM Interface
COS	Common Operations Services, or Class of Service
CP	Control Point
CPI	Common Programming Interface
CSCF	Central Site Control Facility
CSECT	Control Section
CUA	Common User Access
DARPA	Defense Advanced Research Projects Agency
DASD	Direct Access Storage Device
DCE	Data Circuit-terminating Equipment, or Distributed Computing Environment
DDM	Distributed Data Management
DME	Distributed Management Environment
DOM	Delete Operator Message
DOS	Disk Operating System
DSECT	Data Section
DSRB	Data Services Request Block
DST	Data Services Task
DTE	Data Terminal Equipment
EBCDIC	Extended Binary Coded Decimal Interchange Code
EIB	Enterprise Information Base
EN	End Node
EP	Entry Point
ER	Explicit Route
ESA	Enterprise Systems Architecture
FDDI	Fiber-Distributed Data Interface
FDX	Full duplex
FP	Focal Point
GDMO	Guidelines for the Definition of Managed Objects
GDS	General Data Stream
GMF	Graphic Monitor Facility
GUI	Graphical User Interface
HCT	Hard Copy Task
HDX	Half duplex
HLL	High-Level Language
HP	Hewlett-Packard, or High Performance (as in HP transport)
IAB	Internet Architecture Board
IBM	International Business Machines
IEEE	Institute of Electrical and Electronics Engineers
IFR	Internal Function Request

IP	Internet Protocol
ISO	International Standards Organization
JCL	Job Control Language
LAN	Local Area Network
LEN	Low Entry Networking
LU	Logical Unit
LUC	Logical Unit Convergence
MAPI	Method API
MDB	Message Data Block
MIB	Management Information Base
MNT	Main Task
MPF	Message Processing Facility
MPTN	Multi-Protocol Transport Networking
MVS	Multiple Virtual Storage
NAM	Network Asset Manager
NAU	Network Addressable Unit
NCP	Network Control Program
NMVT	Network Management Vector Transport
NN	Network Node
NNT	NetView-to-NetView Task
NPM	NetView Performance Monitor
OMG	Object Management Group
ONM	Open Network Management
OPT	Optional Task
OSI	Model for Open Systems Interconnection
OSI/CS	OSI Communications Subsystem
OSF	Open Software Foundation
OST	Operator Station Task
OS/2	Operating System/2
PC	Personal Computer, or Path Control
PDS	Partitioned Data Set
PIU	Path Information Unit
PPI	Program-to-Program Interface
PPT	Primary Program Operator Interface (POI) Task
PU	Physical Unit
REXX	Restructured Extended Executor
RFC	Request For Comment
RH	Request Header
RMF	Resource Monitor Facility
RMON	Remote Monitoring
RODM	Resource Object Data Manager
RPC	Remote Procedure Call
RPL	Request Parameter List

RTM	Response Time Monitor
RU	Request Unit
SAA	Systems Application Architecture
SDLC	Synchronous Data Link Control
SNA	Systems Network Architecture
SNMP	Simple Network Management Protocol
SNS	Session Network Services
SPS	Session Presentation Services
SSCP	System Services Control Point
SVC	Supervisor Call
TAF	Terminal Access Facility
TCB	Task Control Block
TCP	Transmission Control Protocol
TG	Transmission Group
TH	Transmission Header
TP	Transaction Program
TSCF	Target System Control Facility
TSO	Time Sharing Option
UAPI	User API
UDP	User Datagram Protocol
VM	Virtual Machine
VPD	Vital Product Data
VR	Virtual Route
VSAM	Virtual Storage Access Method
VSE	Virtual Storage Extended
VTAM	Virtual Telecommunications Access Method
WTO	Write-to-Operator
WTOR	WTO with Reply
XA	Extended Architecture
XMP	X/Open Management Protocol

Abstract Syntax Notation One (ASN.1). A formal data definition language issued jointly by ISO and CCITT. ASN.1 is used, for example, to specify the structure of a MIB.

Access Method (AM). An operating system service providing a method for an application to access data. The two major categories of access methods deal with data on a storage device (e.g., disk) or in a communications network.

Access Method Control Block (ACB). A data area created by an application program to share information with and establish a connection to the access method (e.g., VTAM) when accessing data.

Address space. A term used to designate the entire range for a particular value. For example, the local portion of the IP address forms an address space within the assigned network. For the MVS user, an address space refers to a process (e.g., batch job) which, among other things, includes a range of virtual storage addresses.

Advanced Interactive Executive (AIX). The IBM derivative of UNIX. Although AIX runs on several platforms, it is most commonly associated with the RS/6000 workstation.

Advanced Peer-to-Peer Networking (APPN). A dynamic connectivity and routing architecture, based on PU type 2.1, which is designed to augment and eventually replace the traditional, host-centered SNA.

Advanced Program-to-Program Communication (APPC).   IBM's strategic communication model, where transaction programs exchange logical records over a temporary conversation. The underlying LU type 6.2 session is utilized and shared by the programs. APPC forms the basis of several other IBM architectures and products (e.g., SNA/MS).

Advanced Research Projects Agency (ARPA).   The U.S. government agency charged with selecting and funding research which is viewed as strategic to the country's long-term interests. ARPA is part of the Department of Defense, and was subsequently renamed DARPA.

Agent.   A logical entity in the network which manages and controls local resources on behalf of a central manager. The manager-agent model is central to both OSI and TCP/IP network management; also, SystemView has adopted this technique. See manager.

Aggregation.   A technique allowing several resources to be grouped together as one logical entity for the purpose of status display.

Alert.   A high priority event within NetView important enough to justify operator or automation action. An alert is also formally defined by the SNA Management Services architecture. See SNA alert.

American National Standard Code for Information Interchange (ASCII).   A standard for character encoding using seven out of eight bits in a byte.

American National Standards Institute (ANSI).   The major organization for developing and coordinating United States standards; ANSI is also a member of ISO.

Application ID (APPLID).   A VTAM definition parameter through which an application program can gain access to the network, and engage in SNA sessions.

Application Programming Interface (API).   The general name given to a programming interface through which an application gains access to specific services. For example, VTAM includes an API that can be used to establish SNA sessions and exchange data.

ARPANET.   The original packet switching network sponsored by ARPA, which first became operational in 1969. The network was later upgraded to support the TCP/IP protocols, and then dissolved in 1990.

Automated Operator Station Task (AOST). An OST without an associated terminal session, and used primarily for background automation processing. See Autotask and Operator Station Task.

Automation. A technique which, through the use of software such as NetView, allows human intervention in the operation of the enterprise-wide resources to be minimized.

Automation option. One of several products supplied by IBM which enhances NetView operations through a tighter integration with related products.

Automation table. The primary technology used within NetView to implement automation. It is stored as a sequential file in the DSIPARM data set, and contains one of several different types of statements which determine the actions taken for specific messages.

Autotask. A subtask within NetView used to support background automation. An autotask is a special type of Operator Station Task. See Automated Operator Station Task.

Basic Encoding Rules (BER). The ISO-CCITT standard which specifies how ASN.1-encoded data can be transferred.

Batch job. One of the three major types of MVS processes. A job consists of JCL statements, and is submitted through a reader.

Bind. The general process of connecting two NAUs in an SNA session. Also, the BIND data format, which flows between two NAUs during session establishment, is defined and documented by IBM.

Boundary Function (BF). A component of the subarea node designed to support attached peripheral nodes.

Box Error Record (BER). The IBM communication controllers (e.g., 3725) can capture and locally record BERs.

Class. The concept and technique used within object-oriented programming to organize, define, and represent resources with similar characteristics.

Class of Service (COS). The method for allowing sessions to be assigned differing categories of service based on their intended usage. VTAM maintains a COS table with multiple entries.

Command List (CLIST). A program written in a high-level interpretive language, such as REXX.

Command Procedure. The general term used for either a NetView CLIST or command processor.

Command Processor. A "compiled" program, written in C, PL/I, or assembler, which can be scheduled and run within NetView.

Common Management Information Protocol (CMIP). An OSI network management standard precisely defining the format of requests and responses.

Common Management Information Services (CMIS). An OSI standard which precisely defines the services available to network management applications.

Common Operations Services (COS). A set of commonly used operational services which are available to assist in the implementation of the major SNA/MS functional categories (e.g., change management). The SNA/MS architecture defines a COS function set.

Communication controller. A 37xx box (e.g., 3725) which runs the Network Control Program (NCP), and is controlled by the host.

Communication Network Management (CNM). Both an early philosophy and set of formats and protocols designed to enable the management of network resources from a central host.

Communication Network Management Interface (CNMI). A formally defined interface, implemented with VTAM, which allows host applications to manage the network resources.

Communications Manager. Software running under OS/2 which permits network connectivity for the local applications.

Connection. Similar to an SNA session, a connection can be created between two applications using TCP.

Consultative Committee on International Telegraphy and Telephone (CCITT). An important international standards organization which frequently works with ISO to design and publish data communication and connectivity standards.

Control Block. A data area defined as part of a software product which holds parameters and other operational information.

Control Information Base (CIB). One part of the SystemView data model which is defined to contain real-time, operational information.

Control Point (CP). Analogous to the SSCP at the host, the CP provides command and control capabilities for the newer APPN nodes.

Control Section (CSECT). An assembler directive used to designate the beginning of a program or subroutine. Each CSECT must be mapped by a base register in the 370 architecture.

Control unit. The general term given to lower end hardware boxes which support one or more attached terminals (e.g., 3174).

Conversation. A temporary connection between two transaction programs within the LU type 6.2 processing model.

Cross-Domain Resource (CDRSC). A resource, such as an application or terminal, that is defined and owned by another VTAM domain.

Cross-Domain Resource Manager (CDRM). The VTAM component designed to enable resources to be shared among multiple SNA domains (i.e., multiple host machines).

Cross-memory. A programming technique, with supporting hardware and software, allowing a program in one MVS address space to directly access data and code in another process.

DARPA. See Advanced Research Projects Agency.

Data Circuit-terminating Equipment (DCE). A device, such as a modem, which enables a DTE to be connected to a communication link.

Data Section (DSECT). A template used by an assembler language program to map a section of storage containing data fields.

Data Services Task (DST). A special type of optional task provided by IBM to speed NetView-based application development. The DST provides several services, such as access to VSAM and CNMI data.

Data Terminal Equipment (DTE). A node attaching to a communication network, such as a terminal.

Disk Operating System (DOS). The basic, non-preemptive operating system commonly used with Intel-based machines.

Distributed Data Management (DDM). Generally speaking, DDM is the discipline which supports access to local and remote data, as distributed throughout the network. Specifically, it refers to the IBM architecture enabling such access.

Distributed Management Environment (DME). A framework for consistent systems and network management defined by the Open Software Foundation (OSF), with input from its members.

Domain. A term associated with scope of control for a managing entity. Specifically, all of the SNA resources controlled by one instance of an SSCP (i.e., VTAM) is considered to be a domain. Also, each NetView application defines a domain. Most commonly, a VTAM and NetView domain are synonymous.

Element. An individually addressable entity within the SNA network, such as an application or link. Each element is assigned a unique number within a subarea.

End Node (EN). One of the two major node types defined by the APPN architecture. An EN client relies upon the Network Node server for non-adjacent connection establishment and routing.

Enterprise Information Base (EIB). One part of the SystemView data model which is defined to support a set of systems management applications.

Entry Point (EP). Acts as an agent for the controlling Focal Points when carrying out network management functionality within the SNA/MS architecture.

Ethernet. A de facto LAN standard based on the Carrier Sense Multiple Access with Collision Detection (CSMA/CD) model. In 1978, Digital Equipment Corporation, Intel, and Xerox created the DIX Ethernet standard.

Event. An occurrence in the SNA network usually resulting in a data request being sent to the central NetView host. Note that statistics records can become events; also, events can become NetView alerts.

Explicit Route (ER). The physically mapped route within an SNA network. The ERs perform simple node-to-node routing, and leave more advanced functions (e.g., pacing) to the Virtual Routes (VRs).

Extended Binary Coded Decimal Interchange Code (EBCDIC). The encoding standard supported by IBM which uses eight bits to represent a printable or control character.

Filter. An entry, usually set by a NetView command, which acts as a type of screen in order to determine what data should be processed. NetView includes several different types of filters, many of which are defined by the Hardware Monitor.

Focal Point (FP). Acts as a manager for the Entry Point (EP) agents in order to execute the network management functionality within the SNA/MS architecture.

Function set. A grouping of protocols packaged together, and implemented in order to enable a particular feature within the SNA/MS framework.

Generalized Data Stream (GDS). The formally defined data stream used by APPC programs. Each logical record includes a two-byte length field, followed by a two-byte GDSID field. The GDSID conveys the nature and format of the remaining information. GDS also appears as General Data Stream.

Graphic Monitor Facility (GMF). IBM's strategic user interface for NetView. GMF runs under OS/2, and is designed to slowly replace NETCENTER. This is being accomplished through new host technologies such as RODM.

Graphical User Interface (GUI). A general term given to the user display technology based on windowing, graphics, and a pointing device (i.e., mouse).

High Performance (HP) transport. One of two APPC-based transports implemented within NetView as of version 2 release 2. The HP transport includes less rigorous error detection, and other changes, designed to enable improved performance. See Management Services (MS) transport.

International Standards Organization (ISO). An international body which defines a wide range of standards resulting in increased interaction and interoperability. Specifically, ISO has created the OSI model for communications and systems management.

Internet. The large and growing connection of autonomous networks which together form one large Internetwork (i.e., Internet). The services most commonly available to Internet users include mail, remote logon, and file transfer.

Internet Protocol (IP). The lower, network protocol used to transfer data in a TCP/IP network. IP is a "best effort" protocol, with a minimum of error detection and re-transmission.

LAN NetView. A new family of LAN products designed to implement systems management in the LAN arena. LAN NetView can also tie into NetView at the host.

Local Area Network (LAN). A general term given to one of several different technologies which connect PCs, workstations, and other devices within a limited range.

Logical record. The unit of data exchanged between two APPC-based transaction programs.

Logical Unit (LU). One of the three NAUs defined by SNA. An LU enables end users to gain access to the network.

Low Entry Networking (LEN). The basic connection capability provided through the use of PU type 2.1 protocols.

LU type 6.2. The type of LU-to-LU session supporting the APPC processing model.

Major node. A representation, within VTAM and the status monitor, of one or more network resources. See Minor node.

Major vector. One of several well-defined data structures passed between nodes to communicate specific events and other information.

Management Information Base (MIB). A general term given to the collection of data objects, each representing a particular resource in the network. Both OSI and TCP/IP network management use MIBs. Also, RODM can be considered to be a type of MIB containing operational data.

Management Services (MS) transport.   One of two APPC-based transports implemented within NetView as of version 2 release 2. This transport, as its name implies, is designed to carry Management Services data. It places emphasis on the reliable transmission of information.

Manager.   A logical entity in the network which manages and controls remote resources through its assigned agents.   The manager-agent model is central to both OSI and TCP/IP network management.   See Agent.

Member.   A sequential file, identified by a unique name, which is stored in a Partitioned Data Set (PDS).

Message queuing.   A general technique for passing information from one application to another.   At a minimum, a queue will consist of a pointer to the data buffers, as well as an Event Control Block (ECB) that must be posted.

Minor node.   An entry in a VTAM major node defining a single resource.

Multiple Virtual Storage (MVS).   IBM's premier production-oriented operating system.   MVS comes in one of several flavors, such as MVS/XA, and MVS/ESA.

Multi-Protocol Transport Networking (MPTN).   The architecture, with corresponding product support, which IBM has put forth to help solve the interoperability problems among several communication standards.

NETCENTER.   A system for monitoring and managing network resources (including non-SNA) from a DOS-based graphical display. This IBM product, which was originally acquired by U.S. West, is positioned as a tactical solution to be slowly replaced by GMF.

NetView/6000.   An IBM network management product based on HP's OpenView, and designed to monitor and manage network resources using the Simple Network Management Protocol (SNMP) from the RS/6000 workstation.

Network Addressable Unit (NAU).   One of three logical entities that can be individually addressed with a network address that is unique throughout the network.

Network Control Program (NCP). A software product, or more precisely a specialized operating system, which is generated and then loaded into a communication controller (e.g., 3745).

Network management. The processes and procedures defined to support the planning, implementation, administration, monitoring, and control of both hardware and software resources within a communication network.

Network Management Vector Transport (NMVT). An SNA/MS request unit designed to supersede previous network management flows. The NMVT is used primarily within the traditional SNA subarea network.

Network Node (NN). The most sophisticated node within the APPN framework, supporting a variety of services such as intermediate routing.

NetView Performance Monitor (NPM). Originally named the Network Performance Monitor, NPM is IBM's mainframe product designed to collect and display performance information. It was recently enhanced to support VTAM performance data (e.g., buffer pools).

Object. A specific instance of a pre-defined class. Objects are used within the Resource Object Data Manager (RODM).

Object Management Group (OMG). An independent organization, similar to OSF, which focuses on consistent standards development and distribution. Its Common Object Request Broker Architecture (CORBA) has recently received significant attention.

Object-oriented. A term used to describe a system or application that draws on one or more of the attributes commonly associated with object-oriented design and development. These characteristics include, for example, classes, objects, methods, encapsulation, and inheritance.

Open Software Foundation (OSF). A non-profit organization which develops and distributes application frameworks and other technologies designed to support distributed processing. See Distributed Management Environment (DME).

Open Systems Interconnection (OSI). An architectural seven-layer model, created by ISO, designed to promote interconnectivity and interoperability among network and computer resources.

Open Systems Interconnection/Communications Subsystem (OSI/CS). An IBM mainframe product which represents an implementation of OSI protocols.

OpenView. A sophisticated product from HP designed to monitor and manage network resources using the Simple Network Management Protocol (SNMP). The vendor has long claimed that it will support the DME standard from OSF, whenever it finally becomes available.

Operating System/2 (OS/2). A pre-emptive, multi-tasking operating system produced by IBM with assistance from Microsoft. IBM now owns the product, and continues with its enhancements and improvements.

Operator Station Task (OST). One of the several types of NetView subtasks; an OST supports a terminal user.

Packet switching. A network providing a virtual link between two attached nodes. The data accepted for transmission in each direction is divided (e.g., packetized) and then routed depending on network conditions.

Page. A storage frame consisting of 4096 (i.e., 4K) bytes under MVS.

Paging. An operating system feature used to create the illusion of a single, large storage map. This virtual storage is addressed by the application, which the operating system then maps to real storage. If the required page is not resident in real storage, a paging operation occurs to transfer the page from disk to memory.

Partitioned Data Set (PDS). One of several data set organizations provided by the disk access methods on the IBM mainframe. Each PDS has a name, and contains one or more named members. These members, when selected, appear as sequential files.

Path Control (PC) network. The lower layers of the SNA model which, when taken together, provide reliable end-to-end transmission among the nodes.

Path Information Unit (PIU). An SNA data format defined to contain a Transmission Header, followed by a Request Header and Request Unit.

Peripheral node. One of two major categories of nodes in the traditional SNA network. A peripheral node must rely on an attached subarea node for session and routing support.

Physical Unit (PU).   One of three NAUs defined by SNA. Each node contains a PU to manage its local, physical environment.

Proxy agent.   Within the SNMP model, an agent cannot always be integrated with a resource in order to provide management support. In this case, a proxy agent is used, which acts on behalf of such a resource. A proxy agent is similar to the SNA service point.

Real storage.   Generally speaking, this is the hardware memory included with a computer. See Paging and Virtual storage.

Remote Monitoring (RMON).   A recent enhancement to SNMP allowing more of an enterprise-wide management capability for TCP/IP resources.

Remote Procedure Call (RPC).   A technology, supported by several standards organizations and vendors, which allows programs (i.e., procedures) to be invoked on a remote machine. Parameters can be included with the call, and the output is passed back.

Request For Comment (RFC).   A document which is created and submitted to guide and support the evolution of the TCP/IP network architecture.

Resource Object Data Manager (RODM).   An object-oriented data cache containing operational information in support of the SystemView strategy. RODM was first introduced with NetView version 2 release 3.

Restructured Extended Executor (REXX).   A CLIST language supported across a wide variety of IBM and non-IBM platforms. It is the designated SAA procedural language.

Service Point.   One of the three major entities identified within the Open Network Management framework. A service point connects to the SSCP at the central host in order to support non-SNA resources.

Session.   A connection between two NAUs. There are four main categories of SNA sessions (e.g., LU-to-LU).

Simple Network Management Protocol (SNMP).   The framework and data definitions, as well as protocol exchanges, which have become the de facto standard for TCP/IP-based network management.

SNA Alert. A formally defined data structure used to communicate problem management information. SNA alerts are sent from an Entry Point to a Focal Point, always in an unsolicited fashion. See Alert, and Chapter 3.

SNA Management Services (SNA/MS). The detailed format and protocol definitions included with SNA which enable the management of SNA communication networks. See Chapter 2.

Socket. A programming abstraction, originally developed in the UNIX community, which allows an application to communicate with other applications. The socket API is supported within the TCP/IP framework, and has become the de facto standard.

Started task. One of three major types of MVS processes. The started task JCL is stored in a system procedure library (PROCLIB), and is created with the start command.

Statistic. A record sent in either a solicited or unsolicited fashion to a central Focal Point. The information can describe traffic and error counts.

Subarea. A section of the SNA network which is identified by a unique number.

Subarea node. An SNA type 4 (e.g., NCP) or type 5 (e.g., VTAM) node which when combined together form the network backbone. See Peripheral node.

Supervisor Call (SVC). A machine instruction in the System/370 architecture which generates an SVC interrupt and a subsequent branch to a pre-defined program based on the provided number.

Swappable. An MVS address space can be either marked as swappable or non-swappable. If swappable, it can be disabled, usually due to lack of activity, and moved (almost) completely out of real storage.

System Services Control Point (SSCP). One of three NAUs defined by SNA. The SSCP, usually implemented within VTAM, manages an SNA domain.

Systems Application Architecture (SAA). The IBM framework, consisting of three major components, designed to guide application development. The benefits of SAA include application portability and consistent skills development.

Systems Network Architecture (SNA). The proprietary communication architecture introduced by IBM in 1974 to guide its product development.

SystemView. The IBM framework designed to support consistent, enterprise-wide systems management.

Time Sharing Option (TSO). One of three major types of MVS processes. A TSO user logs on to the system, which then creates a new address space. Among other things, TSO provides the terminal user with an interactive window into the MVS batch-oriented system.

Token ring. A type of Local Area Network (LAN) that IBM has adopted as its primary PC and workstation connectivity technology. The IBM token ring is based on the IEEE 802 architecture.

Transaction Program (TP). A temporary instance of a program or procedure which is initialized, executes, and then terminates. TP processing forms the basis for APPC.

Transmission Control Protocol (TCP). One of two transport layer protocols included with the TCP/IP architecture. TCP is connection-oriented. See User Datagram Protocol (UDP).

Transmission Control Protocol/Internet Protocol (TCP/IP). A de facto communication standard widely used in the growing LAN, PC, and workstation area.

Trap. An unsolicited event in the TCP/IP network, represented as an SNMP message sent from an agent to its manager.

User Datagram Protocol (UDP). One of two transport layer protocols included with the TCP/IP architecture. UDP is connectionless. See Transmission Control Protocol (TCP).

Virtual Route (VR). A logical, end-to-end path which sessions utilize in order to route data between the SNA nodes. The VR protocols include error detection and pacing, and are based on the underlying ERs.

Virtual storage. Memory, containing both data and code, which is addressed by system and application programs. Each virtual page must be mapped to a real page frame before it can actually be used.

Virtual Storage Access Method (VSAM). A sophisticated disk access method, with several different implementation options (e.g., keyed sequential access). VSAM is widely used by mainframe software, such as NetView.

Virtual Telecommunications Access Method (VTAM). A telecommunications access method based on the SNA model. An instance of VTAM includes the SSCP, and therefore defines an SNA domain.

X/Open. An open systems standards organization based in England; IBM has adopted the X/Open Management Protocol (XMP) interface within its SystemView framework.

X.25. A standard, created by CCITT, which defines how computer equipment can connect to a packet switching network.

Bibliography

GraphicsView/2

GC31-6116   GraphicsView/2 General Information

NETCENTER

GC31-6100   NETCENTER At a Glance

NetView Version 2 Release 3

GC31-7016   NetView At a Glance
LY43-0014   NetView Problem Determination and Diagnosis
LY43-0015   NetView Automation Implementation
SC31-6125   NetView Installation and Administration Guide
SC31-6127   NetView Operation
SC31-6128   NetView Administration Reference
SC31-6129   NetView Application Programming Guide
SC31-6130   NetView RODM Programming Guide
SC31-6131   NetView Bridge Implementation
SC31-6132   NetView Customization Guide
SC31-6133   NetView Customization: Using Assembler
SC31-6134   NetView Customization: Using PL/I and C
SC31-6135   NetView Customization: Writing CLISTs

SC31-6138   NetView Messages
SC31-6139   NetView GMF User's Guide
SC31-6141   NetView Automation Planning

NetView/PC

GG22-9119   NetView/PC Version 1.2
SC31-6002   NetView/PC V1.2.1 Planning, Installation,
             Customization

NetView/6000

GC31-6179   NetView/6000 Version 2 Concepts

Network Configuration Application

SC31-6149   NCA/MVS User's Guide
SC31-6150   NCA/MVS Analyst's Guide

Network Management

GC31-6809   SNA/MS Alert Implementation Guide
GC30-3431   Introduction to Open Network Management

REXX

SH19-8160   IBM Compiler and Library for REXX/370:
             User's Guide and Reference

Systems Network Architecture

GA23-0059   3270 Data Stream Programmer's Reference
GC30-3073   SNA Technical Overview
SC30-3112   SNA Format and Protocol Reference: Architecture
             Logic
SC30-3269   SNA Format and Protocol Reference: Arch. Logic for
             LU 6.2
SC30-3346   SNA Management Services Reference
SC31-6808   SNA LU 6.2 Peer Protocol Reference

SystemView

GC23-0576	SAA: An Introduction to SystemView
GC28-1383	Guide for Evaluating SystemView Integration
GC34-4354	SystemView Data Model Concepts and Planning

VTAM Version 4 Release 1

GC31-6416	VTAM Migration Guide
GC31-6441	VTAM Release Guide

Textbooks and References

Ranade, Jay and Sackett, George, *Introduction to SNA Networking: Using VTAM/NCP*, McGraw-Hill, 1989.

Ranade, Jay and Sackett, George, *Advanced SNA Networking: A Professional's Guide to VTAM/NCP*, McGraw-Hill, 1991.

Black, Uyless, *Network Management Standards: The OSI, SNMP, and CMOL Protocols*, McGraw-Hill, 1992.

Feit, Sidnie, *TCP/IP: Architecture, Protocols, and Implementation*, McGraw-Hill, 1993.

Index

About the Author

David Peterson is an independent instructor, writer, and consultant assisting companies in their transition to a more distributed processing environment. He has extensive experience in the design and development of system software products, with a focus on data communications, network management, and some of the recent client/server technologies.

As a product author at Peregrine Systems, Peterson designed and produced NV/Monitor with the assistance of one developer. It became generally available on May 1, 1992, and is the first complete performance monitoring product for NetView on the MVS platform.

Before joining Peregrine, he spent three and a half years on the R&D staff at Candle Corporation. As part of the network group, he focused on researching VTAM internals processing and control block structures. This experience allowed him to design a large number of the VTAM-specific data collection routines, which formed the basis of the Omegamon II for VTAM product. He gradually assumed a project leadership role for the group, with influence on the product's overall quality and direction.

Peterson has published a dozen technical articles and made numerous conference presentations, covering topics such as OS/2, APPC, NetView, VTAM, and MVS. He has developed and taught several different courses through various university extension programs. Most recently, he has created a series of classes on client/server computing for the University of California at Irvine.

Before beginning work in the software development industry, Peterson spent several years as a systems and graphics programmer. He can be reached through the Internet at peterson@cerf.net.

DATE DUE

24 93 493	
4/1/97	